Financing Government
in a Federal System

Studies of Government Finance: Second Series

TITLES PUBLISHED

Financing Government in a Federal System

GEORGE F. BREAK

Studies of Government Finance

THE BROOKINGS INSTITUTION

WASHINGTON, D.C.

Copyright © 1980 by
THE BROOKINGS INSTITUTION
1775 Massachusetts Avenue, N.W., Washington, D.C. 20036

Library of Congress Cataloging in Publication Data:

Break, George F

   Financing government in a Federal system.

   (Studies in government finance: Second series)
   Includes bibliographical references and index.
     1. Intergovernmental fiscal relations—United States.
2. Finance, Public—United States.   I. Title.
II. Series.
HJ275.B66   336.1'85'0973   79-3775
ISBN 0-8157-1068-2
ISBN 0-8157-1067-4 (pbk.)

9 8 7 6 5 4 3 2

THE BROOKINGS INSTITUTION is an independent organization devoted to nonpartisan research, education, and publication in economics, government, foreign policy, and the social sciences generally. Its principal purposes are to aid in the development of sound public policies and to promote public understanding of issues of national importance.

The Institution was founded on December 8, 1927, to merge the activities of the Institute for Government Research, founded in 1916, the Institute of Economics, founded in 1922, and the Robert Brookings Graduate School of Economics and Government, founded in 1924.

The Board of Trustees is responsible for the general administration of the Institution, while the immediate direction of the policies, program, and staff is vested in the President, assisted by an advisory committee of the officers and staff. The by-laws of the Institution state: "It is the function of the Trustees to make possible the conduct of scientific research, and publication, under the most favorable conditions, and to safeguard the independence of the research staff in the pursuit of their studies and in the publication of the results of such studies. It is not a part of their function to determine, control, or influence the conduct of particular investigations or the conclusions reached."

The President bears final responsibility for the decision to publish a manuscript as a Brookings book. In reaching his judgment on the competence, accuracy, and objectivity of each study, the President is advised by the director of the appropriate research program and weighs the views of a panel of expert outside readers who report to him in confidence on the quality of the work. Publication of a work signifies that it is deemed a competent treatment worthy of public consideration but does not imply endorsement of conclusions or recommendations.

The Institution maintains its position of neutrality on issues of public policy in order to safeguard the intellectual freedom of the staff. Hence interpretations or conclusions in Brookings publications should be understood to be solely those of the authors and should not be attributed to the Institution, to its trustees, officers, or other staff members, or to the organizations that support its research.

Foreword

IT IS IRONIC to recall that the Brookings conference in 1965 that gave rise to the first version of this study (*Intergovernmental Fiscal Relations in the United States,* by George F. Break, published by Brookings in 1967) was organized in the belief that "both state and local governments will need assistance from the national government if they are to perform their traditional roles in our federal system." As it happened, it was only a matter of months before federal assistance began flowing in such abundance that the resulting changes in the fiscal environment, in the opinion of many observers, constituted a serious threat to those very roles. The Great Society's War on Poverty poured billions into categorical grants that established a multitude of fiscal links not only with state and local governments but also with paragovernmental agencies. Dissatisfied with the results of this effort to solve problems by identifying them from Washington and showering money on them, the New Federalists tried channeling money to governments under revenue sharing programs and also to broad problem areas under block grant programs. These activities have altered intergovernmental relations significantly, but few problems have disappeared.

Fifteen years later, it now seems time for a systematic reassessment of the problems of financing government in a federal system. How should spending responsibilities be assigned among levels of government? How should taxing sources and powers be coordinated? What are the uses and misuses of intergovernmental grants-in-aid?

What are the best means of confronting the special financial difficulties of large urban areas? The inauspicious beginnings of the 1980s—high inflation, sluggish economic growth, and worrisome international tensions—may give way to better times, but it is certain that the nation will have a continuing need for a productive and resilient fiscal system. It is with the hope of helping to improve the design of that system that this study, which examines the anatomy of the present structure and the principles and trade-offs that have determined its evolution, is offered.

George F. Break is professor of economics at the University of California (Berkeley). He acknowledges the many helpful comments of Richard A. Musgrave of Harvard University, Will Myers of the Advisory Commission on Intergovernmental Relations, Earl R. Rolph and Michael Wiseman of the University of California (Berkeley), and Joseph J. Minarik of the Brookings staff. He is also grateful to Alice M. Carroll, who edited the manuscript, to Ellen W. Smith, who verified its factual content, and to Florence Robinson, who prepared the index. He adds that the help and encouragement of his wife, Helen S. Break, while the manuscript was in preparation were essential to its completion.

This is the twelfth volume in the second series of Brookings Studies of Government Finance. Both series are devoted to examining issues in taxation and public policy.

The views expressed in this book are those of the author and should not be ascribed to the trustees, officers, or other staff members of the Brookings Institution.

BRUCE K. MACLAURY
President

June 1980
Washington, D.C.

Contents

Tables

Figures

CHAPTER ONE

Fiscal Relations
in the Federal System

SINCE the Great Depression the term *intergovernmental relations* has
become an indispensable fixture in that special language by which
governments in the United States conduct their business and scholars
study it. The philological origins of the term are obscure[1] and its
definitional boundaries, as years of use have proved, are imprecise.
Yet it has been an essential part of the vocabularies of scholars, public
officials, and ordinary citizens since the New Deal built it into government's fiscal framework.

Whether categorized intriguingly as the "hidden dimension of government" or mundanely as "an important body of activities or interactions occurring between governmental units of all types and levels
within the federal system,"[2] intergovernmental relations is the key-
stone of economic and fiscal policymaking in the United States. It has
come a long way since W. Brooke Graves edited a special issue of

---

1. Deil S. Wright, *Understanding Intergovernmental Relations: Public Policy
and Participants' Perspectives in Local, State, and National Governments* (Duxbury
Press, 1978), p. 6.
2. The first term was used by Senator Edmund Muskie in 1962, and the second
by Professor William Anderson in 1960. Ibid., p. 5.

Table 1-1. Government Output and Own-Financed Expenditures as a Percent of GNP, Selected Years, 1940–78

	Government purchases of goods and services			Own-financed government expenditures[a]		
Year	Federal	State and local	Total	Federal	State and local	Total
1940	6.1	8.1	14.2	10.0	8.5	18.4
1950	6.5	6.9	13.5	14.3	7.0	21.3
1960	10.6	9.2	19.8	18.4	8.6	27.0
1970	9.7	12.5	22.3	20.8	11.0	31.8
1975	8.0	14.1	22.1	23.3	11.5	34.9
1977	7.6	13.3	20.9	22.2	10.8	33.0
1978	7.2	13.3	20.5	21.6	10.6	32.2

Source: *The National Income and Product Accounts of the United States, 1929–74, Statistical Tables*, supplement to the *Survey of Current Business* (U.S. Government Printing Office, 1977), pp. 2–3, 99–103, 108–09, 340–41; *Survey of Current Business*, vol. 59 (July 1979), pp. 26, 39–40. Figures are rounded.

a. Federal grants are included in federal expenditures and deducted from state and local expenditures.

The Annals of the American Academy of Political and Social Science entitled "Intergovernmental Relations in the United States."[3] Federal expenditures then were 10 percent of gross national product (GNP) and state and local expenditures 8.5 percent; not quite forty years later they were 22 percent and 11 percent, respectively (table 1-1). That the public sector has grown dramatically is hardly news. Less obvious, however, are the intricate, ever-changing intergovernmental complexities of its growth pattern and their impact on the nation's basic fiscal development.

Trends in Government Output, Expenditures, and Revenues

Broadly speaking, government expenditures are made to provide the collective goods and services that make up government output or to make transfer payments to individuals, businesses, or other governments.[4] Between 1940 and 1978 the government share of total national output increased from 14 percent to over 20 percent (table 1-1). Most of this relative growth in government output occurred at the state and local level. Transfer payments, especially at the federal

3. Vol. 207 (January 1940).

4. Another kind of spending, the host of direct lending and loan guaranty operations carried out by the federal government, has a very high economic impact. See, for example, "Federal Credit Programs," *Special Analyses, Budget of the United States Government, Fiscal Year 1980*, pp. 132–82. The burgeoning federal regulatory programs also typically induce large amounts of private spending.

level, became increasingly important during this period. Whereas in 1940 total federal expenditures were higher than output expenditures alone by only 4 percent of GNP, in 1978 that difference was 14 percent of GNP. State and local governments' expenditures financed by their own revenue collections, in sharp contrast, were only slightly larger than their purchases of goods and services in 1940 and smaller in 1978 (table 1-1). In the latter year, federal grants were large enough to cover not only all state and local transfer payments but a significant portion of output spending at the lower levels as well.[5]

A high and rising level of government expenditures is not likely to arouse widespread public opposition in a world that is seen to be coping well with its most important social and economic problems. When these problems appear to be worsening, however, government is likely to be perceived as self-serving, uncontrolled, and unproductive instead of seeming a responsive, productive, and helpful institution. The rising incidence of unflattering views became one of the most notable features of the 1970s when sunset laws, balanced-budget proposals, and spending limitations emerged as household phrases. Some effects of these constraining pressures, as seen in chapter 5, have already been felt at the local level. If these pressures intensify and spread, intergovernmental fiscal relations will be in for an exciting time. The Great Tax Revolt may yet rank with the Great Depression and the Great Society as critical molders of the shape of U.S. fiscal federalism.

Intergovernmental Grants and Relative Spending Shares

An outstanding feature of intergovernmental relations since World War II has been the rapid increase in the importance of intergovernmental grants. Federal aid, for example, has much more than kept up with the economy's growth, rising from a mere 0.5 percent of GNP in 1946 to 1.3 percent in 1960, 2.5 percent in 1970, and 3.6 percent in the late 1970s (table 1-2). Federal grants are now such an important source of revenue to state and local governments, and especially to the nation's largest cities, that what Washington does, and can be made to do, is a major preoccupation of governors and mayors. State

5. In 1978, federal purchases of goods and services were only 33 percent of total federal expenditures. For state and local governments the comparable figure was 93 percent. Federal grants of $77 billion financed 25 percent of total state and local expenditures. As a result, purchases of goods and services by state and local governments in 1978 were 125 percent of their own-financed expenditures. *Survey of Current Business*, vol. 59 (July 1979), pp. 39–40.

Table 1-2. Federal and State Intergovernmental Grants as a Percent of GNP, Selected Years, 1946–78

Year	Federal grants	State grants
1946	0.5	1.0
1950	0.8	1.5
1955	0.8	1.5
1960	1.3	1.9
1965	1.6	2.2
1970	2.5	3.0
1975	3.6	3.4
1976	3.6	3.3
1978	3.6	a

Sources: *National Income and Product Accounts*, pp. 2–3, 96–97, 108–09, 340–41; David J. Levin, "Receipts and Expenditures of State Governments and of Local Governments, 1959–76," *Survey of Current Business*, vol. 58 (May 1978), p. 16; *Survey*, vol. 59 (July 1979), pp. 26, 39; U.S. Advisory Commission on Intergovernmental Relations (ACIR), *The States and Intergovernmental Aids: The Intergovernmental Grant System: An Assessment and Proposed Policies*, Report A-59 (GPO, 1977), p. 9.
a. Data for 1978 are not available. In 1976–77, state grants were 3.4 percent of GNP.

grants to local governments have also outpaced the economy's growth, rising from 1 percent of GNP in 1946 to 3.4 percent in 1977 (table 1-2).[6]

This greatly increased use of intergovernmental grants complicates the task of studying the changing importance of different levels of government. One picture is shown by federal, state, and local expenditures made for general government purposes and directly benefiting the private sector—what the Census Bureau calls direct general expenditures. Another, and increasingly different, picture is obtained from studies of the own-financed expenditures of each level of government.[7] From 1940 to 1965 the state share of direct general ex-

6. The rising importance of intergovernmental grants in federal, state, and local budgets is traced in chap. 4.

7. In the U.S. Census Bureau's fiscal tabulations, total government expenditures are divided into three broad categories—insurance trust expenditures, intergovernmental expenditures, and direct general expenditures. In the bureau's tabulations, own-financed general expenditures are the sum of direct general expenditures and intergovernmental expenditures minus intergovernmental revenue, which is equal to general expenditures minus intergovernmental revenue. The term *own-financed* does not imply that intergovernmental grants induce an equal amount of additional spending on the part of grantees. Intergovernmental revenues are subtracted from grantee expenditures since the grants are included in grantor expenditures. The implicit assumption, of course, is that the transfer of funds between levels of government creates no measurable benefit to society. A more cumbersome set of terms that might be freer of conceptual ambiguities would be general expenditures, by level of final disbursement, and general expenditures, by originating level. See James A. Maxwell and J. Richard Aronson, *Financing State and Local Governments,* 3d ed. (Brookings Institution, 1977), chap. 1.

Table 1-3. Percentage Shares of Direct and Own-Financed General Expenditures by Federal, State, and Local Governments, Selected Fiscal Years, 1940–77

Fiscal year	Direct general expenditures			Own-financed general expenditures		
	Federal	State	Local	Federal	State	Local
1940	49	15	36	54	20	25
1950	62	13	24	67	16	17
1960	65	15	20	71	17	12
1966	56	15	28	63	18	19
1971	51	19	31	59	22	20
1976	46	20	34	59	22	19
1977	47	20	33	60	22	18

Sources: George F. Break, "Changing Roles of Different Levels of Government," in Julius Margolis, ed., *The Analysis of Public Output* (Columbia University Press for National Bureau of Economic Research, 1970), pp. 198–99; U.S. Census Bureau, *Census of Governments, 1972*, vol. 6: *Topical Studies*, no. 4: *Historical Statistics on Governmental Finances and Employment* (GPO, 1974), pp. 35–36, 41–42, 44–45; Census Bureau, *Governmental Finances in 1975–76*, series GF76, no. 5 (GPO, 1977), pp. 19, 21, and *1976–77*, series GF77, no. 5 (GPO, 1978), pp. 19, 27. Figures are rounded.

penditures was relatively stable, at close to 15 percent; it then rose moderately to 20 percent by 1976–77 (table 1-3). Federal and local shares were more or less mirror opposites. Each began and ended the period in about the same relative position—the federal government with just under 50 percent of direct general expenditures and local governments with 33 percent. In the interim, however, the federal share rose to 65 percent in 1960 and then declined while the local share fell to 20 percent in 1960 and then rose again. Throughout the period the federal government was the dominant partner in the provision of services and transfers to the private sector, local governments a strong second, particularly at the beginning and the end of the period, and states the least important.

That picture changes significantly when the sources of the funds spent are taken into account. The federal government has increasingly been in the business of providing aid, with local governments as major recipients, while state governments act as middlemen, both receiving and paying out large amounts of grant funds. When relative importance is measured by own-financed general expenditures, the state's role remains about the same as its share of direct expenditures, but the federal share is considerably larger and the local share correspondingly smaller. In recent years, as table 1-3 shows, the local and state shares of own-financed expenditures have each been close to 20 percent while the federal share stood at 60 percent.

Table 1-4. Baseline Federal Budget Expenditures as a Percent of Nonrecession GNP, Selected Fiscal Years, 1955–77

Category	1955	1960	1965	1970	1975	1977
Total baseline expenditures	18.2	18.1	18.1	19.0	19.9	20.1
National defense and foreign affairs	11.2	9.5	8.1	6.9	5.7	5.4
Domestic programs	7.0	8.6	10.0	12.1	14.2	14.7

Source: Charles L. Schultze, "Federal Spending: Past, Present, and Future," in Henry Owen and Charles L. Schultze, eds., *Setting National Priorities: The Next Ten Years* (Brookings Institution, 1976), p. 328.

Expenditure Patterns

Basic trends in federal spending are more easily discerned if reported expenditures are adjusted both for the temporary effects of recurring recessions and for the direct impact of such episodic events as the Vietnam War. The baseline budget expenditures calculated by Charles Schultze with those adjustments indicate relative stability in the ratio of the series to nonrecession GNP—18 percent in the 1960s, 19–20 percent in the 1970s. They conceal two sharply divergent trends, however.[8] Whereas spending for national defense and foreign affairs fell from 11 percent of nonrecession GNP in 1955 to 5 percent in 1977, domestic expenditures rose from 7 percent to nearly 15 percent over the same period (table 1-4). Nearly all of that twenty-two-year growth in the domestic expenditure ratio is accounted for by the increase in transfer payments to individuals, from 3 percent to 8 percent of nonrecession GNP, and by intergovernmental grants, from 0.5 percent to 2 percent of nonrecession GNP (table 1-5). Each of the remaining broad groups of domestic expenditures stood at just over 2 percent of nonrecession GNP in 1977. Social services and investment, however, experienced much the greatest rate of growth during the 1955–77 period, as table 1-5 shows.[9]

Where growth in federal domestic expenditures did occur between 1955 and 1977, a major cause was discretionary legislation creating new programs or expanding old ones rather than expansionary pres-

8. "Federal Spending: Past, Present, and Future," in Henry Owen and Charles L. Schultze, eds., *Setting National Priorities: The Next Ten Years* (Brookings Institution, 1976), pp. 323–69.

9. About 40 percent of the expenditures for the physical and economic environment and two-thirds of those for social services and social investment are made in the form of intergovernmental grants. General revenue sharing is not included in the figures given in table 1-5. However, that program became significant only in 1977 when it was 0.4 percent of nonrecession GNP. Ibid., pp. 334–35.

Table 1-5. Baseline Federal Domestic Expenditures as a Percent of Nonrecession GNP, by Major Category, Fiscal 1955 and 1977

Category	1955	1977
Transfer payments to individuals	3.2	8.4
Retirement, disability, and unemployment	2.8	6.9
Low-income assistance	0.5	1.5
Physical investment and economic subsidies	1.6	2.1
Social services and investment	0.6	2.1
Overhead and net interest	1.6	2.2
Addendum: Grants to state and local governments	0.5	2.2

Source: Schultze, "Federal Spending," pp. 333–34.

sure on established programs.[10] The picture of growth in state and local general expenditures is quite different when spending is allocated among three major factors—increasing work loads (such as rising school and welfare populations), higher prices, and improvements in the scope and quality of services. Between 1955 and 1969 they contributed 26 percent, 44 percent, and 30 percent, respectively, to the growth of state and local general expenditures. Between 1962 and 1972 the comparable allocations were 13 percent, 52 percent, and 35 percent. Table 1-6 shows how variable the influences of these three causes of growth were among the major functional categories of state and local expenditures. Nevertheless, it is clear that, on the average, exogenous factors were more important determinants of growth at the state and local than at the federal level.

The rapid growth in federal grants has, of course, had a major influence on intergovernmental relations, but one that is already showing signs of decline. The significant federal fiscal dividends that the Brookings Institution's annual analyses of the federal budget projected in the early 1970s[11] have been harder and harder to find in recent years.

The rapid growth in federal aid to low-income families and in ex-

10. Ibid., p. 346.

11. The first of the series was Charles L. Schultze, with Edward K. Hamilton and Allen Schick, *Setting National Priorities: The 1971 Budget* (Brookings Institution, 1970). Owen and Schultze, *Setting National Priorities: The Next Ten Years,* and Joseph A. Pechman, ed., *Setting National Priorities: Agenda for the 1980s* (Brookings Institution, 1980) differed from the others by focusing on longer run issues, in many of which intergovernmental relations are an important dimension. Also of special interest here are the discussions of urban problems in the 1973, 1978, and 1979 budget analyses and of intergovernmental grants in the 1972 and 1974 budget volumes and in the 1980 agenda volume.

Table 1-6. Percentage Increase in General Expenditures of State and Local Governments, by Function and Factor, 1955–69 and 1962–72

Period and function	Increase during period	Share of increase attributed to		
		Work load	Price	Scope and quality
1955–69				
General expenditures	246	26	44	30
Local schools	233	32	52	16
Higher and other education	658	25	36	39
Public welfare	282	...	30	70
Highways	139	51	42	7
Hospitals and health	238	19	44	37
Basic urban services	244	23	51	27
Administration and other	247	18	38	44
1962–72				
General expenditures	177	13	52	35
Local schools	157	10	59	32
Higher and other education	329	26	38	36
Public welfare	314	−6	16	90
Highways and parking	84	37	81	−18
Hospitals and health	196	37	55	9
Police and fire protection	163	39	63	−1
Sewerage and sanitation	142	11	71	18
Financial administration and general control	152	10	65	25
Other and unallocable	178	10	52	37

Sources: Charles L. Schultze and others, *Setting National Priorities: The 1972 Budget* (Brookings Institution, 1971), p. 139; Emil M. Sunley, Jr., "State and Local Governments," in Owen and Schultze, *Setting National Priorities: The Next Ten Years*, p. 379.

penditures on social services and investment since 1945 is a development consistent with the widely supported goal of concentrating financial responsibility for redistributive programs at the federal level. Even so, state and local governments still have an important fiscal commitment to this basic function of government. Nearly half of the money for public welfare expenditures still came from state and local governments in 1976–77, for example, and numerous other state and local programs provide important kinds of support to low-income groups.[12]

12. In 1976–77, 53 percent of the public welfare and medicaid expenditures made by state and local governments were from federal sources, 37 percent from state, and 10 percent from local, with wide variations in these shares from one state to another. U.S. Advisory Commission on Intergovernmental Relations (ACIR), *Significant Features of Fiscal Federalism, 1978–79 Edition,* Report M-115 (U.S. Government Printing Office, 1979), p. 24.

Table 1-7. Major Sources of U.S. Tax Revenue, 1948, 1950, and 1978

Type of tax	Total tax revenue[a]			General tax revenue[a,b]		
	1948	1950	1978	1948	1950	1978
	Percent					
Individual income	32.4	27.0	34.6	35.7	30.2	46.3
Corporation income	21.3	26.4	11.9	23.5	29.5	15.9
Sales and excise	20.8	20.1	14.9	22.9	22.5	19.9
Property	10.7	11.0	10.0	11.8	12.2	13.4
Estate and gift	1.9	1.3	1.1	2.1	1.4	1.5
Social insurance	9.3	10.5	25.2	...	...	...
Other	3.6	3.7	2.2	3.9	4.2	3.0
	Billions of dollars					
Total amount	57.4	67.2	650.1	52.1	60.2	486.0

Source: *National Income and Product Accounts*, pp. 96, 108; *Survey of Current Business*, vol. 59 (July 1979), pp. 39–40. Figures are rounded.
a. Excludes Federal Reserve Banks' corporate profits tax accrual.
b. Excludes contributions for social insurance.

Some difficult policy trade-offs in the future between federal defense and domestic programs are also suggested by past spending trends, quite apart from the influence of international events. Simple fiscal arithmetic indicates that domestic federal programs cannot continue to expand at the expense of defense spending, as they did between 1955 and 1977. Any stabilization or reversal of these two broad expenditure trends will inevitably shift the focus in intergovernmental relations from the design of intergovernmental grants to the regional location of defense facilities and production operations.

Tax Systems

The U.S. tax system has grown and changed significantly in structure since 1948; by 1978, total tax revenues at all levels of government had increased more than eleven times, from $57 billion to $650 billion. Some parts of the system outpaced even that high average growth rate (table 1-7). Social insurance contributions rose sharply from 9 percent of the total to 25 percent, and the individual income tax also increased. The property tax more or less maintained its relative position, while sales and excise taxes fell and corporation profits taxes plummeted from 21 percent to 12 percent of the total.

Another view of the U.S. tax structure, which excludes social insurance contributions, concentrates on taxes used to finance general

Table 1-8. Major Sources of Federal, State, and Local Tax Revenue, 1948 and 1978

	General tax revenue					
	Federal		State		Local	
Type of tax	1948	1978ᵃ	1948	1978ᵃ	1948	1978ᵃ
	Percent					
Individual income	51.0	65.8	7.4	26.1	0.7ᵇ	5.3ᵇ
Corporation income	25.6	21.7	8.7	9.0	...	...
General sales	...	...	21.9	30.3	3.2	7.7
Selective sales and excise	20.2ᶜ	9.9ᶜ	34.2	17.9	2.9	3.3
Property	...	...	4.1	2.0	88.6	80.1
Estate and gift	2.3	2.1	2.7	1.8	...	...
Motor vehicle	...	...	8.8	4.3	...	...
Other	0.9	0.6	12.3	8.6	4.6	3.6
	Billions of dollars					
Total amount	37.9	271.8	6.7	114.0	6.6	81.5

Source: ACIR, *Significant Features of Fiscal Federalism, 1978–79 Edition*, Report M-115 (GPO, 1979), pp. 44, 53, 55. Figures are rounded.
a. Estimate.
b. Includes minor amounts of corporation income tax revenue.
c. Includes customs duties.

government operations.[13] Here the individual income tax stands out as the major gainer, its relative share rising from 36 percent to 46 percent between 1948 and 1978 (table 1-7). The property tax gained moderately in relative importance, sales and excise taxes declined moderately, and the corporation income tax fell off sharply.

The growing importance of the individual income tax shows up at all levels of government (table 1-8). For the federal government this tax became even more of a mainstay, rising to 66 percent of general tax revenues by 1978. For state governments the trend toward greater use of the income tax meant more diversification of the tax structure. While excises dropped from first to third position, general sales taxes rose from 22 percent of the total in 1948 to 30 percent in 1978, and individual income taxes shot up from 7 percent to 26 percent. The property tax maintained its unchallenged preeminence as a source of local revenue throughout the period, but with a slightly reduced

13. Gasoline taxes might also be excluded in principle, but the national income and product accounts provide separate tabulations only for state taxes.

margin—89 percent of local taxes in 1948, 80 percent in 1978. General sales taxes expanded their share and the individual income tax moved from virtual obscurity in 1948 to a 5 percent relative position in 1978.

These tax trends resolved some problems but created others. State and local tax systems were strengthened in a number of ways. Their scope was broadened, their responsiveness to economic growth increased, and their equity rating in general improved. The general move toward greater reliance on the individual income tax, however, did not come about without challenge. Structural weaknesses that were bearable when less was demanded of the tax became more and more irritating, and inflationary pressures served only to intensify the complaints. Some observers viewed these pressures as welcome incentives for individual income tax reform, while others turned their attention to alternative sources of federal revenue. The late 1970s witnessed an unprecedented resurgence of interest in federal tax reform proposals that had been frequent topics of discussion but typically not taken seriously as active policy options. These included integration of the individual and corporation income taxes, conversion of the existing income tax into a levy on personal consumption expenditures through exclusion of all forms of saving from its base, and adoption of a value-added tax.[14] Whether the country will turn to such radical reforms to relieve the mounting pressure on the weak points of the income tax remains to be seen. Whatever course is taken at the federal level, however, is bound to affect all the aspects of intergovernmental relations that this study examines—state and local tax coordination, intergovernmental grants, and urban fiscal systems.

Structural Aspects of Intergovernmental Relations

The optimal design of governments in a federal system is a subject that is both fascinating and frustrating. Few can aspire to expertise in more than one or two of its many dimensions—political, social, cultural, linguistic, religious, historical, and economic. Though the economic gains and losses from restructuring government are frequently

14. See Charles E. McLure, Jr., *Must Corporate Income Be Taxed Twice?* (Brookings Institution, 1979); Joseph A. Pechman, ed., *What Should Be Taxed: Income or Expenditure?* (Brookings Institution, 1980). The relevance of such tax policies to the design of urban revenue systems is discussed in chap. 5 below.

dwarfed by other considerations, they are nonetheless important enough to matter. Some of the factors determining these economic benefits and costs are volatile and uncertain. Others are more certain in their manner of operation but frequently productive of conflicting effects. Difficult trade-offs must be considered, and simple, unambiguous answers are not to be expected.

Strong professional interest in economic theories of fiscal federalism has led to the development of various approaches to the question. One of the most influential—Musgrave's multiple theory of the public household—divides governmental objectives into three broad groups or branches.[15] The stabilization branch seeks to keep the economy on a stable growth path that reflects the society's relative preferences for present and future consumption and minimizes the occurrence of excess unemployment and inflation. The distribution branch concentrates on the achievement of an optimal distribution of income and wealth in the society. Both of these branches, Musgrave argues, should perform their functions primarily at the central, or national, level of government.[16] This does not mean, of course, that other governmental levels have no role to play in these two fiscal areas.[17]

Indeed, recent history provides many illustrations of the eternal ambivalence in a federal system of government. On the one hand, a recognition that national economies are increasingly interdependent, restricting the capacity of individual nations to pursue independent stabilization policies without regard to what is occurring elsewhere, has led to the creation of such coalitions as the European Monetary System and the European Economic Community. On the other hand, the frustrations that come with being a part of a large federal system caused states like California to give serious thought during the recession of 1974–75 to the possibility of taking matters into their own hands and initiating state policies designed to stimulate economic

15. Richard A. Musgrave, *The Theory of Public Finance: A Study in Public Economy* (McGraw-Hill, 1959), pt. 1.

16. Ibid. See also Stanley Engerman, "Regional Aspects of Stabilization Policy," in Richard A. Musgrave, ed., *Essays in Fiscal Federalism* (Brookings Institution, 1965), pp. 7–62; Wallace E. Oates, "The Theory of Public Finance in a Federal System," *Canadian Journal of Economics,* vol. 1 (February 1968), pp. 37–54, and *Fiscal Federalism* (Harcourt Brace Jovanovich, 1972), chaps. 1, 2.

17. The theoretical case for not allocating all stabilization and distribution responsibilities to the national government is presented by Albert Breton and Anthony Scott, *The Economic Constitution of Federal States* (University of Toronto Press, 1978), chaps. 10, 11.

recovery. The same tensions are found in the operation of distribution policies. The worldwide mobility of wealthy individuals and multinational corporations is both a constraint on independent national behavior and an incentive for international cooperation.[18] While such problems may be particularly bothersome for small countries, others of a different nature perplex large nations with heterogeneous populations. For them the challenge is to find a policy for redistributing income that does not displease any one group too much or, failing that, to provide an escape valve by decentralizing the distribution branch without creating the same mobility distortions that plague small countries.[19]

Finding a satisfactory design by which the stabilization and distribution functions can be effectively handled is important not only to those two branches but also to the third, the allocation branch, which is responsible for carrying out the classical functions of government. Its prime task is to secure the best possible use of society's scarce resources. This is done directly by allocating these resources between the private and public sectors of the economy and indirectly by regulating and controlling the use of resources in the private sector. There is no presumption that either of these two kinds of activity should be the sole responsibility of any one level of government. Some sensible division must be made, and there are many conflicting factors to be considered in attempting to determine an optimal design of governments.[20]

The geographical incidence of the benefits of a government program ideally should be uniform throughout the jurisdictional area covered by the government operating the program and zero everywhere else. Programs with nationwide benefits should be assigned to the central government; those with regional benefits should be operated by regional governments; and so on down the geographical

18. See, for example, C. Fred Bergsten, Thomas Horst, and Theodore H. Moran, *American Multinationals and American Interests* (Brookings Institution, 1978); J. A. Kay and M. A. King, *The British Tax System* (Oxford: Oxford University Press, 1978), pp. 234–36; Jagdish N. Bhagwati and Martin Partington, eds., *The Taxing Brain Drain,* vol. 2: *The Brain Drain and Taxation* (Amsterdam: North-Holland, 1976).

19. Mark V. Pauly, "Income Redistribution as a Local Public Good," *Journal of Public Economics,* vol. 2 (February 1973), pp. 35–58.

20. See Richard M. Bird and Douglas G. Hartle, "The Design of Governments," in Richard M. Bird and John G. Head, eds., *Modern Fiscal Issues: Essays in Honor of Carl S. Shoup* (University of Toronto Press, 1972), pp. 45–62.

scale. The geographical confines of benefits, however, are not always easy to pin down. Moreover, creating a separate governmental unit for each benefit area would undoubtedly result in an excess of governments. In any case, the geographical concentration of particular program benefits creates a presumptive case for fiscal decentralization, with due account being taken of the spillover of benefits and of ways of mitigating its distorting effects.[21]

The fact that different people have different views concerning the public goods government should provide is another factor favoring decentralization.[22] Even where there is little disagreement as to the amounts and kinds of public services that should be provided, tastes may well differ as to what decisionmaking process should be used, how the chosen programs should be financed, and how much relative importance should be attached to them.[23] Whatever the differences are, a decentralized system of governments can accommodate them by enabling people with like tastes to live together and design their public sectors accordingly. Such an arrangement makes possible a higher level of economic and political welfare than does a centralized system that requires everyone to consume the same menu of public goods and to choose and produce it in the same way.

Even if there are few material differences in taste concerning local public goods, a decentralized system of independent governments offers protection against the use of the public sector by one group to enhance its private interests at the expense of other groups. Each

21. William C. Brainard and F. Trenery Dolbear, Jr., "The Possibility of Oversupply of Local 'Public' Goods: A Critical Note," *Journal of Political Economy,* vol. 75 (February 1967), pp. 86–90; Werner Z. Hirsch, Elbert W. Segelhorst, and Morton J. Marcus, *Spillover of Public Education Costs and Benefits* (Institute of Government and Public Affairs, University of California, Los Angeles, 1964); Werner Z. Hirsch and Morton J. Marcus, "Intercommunity Spillovers and the Provision of Public Education," *Kyklos,* vol. 22, no. 4, pp. 641–60; Alan Williams, "The Optimal Provision of Public Goods in a System of Local Government," *Journal of Political Economy,* vol. 74 (February 1966), pp. 18–33, and "Local Autonomy and Intercommunity Spillover Effects," in Ernesto d'Albergo, ed., *Scriti "In Memoria" di Antonio de Viti de Marco,* vol. 2: *Studies "In Memoriam" of Antonio de Viti de Marco* (Bari, Italy: Cacucci Editore, 1972), pp. 623–41.

22. Oates, *Fiscal Federalism,* chap. 2.

23. Lyle C. Fitch, among others, has stressed the fact that in the city government game, which has many players with many different objectives, output is only one, and not necessarily the most important, objective. "Scale and Effectiveness of Urban Government: A Commentary," in Bird and Head, *Modern Fiscal Issues,* p. 181.

citizen may have a greater influence on government, in other words, when the option to exit is available.[24]

Competition among governments may also be a means of controlling the level, as well as the composition, of public spending. A large number of independently operating units, like a large number of separate business enterprises, is likely to be more responsive to consumer demands, and more efficient in satisfying them, than a small number of units each with significant monopoly powers.

Minimization of costs in the public sector requires, among other things, a careful design of governments so that each can operate at or near its most efficient output level. Some programs requiring large initial investments or highly specialized labor services may be impossible for small units to operate efficiently. Other programs may deteriorate rapidly in quality as the size of the clientele served increases beyond some point. These general rules are clear enough, but their implementation is no easy matter. Difficulties in measuring program outputs make the cost of operation hard to identify. Even when cost ranges can be estimated, it may well turn out that they are so different for different programs that there is no optimal size for a government that has to operate all of them.[25] Program assignment fortunately is not the only way of dealing with economies and diseconomies of scale. Governments that are too small to operate certain programs may still be able to buy their services from governments that are large enough. Governments that are too large to provide some services well on a unified basis may retain general responsibility for them but decentralize their management to appropriate subunits.

In addition to attaining efficiency in the production and delivery of a given set of government services, it is also important to minimize the costs of deciding what those services should be. Channels of communication between citizens and government are vital. The government needs information about voter tastes and voters must communicate those tastes. The costs not only of providing services but of getting public feedback on them are likely to rise with increased

24. Albert O. Hirschman, *Exit, Voice, and Loyalty: Responses to Decline in Firms, Organizations, and States* (Harvard University Press, 1970).

25. A summary of the findings of empirical studies of scale economies and diseconomies in different local government programs is given in Werner Z. Hirsch, *The Economics of State and Local Government* (McGraw-Hill, 1970), p. 183.

government centralization. Where personal interrelationships are an important determinant of program quality, assignment to small government units has important advantages. Moreover, direct political access to small local units of government appears to be valued by many people.[26] On the other hand, the quality of some government services, particularly those of a highly specialized nature, is more likely to be impaired than improved by extensive public participation in the programs. In addition, political realities may mean that certain public sector goals can be more successfully pursued at federal or state than at local levels.

Resolution of the conflicts in voter tastes and views is also important. Both big and small governments may have difficulty here—the former because taste diversities are likely to be greatest for them, the latter because their opportunities for compromise may be too limited. Medium-sized units may have an advantage here because they operate enough different programs to achieve consensus through a package of benefits.[27] Of course, such logrolling may simply convert the conflict among competing beneficiary groups into one between those groups and taxpayers.

Would-be architects of an optimal structure of governments, then, must deal with a complex set of conflicting criteria.[28] Since some favor centralization and some decentralization, and since few government functions fall clearly at either end of that spectrum,[29] some kind

26. Amos H. Hawley and Basil G. Zimmer, *The Metropolitan Community: Its People and Government* (Sage, 1970).

27. Julius Margolis, "Metropolitan Finance Problems: Territories, Functions, and Growth," in *Public Finances: Needs, Sources, and Utilization,* A Conference of the Universities–National Bureau Committee for Economic Research, A Report of the National Bureau of Economic Research (Princeton University Press, 1961), pp. 229–70.

28. In its discussion of the subject, the ACIR deals with twelve criteria divided into four target areas of economic efficiency, equity, political accountability, and administrative effectiveness. *Substate Regionalism and the Federal System,* vol. 4: *Governmental Functions and Processes: Local and Areawide,* Report A-45 (GPO, 1974), pp. 82–99. See also Russell L. Mathews, ed., *Fiscal Federalism: Retrospect and Prospect,* and *Responsibility Sharing in a Federal System,* Research Monographs 7 and 8 (Canberra: Centre for Research on Federal Financial Relations, Australian National University, 1974 and 1975).

29. See, for example, the ACIR's discussion of community schools, family social assistance, police protection, and land-use controls in *Governmental Functions and Processes,* pp. 52–67. See also their general discussion of assignment policies, pp. 1–25.

of intermediate, federated model with shared powers is strongly suggested. Today's world provides numerous examples of movements toward a federated model from both directions as well as movements of federated systems toward either pole. Devolution of power in a centralized, unitary system is an important policy issue in such countries as Belgium, Nigeria, Iran, and the United Kingdom.[30] Greater coordination and consolidation of decentralized governments, in contrast, has long been a goal of urban fiscal reformers,[31] and federated metropolitan systems of varying kinds have been set up in Canada and in parts of the United States. Paradoxically, while centralization may have made Canada's city governments more efficient and equitable, further decentralization of power from the federal to the provincial governments may well be the price of national survival. The same conflicting forces may be seen, in less virulent forms, in the United States. They show up in the debates between advocates of federal categorical grants and supporters of general revenue sharing and also in the struggles of urban experts to strike a viable compromise between demands for greater neighborhood independence and desires for stronger regional governance.

The most ambitious approach to the design of governments would be to specify a mix of public goals and analyze the cost effectiveness of alternative functional assignments, jurisdictional sizes, and intergovernmental fiscal relations. Though the analytical results of such general theoretical models could not be expected to be very specific, the models might provide a helpful reference framework for policymakers. Breton and Scott base their least-cost and representative-government models of federalism on the rationale that any specific public sector structure stems from the need to economize on various kinds of organizational costs, which are typically neglected in orthodox economic theories of federalism.[32] On the supply side

30. Alan Peacock, "The Political Economy of Devolution: The British Case," in Wallace E. Oates, ed., *The Political Economy of Fiscal Federalism* (Lexington Books, 1977), pp. 49–63.

31. Alan K. Campbell and Roy W. Bahl, eds., *State and Local Government: The Political Economy of Reform* (Free Press, 1976); Thomas P. Murphy and Charles R. Warren, eds., *Organizing Public Services in Metropolitan America* (Lexington Books, 1974); Committee for Economic Development, Research and Policy Committee, *Reshaping Government in Metropolitan Areas* (New York: CED, 1970).

32. *Economic Constitution of Federal States,* chaps. 7, 8.

there are the costs of setting up and operating governmental institutions and the costs of coordinating the activities of different units. On the demand side, citizens are seen as engaging in two main types of activity designed to secure for them the bundle of government services they most want. They use their voices in every way possible to influence the way things are run (signaling), and then if necessary their feet, to make their exit from units providing inferior public good packages (mobility). In their least-cost model, functions are assigned and jurisdictional boundaries drawn solely in order to minimize the investment of scarce resources in the administration and coordination of activities by governments and the signaling and mobility of citizens. One question of interest is how these costs vary as the structure of governments is moved toward centralization or decentralization. Though some qualitative a priori deductions can be made—for example, that the costs of citizen mobility and government coordination are both inversely related to the degree of centralization—other relationships are indeterminate. That few definite conclusions can be drawn[33] becomes even more apparent when the utility-maximizing goals of politicians and bureaucrats are added to the picture in the representative-government model. However, the models do provide a carefully integrated way of thinking about public sector structures.

Even in a completely static economic and social environment the optimal design of governments would be an elusive target. In the rapidly changing real world, the quest will probably be even more frustrating, except in the unlikely event that all major developments point in the same direction.[34] Indeed, a prime consideration in the design of governments is surely the adaptability of different structures to unexpected events. By this test, precision in the assignment of functions is no virtue. The very vagueness, ambiguity, and complexity of the federal system that trouble many critics may well be its great strength.[35]

Such a conclusion certainly does not mean that there is not plenty of room for improvement, and the country does not lack for activity

33. Ibid., chap. 5. One definite conclusion is that failure to take full account of organizational costs will seriously bias and frustrate the search for optimal government structures.

34. See Oates, *Fiscal Federalism*, chap. 6.

35. Bird and Hartle, for example, conclude that "the main problem with present governmental structures is not that they are complex, but rather that they are too *rigid*." "Design of Governments," p. 61.

in this area. Nearly one-third of the over thirty-three hundred municipalities responding to a 1975 survey conducted by the Advisory
Commission on Intergovernmental Relations had transferred a function to another governmental unit between 1965 and 1975.[36] The
great variety and flexibility of the instruments used to assign and
reassign functions below the state level is vividly shown in a series of
studies by the ACIR.[37] They examine the utility of three procedural
measures now in use—intergovernmental service agreements, the
transfer or consolidation of specific functions, and the A-95 federal-
aid review process[38]—and the viability of four types of basic structural units.[39] The substate districts and regional councils that help
carry out the A-95 reviews typically exert an indirect influence on
functional assignments through their funding, planning, and coordination activities.[40] The more traditional regional special districts,
which doubled their numbers in the seventy-two largest metropolitan
areas between 1957 and 1972,[41] are important in such functional
areas as health, sewerage, and utilities. To some, these areawide
districts are insulated and unresponsive bureaucracies that tend to
impede the restructuring of local government; to others, they are

36. ACIR, *Pragmatic Federalism: The Reassignment of Functional Responsibility*, Report M-105 (GPO, 1976), p. 27.

37. *Performance of Urban Functions: Local and Areawide*, Report M-21 (GPO,
1963). *Substate Regionalism and the Federal System*, vol. 1: *Regional Decision
Making: New Strategies for Substate Districts*, Report A-43 (GPO, 1973); vol. 2:
Regional Governance; vol. 3: *The Challenge of Local Governmental Reorganization*,
Report A-44 (GPO, 1974); vol. 4: *Governmental Functions and Processes;* vol. 5:
A Look to the North; vol. 6: *Hearings on Substate Regionalism* (GPO, 1974). *Prag-
matic Federalism.*

38. Circular A-95 was issued by the Office of Management and Budget in 1969
to implement title IV of the Intergovernmental Cooperation Act of 1968. Its goals
were, through planning and coordination, to improve the whole process by which
federally funded projects are initiated, reviewed, and implemented by state and local
governments. Its functions are advisory and supportive, but understanding of its
processes has been slow in developing. In May 1978, an OMB evaluation concluded
that much of its potential was still unrealized. ACIR, *Governmental Functions and
Processes*, p. 40, and "In Washington: Not Many Answers," *Intergovernmental Perspective*, vol. 5 (Winter 1979), p. 38. See also ACIR, *Regional Decision Making*,
chap. 5; Darryl M. Bloom, "A-95: What's It all About?" *Planning for Progress*
(North Carolina Office of State Planning), vol. 7 (Winter/Spring 1975), pp. 12–14,
25, reprinted in Wright, *Understanding Intergovernmental Relations*, pp. 377–87.

39. ACIR, *Governmental Functions and Processes*, pp. 31–69.

40. ACIR, *Regional Decision Making*, chaps. 3, 4, 6, 7.

41. ACIR, *Governmental Functions and Processes*, p. 46.

an important transition en route to better regional governance structures.[42]

The county, the largest general-purpose local governmental unit in
most urban areas, has been the focus of reformers seeking an alternative to single-purpose special districts. Their aim is to create comprehensive urban counties by assigning all major responsibilities for
regional services to them. Though this choice of multi- over single-
function governmental units has long been favored by the ACIR,[43]
its research shows that most urban counties have yet to become very
effective providers of regional services.[44] Clearly, special districts
and urban counties have disadvantages as well as advantages, and
it may be that neither is a satisfactory solution in the long run to the
problem of providing services over a wide area. A better vehicle may
be the comprehensive city-county consolidations and federations
created in Miami, Jacksonville, Indianapolis, and Nashville in the
1950s and 1960s,[45] and elected regional councils like that created in
Portland, Oregon in May 1978.[46]

Local government restructuring, then, has mainly been a process of
pragmatic incrementalism and is likely to continue in that vein. Economists can contribute to its improvement at the micro level by making
benefit-cost analyses of specific proposals, though the redistributive
(equity) effects of changes are likely to be of greater consequence
than gains and losses in efficiency. At the macro level a general theoretical framework, such as the least-cost models of Breton and Scott,
can provide valuable guidance and might impart some degree of order
to the ad hoc procedures by which functional reassignments are carried out.[47] Adoption of the ACIR's recommendations in this area
would provide the political and institutional means for bringing

42. ACIR, *Challenge of Local Governmental Reorganization*, p. 2. See also
ACIR, *Regional Decision Making*, chap. 2.
43. ACIR, *The Problem of Special Districts in American Government*, Report
A-22 (GPO, 1964).
44. ACIR, *Challenge of Local Governmental Reorganization*, chap. 4.
45. ACIR, *Regional Governance*, chaps. 1, 2.
46. "States Tackle Tough Federal Issues," *Intergovernmental Perspective*, vol. 5
(Winter 1979), p. 27. The voters authorized a three-county metropolitan service
district with the usual areawide planning and A-95 review responsibilities and with
the prospect of providing selected services if further approval of a district tax source
were forthcoming.
47. ACIR, *Pragmatic Federalism*, p. 70.

systematic direction and analyses to bear on this important aspect of intergovernmental relations.[48]

The design of governments is not a topic suited to many tastes. Few aspire to understand its theoretical refinements, and it is seldom suggested as an electoral issue of consequence. Yet the fiscal world is far from static in its intergovernmental dimensions. Seemingly small incremental changes can eventually add up to major structural alterations. It is well to keep them in mind and to test their effects and promise.

The Rise of Competitiveness in Fiscal Relations

Intergovernmental relations have passed a number of milestones and gone through several distinct phases since 1953 when the U.S. Commission on Intergovernmental Relations, widely known as the Kestnbaum Commission, made the first official broad-based study of U.S. federalism since adoption of the Constitution. In 1959 the Advisory Commission on Intergovernmental Relations was created to study all dimensions of that important area of public finance and to make policy recommendations. In 1967 the ACIR, in a report on fiscal balance, identified three important sources of tension in the federal system.[49]

One source of trouble was the rapid growth of federal aid to state and local governments. As it turned out, the report provided an early and prescient assessment of an accelerating and diversifying trend in intergovernmental relations. The role of intergovernmental grants, discussed in chapters 3 and 4 below, bears little resemblance to what it was only a few years ago. To keep abreast of the changes, the ACIR undertook in 1974 a comprehensive study of the whole grant system that lasted several years and resulted in thirteen volumes of analysis, findings, and recommendations.[50]

A second source of tension spotted in 1967 was the rash of fiscal crises then besetting some of the nation's largest cities. Finding a

48. ACIR, *Governmental Functions and Processes*, pp. 19–25.

49. ACIR, *Fiscal Balance in the American Federal System*, Report A-31, 2 vols. (GPO, 1968), and a summary article with the same title by Will S. Myers, Jr., in *State Government*, vol. 4 (Winter 1968), pp. 57–64.

50. For a short summary of the work see ACIR, *In Brief: The Intergovernmental Grant System: An Assessment and Proposed Policies* (ACIR, 1978), and for a more detailed one *Summary and Concluding Observations: The Intergovernmental Grant System: An Assessment and Proposed Policies*, Report A-62 (GPO, 1978).

solution to these serious ailments was complicated, then as now, by
the multiform character of the troubles confronting urban America,
by uncertainty over the extent to which the cities might reasonably
be expected to handle matters on their own, and by controversy over
the particular ways in which state and federal governments could
help. These issues are discussed in chapter 5 below. The problem is
big and persistent.

The third source of tension cited by the ACIR was the greater
productivity and equity of the federal government's revenue system,
as compared to those generally characteristic of state and local governments. Throwing the spotlight on these disparities focused attention on ways of strengthening and improving the coordination of the
many components of the nation's tax system. Chapter 2 deals with
these aspects of intergovernmental relations. This, at least, is one
area in which definite progress has been made since 1967. Not only
are state and local revenue systems more productive and equitable
than they were, but the rate of growth in some of the factors that
pushed state and local expenditures relentlessly upward, such as
school enrollments and welfare caseloads, is now moderating or even
declining. In sharp contrast to the 1962–72 decade when state and
local expenditures had to rise faster than GNP simply to maintain the
1962 level and quality of services, there appears to be a reasonable
likelihood that between 1973 and 1986, significant improvements in
quality can be made without increasing state and local tax burdens or
that taxes can be reduced without a sacrifice in the flow of services.[51]
Projections of future fiscal conditions, of course, are subject to wide
margins of error. There is no doubt, however, that many state and
local governments enjoyed comfortable budgetary positions in the
1970s. The sector as a whole showed an operating surplus in the
national income and product accounts during 1972–73 and 1976–
78.[52] There is considerable evidence that these palmy days ended with

51. Emil M. Sunley, Jr., estimates that "in 1986 the 1973 revenue system will
produce 18.3 percent more than is required to maintain 1973 service levels." "State
and Local Governments," in Owen and Schultze, *Setting National Priorities: The
Next Ten Years*, p. 408.

52. *National Income and Product Accounts of the United States, 1929–74, Statistical Tables*, supplement to the *Survey of Current Business* (GPO, 1977), and
Survey, subsequent issues, table 3.4. During the decade, surpluses in state and local
social insurance funds rose steadily—from $6.8 billion in 1970 to over $23 billion
in 1978. These surpluses, however, are not ordinarily a direct source of funds for
operating expenditure programs, New York City to the contrary notwithstanding.

the decade, for the 1980s began amid indications of deteriorating surpluses and the reappearance of deficits.[53] The decline, however, may not be general. Budgetary ease for the sector as a whole is perfectly consistent with severe fiscal stringencies in particular states and cities, and vice versa.

Tension in intergovernmental relations is an essential condition of fiscal progress in federal systems. For the most part the changes it induces are too subtle and recondite to make much impression on the casual observer. This is not to say that no events of major significance ever occur. They do, but their effects are likely to be spread out over many years. Consider, for example, such important milestones as the passage of the State and Local Fiscal Assistance Act of 1972, the rendering of the Serrano and Rodriguez court decisions on school finance in 1971, 1973, and 1977,[54] and the approval, by nearly a two-thirds vote, of California's Proposition 13 in June 1978. The broad directional changes that such events are likely to set in motion may take years to develop fully. The early effects of revenue sharing are reasonably clear, but uncertainties created by the necessity of periodic renewal hover over the program and prevent its taking the course that it might if it were established as a permanent part of the federal grant system. School finance reform is still a largely unresolved issue, and the rising tide of tax and expenditure limitation movements may inaugurate an entirely new era in the history of intergovernmental fiscal relations.

Hard as the direct effects of such developments are to foretell, the indirect economic and political reactions present an even more baffling problem as they often follow Newtonian lines, producing effects directly opposite to those intended. Tracing these complex interactions requires skills in which economists and political scientists are becoming increasingly proficient.[55]

Whatever its future, the course of intergovernmental relations since World War II has been a complex, slow evolution, in which the prac-

53. "A Crunch Is Coming for State and Local Budgets," *Fortune*, February 12, 1979, p. 12. State and local operating deficits reappeared in the national income accounts in the second and third quarters of 1979.

54. *Serrano* v. *Priest*, C.3d 584, 487 P.2d 1241 (1971), *San Antonio Independent School District* v. *Rodriguez*, 411 U.S. 1 (1973), and *Serrano* v. *Priest*, 557 P.2d 929 (1977).

55. See, for example, Robert P. Inman and Daniel L. Rubinfeld, "The Judicial Pursuit of Local Fiscal Equity," *Harvard Law Review*, vol. 92 (June 1979), pp. 1662–1750.

tised eye can discern several distinct, though overlapping, phases.
Deil Wright has described the early stages as "increasingly specific,
functional and highly focused—in short, concentrated."[56] This pattern changed rather abruptly when Sputnik prodded the nation into
reexamining its goals. Finding itself well short of their achievement,
the country gave broad support to reformers with plausible programs
to offer. A guiding framework was provided by President Eisenhow-
er's Commission on National Goals, created in 1959. Its report,
ranging over a wide area, included Morton Grodzins' now famous
assessment of the federal system:

The American form of government is often, but erroneously, symbolized
by a three-layer cake. A far more accurate image is the rainbow or marble
cake, characterized by an inseparable mingling of differently colored in-
gredients, the colors appearing in vertical and diagonal strands and unexpected whirls. As colors are mixed in the marble cake, so functions are
mixed in the American federal system.[57]

Mixed up or not, the system proceeded to embark on a feverish phase
of creative energy that led to President Johnson's Great Society, then
to even greater expectations, and inevitably, to equally great disap-
pointments. "No administration since Franklin Roosevelt's first," as
Henry Aaron notes, "had operated subject to fewer political constraints than President Johnson's. . . . The result was a deluge of
legislation poorly planned, hastily enacted, and beyond the capacities
of the federal or state governments to administer."[58]

Reactions to this creative phase, again exacerbated by foreign
events, were not long in coming. Between 1965, when the Vietnam
War was just beginning to emerge as a controversial issue, and 1975
a remarkable change occurred; the national mood moved in effect
from overenthusiastic support for government spending aimed at
broad social reforms to overpessimistic rejection of all such efforts.[59]
In the process, intergovernmental relations moved to a new competi-

56. Wright, *Understanding Intergovernmental Relations*, p. 48.
57. "The Federal System," in U.S. President's Commission on National Goals,
Goals for Americans: Programs for Action in the Sixties, Report of the President's
Commission on National Goals and Chapters Submitted for the Consideration of the
Commission (Prentice-Hall for the American Assembly, Columbia University,
1960), p. 265.
58. Henry J. Aaron, *Politics and the Professors: The Great Society in Perspective*
(Brookings Institution, 1978), pp. 3–4.
59. Aaron provides a vivid analysis of the nature of these changes and the reasons for them. Ibid.

tive stage marked by divisiveness and multidimensional conflict. In the public sector, functional specialists competed for power with one another and also with policy generalists; suburbs competed with central cities for jobs, residents, and intergovernmental aid; the Frost-belt eyed developments in the Sunbelt with a cold and skeptical eye and the Sunbelt stared back through darkening glasses; and the all-important general taxpayer became restive and increasingly recep-tive to the idea of placing limits on the rate of growth of government activity. The response of the nation to these shifts in mood will determine the course of intergovernmental relations in the 1980s.

Regional Conflicts and Urban Crises

Two prominent features of the current, competitive phase of inter-governmental relations are the vigorous regional rivalries and the continuing fiscal shakiness of some of the largest cities. While these problems are probably not as serious as the melodramatic rhetoric of the times often suggests, they are serious challenges to the adapt-ability and rationality of the American federal system.

Active regional competition for labor, capital, and federal govern-ment benefits is one of the basic facts of economic and fiscal life in a large country. While this competitiveness is never absent from the scene, it does attract more public attention at certain times than at others. In the early 1960s Edwin C. Gooding, for example, saw the increasingly active competition by state and local governments for business as serious enough to constitute a "New War Between the States."[60] Important as these concerns were to Gooding and other fiscal experts, their highly technical nature gave them low public visibility for a number of years, but they became front-page news in 1975 when New York City embarked on its long and difficult strug-gle to stave off bankruptcy.[61] National attention was then drawn to the problems faced by some of the other older metropolitan areas in

60. See his four-part article with that title in the Federal Reserve Bank of Bos-ton's *New England Business Review,* October and December 1963, and July and October 1964.

61. Ken Auletta, *The Streets Were Paved With Gold* (Random House, 1979); Edward M. Gramlich, "The New York City Fiscal Crisis: What Happened and What is to be Done?" *American Economic Review,* vol. 66 (May 1976, *Papers and Proceedings, 1975*), pp. 415–29 (Brookings Reprint 319); and Ralph Schlosstein, *New York City's Financial Crisis: An Evaluation of Its Economic Impact and of Proposed Policy Solutions,* prepared for the Joint Economic Committee, 94 Cong. 1 sess. (GPO, 1975).

the Northeast and Great Lakes regions. Regional consciousness sharpened, and suddenly intergovernmental relations took center stage. The editors of *Business Week,* concerned about potential threats to national prosperity, concluded a special report on "The Second War Between the States: A Bitter Struggle for Jobs, Capital, and People" with a proposal that envisaged some fundamental changes in the nature of the federal system.[62] At about the same time the ACIR began a major study of regional growth problems.

It is no small irony that the rumors of regional conflicts began circulating widely at a time when regional differences in per capita incomes and in federal expenditures and revenues had narrowed to an unprecedented degree.[63] In 1929, per capita income in the richest region (the Mideast) was nearly 140 percent of the national average while in the poorest region (the Southeast) it was barely above 50 percent. By 1950, as figure 1-1 shows, the richest region (the Far West) was down to about 120 percent of the national average and the poorest (the Southeast) up to 68 percent. Thereafter this converging trend continued, but at a slower pace. In 1978 the regional differences ranged only from 112 percent to 87 percent of the national average.[64]

The patterns of regional incidence of federal expenditures and revenues have also been growing increasingly similar. Even determining what they are in a single year is a daunting task, but I. M. Labovitz, who has been dealing with these problems for many years, has estimated and compared these patterns for 1952, 1965–67, and 1974–76.[65] Tax revenues are allocated to the state of residence of the person bearing the tax burden,[66] and expenditures to the state where the

---

62. *Business Week,* May 17, 1976, pp. 92–114. Their proposals included a redirection of federal government programs to help slow-growth areas; more state financial support, and less local autonomy, for schools; and federalization and greater standardization of welfare. Ibid., pp. 112–14.

63. Janet Rothenberg Pack, "Frostbelt and Sunbelt: Convergence Over Time," *Intergovernmental Perspective,* vol. 4 (Fall 1978), pp. 8–15.

64. Among states the range in 1978 was from 73 percent and 79 percent in Mississippi and Arkansas, respectively, to 116 percent and 139 percent in Wyoming and Alaska. *Survey of Current Business,* vol. 59 (April 1979), p. 20. In these tabulations the Far West region excludes Alaska and Hawaii.

65. I. M. Labovitz, "Federal Expenditures and Revenues in Regions and States," *Intergovernmental Perspective,* vol. 4 (Fall 1978), pp. 16–23.

66. They are based on standard assumptions about tax incidence; for example, the corporation income tax is allocated half to shareholders and half to consumers. Ibid., p. 23.

Figure 1-1. Per Capita Personal Income as a Percent of the National Average, by Region, Selected Years, 1929–77

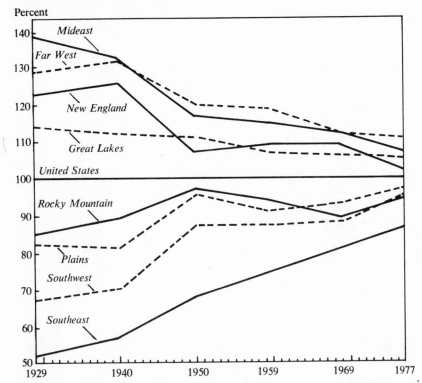

Source: Howard L. Friedenberg, "Regional Differences in Personal Income Growth, 1929–77," *Survey of Current Business*, vol. 58 (October 1978), p. 27. The Far West includes Alaska and Hawaii.

goods and services purchased by the government are produced or to the state of residence of persons receiving federal wage payments or transfers. When these distributions are converted into expenditure-revenue ratios (table 1-9), a definite narrowing of regional disparities is again apparent.[67] In 1952 the range was from a ratio of 0.75 in the Mideast to 1.51 in the Southeast; in 1974–76 it was from 0.75 in the Great Lakes to 1.13 in the Far West.

Interesting as these estimates are in their own right, they do not have any direct policy significance. A more progressive set of federal taxes and transfers, for example, could widen or narrow the differentials depending on the geographical location of taxpayers and beneficiaries. Such a policy change, however, should be evaluated on the

67. A narrowing of per capita income differentials implies, of course, a narrowing in some federal expenditure and revenue differentials.

Table 1-9. Ratio of Estimated Federal Expenditures to Estimated Federal Revenues, by State and Region, Fiscal 1952, 1965–67, and 1974–76

State	1952	1965–67	1974–76
United States	1.00	1.00	1.00
New England	0.78	0.95	1.01
Connecticut	0.86	0.92	0.90
Maine	0.96	1.14	1.20 ·
Massachusetts	0.74	0.90	1.06
New Hampshire	0.64	0.83	0.90
Rhode Island	0.68	1.17	1.08
Vermont	0.74	1.11	1.18
Mideast	0.75	0.75	1.02
Delaware	0.53	0.54	0.70
District of Columbia	1.10	2.16	4.48
Maryland	1.09	1.34	1.12
New Jersey	0.90	0.71	0.80
New York	0.61	0.62	0.95
Pennsylvania	0.86	0.71	0.95
Great Lakes	0.87	0.64	0.75
Illinois	0.69	0.59	0.71
Indiana	1.34	0.75	0.74
Michigan	0.87	0.58	0.78
Ohio	0.95	0.70	0.76
Wisconsin	0.85	0.67	0.77
Plains	1.20	1.15	0.97
Iowa	1.05	1.00	0.81 ·
Kansas	1.73	1.44	0.95
Minnesota	1.26	0.93	0.86
Missouri	1.01	1.09	1.10
Nebraska	1.12	1.26	0.90
North Dakota	1.56	2.04	1.30
South Dakota	1.52	1.67	1.32
Southeast	1.51	1.36	1.11
Alabama	2.03	1.52	1.28
Arkansas	2.15	1.29	1.18
Florida	0.82	1.15	0.94
Georgia	1.41	1.52	1.08
Kentucky	1.55	1.32	1.17
Louisiana	1.50	1.33	1.06
Mississippi	2.16	1.68	1.62
North Carolina	1.07	1.21	0.99
South Carolina	2.30	1.58	1.22
Tennessee	2.15	1.12	0.97
Virginia	1.57	1.73	1.36
West Virginia	1.15	1.02	1.19

Table 1-9 (continued)

State	1952	1965–67	1974–76
Southwest	1.46	1.37	1.03
Arizona	1.39	1.33	1.15
New Mexico	2.99	1.68	1.48
Oklahoma	1.56	1.36	1.21
Texas	1.34	1.35	0.94
Rocky Mountain	1.20	1.34	1.09
Colorado	0.98	1.33	1.04
Idaho	1.55	1.15	1.04
Montana	1.04	1.53	1.12
Utah	1.67	1.32	1.27
Wyoming	1.35	1.50	1.02
Far West	1.12[a]	1.27	1.13
California	1.06	1.32	1.15
Nevada	0.77	0.86	0.84
Oregon	0.96	0.80	0.91
Washington	1.58	1.24	1.19
Alaska	. . .	4.54	1.79
Hawaii	. . .	2.27	1.55

Source: I. M. Labovitz, "Federal Expenditures and Revenues in Regions and States," *Intergovernmental Perspective*, vol. 4 (Fall 1978), p. 17.

a. Omits Alaska and Hawaii, which were territories in 1952.

basis of its national equity and efficiency effects and not by its incidental geographical patterns. Federal procurement programs may have a highly concentrated or a highly diversified regional impact, depending on the relative importance of primary contractors and subcontractors. The one federal expenditure category for which interstate allocations are both statistically reliable and of some policy interest is aid to state and local governments. Table 1-10 compares the regional distribution of federal grants with those of the other major categories of federal spending in 1974–76.

Economic and fiscal convergence or not, regional rivalries and urban crises are not likely to disappear. Crises created by inflation, energy shortages, faltering economic growth, urban fiscal insolvency, and taxpayer restiveness and rebellion only add to the tensions. While these intensify the strains that make for pulling and pushing among regions and interest groups, the only peaceable long-term solutions lie in establishing the supremacy of such principles as self-reliance, efficiency, coordination, and equity. The recipe is old-fashioned, but history has often demonstrated its effectiveness. Without strong doses of it our federal Constitution could never have won approval.

Table 1-10. Distribution of Major Federal Government Expenditures, by Region, Fiscal 1974-76

Region	Total allocated expenditures	Aid to state and local governments	Personal income payments[a]			Military outlays except personnel	Interest on debt[b]	All other[c]
			Total	Civilian and military personnel	All other			
			Percent					
New England	6.2	6.3	5.6	3.8	6.2	10.8	5.4	2.8
Mideast	22.2	23.6	22.1	22.0	22.1	21.0	25.6	12.8
Great Lakes	15.1	16.4	15.7	9.8	17.9	9.6	19.3	5.5
Plains	7.1	7.2	7.1	6.0	7.6	7.2	7.5	4.5
Southeast	21.7	21.3	22.8	25.6	21.7	16.2	18.9	20.4
Southwest	8.4	7.6	8.5	10.6	7.7	8.9	7.8	7.8
Rocky Mountain	2.7	3.0	2.8	3.9	2.3	1.8	2.2	5.2
Far West	15.5	13.5	14.4	15.8	13.9	23.2	12.9	40.5
Alaska, Hawaii	1.1	1.1	1.0	2.4	0.6	1.3	0.4	0.5
			Billions of dollars					
Amount allocated	969.9	148.6	672.3	187.7	484.6	103.4	34.0	11.5

Source: Labovitz, "Federal Expenditures," p. 21.
a. Federal wage, transfer, and other expenditures that are personal income to recipients.
b. Excludes interest paid to individuals and nonprofit institutions, which is included in "personal income payments, all other." Also excludes interest paid to foreign holders of U.S. obligations.
c. Comprises research and development contracts of the National Aeronautics and Space Administration, civil prime contracts of the Department of Defense, and hospital and domiciliary construction contracts of the Veterans Administration.

CHAPTER TWO

Tax Coordination

A FEDERAL fiscal system faces two kinds of tax coordination problems. One is concerned with different levels of government using the same tax base, the other with businesses or individuals carrying out economic activities in different taxing jurisdictions at the same level of government. Both vertical overlapping, as of the federal and a state government taxing the same income, and horizontal overlapping, as between taxing authorities of different states, are widespread in the United States. The economic inefficiencies and taxpayer inequities that they are capable of creating can seriously impair the general welfare.

Those conditions that make for a large amount of horizontal tax overlapping—businesses operating in many state and taxpayers living in one community and working in another—have long been familiar characteristics of the American economy. Nor is vertical tax overlapping unfamiliar to the average taxpayer—in 1980 individual income taxes were being collected by the federal government, forty-five states and the District of Columbia, and a large number of local governments;[1] corporation profits taxes were levied by the federal

1. While most states levied taxes on the total income of all taxpayers, Connecticut, New Hampshire, and Tennessee restricted them to certain kinds of income or to special taxpayer groups. See U.S. Advisory Commission on Intergovernmental Relations (ACIR), *Significant Features of Fiscal Federalism, 1976–77 Edition*, vol. 2: *Revenue and Debt* (U.S. Government Printing Office, 1977), pp. 99, 194–201. No changes occurred between 1976 and 1980.

Table 2-1. Federal, State, and Local Tax Collections, by Major Type of Tax, 1976–77

Instrument	Federal	State	Local	Total yield (billions of dollars)
Customs duties	100	0	0	5.4
Property tax	0	4	96	62.5
Corporation income tax	86	14	a	64.1
Individual income tax	84	14	2	186.0
Motor vehicle and operators' license fees	0	93	7	4.9
General sales and gross receipts taxes	0	85	15	36.3
Alcoholic beverage excises	70	28	2	7.7
Tobacco excises	40	58	2	6.0
Motor fuel excises	35	65	1	14.1
Public utility excises	40	34	26	6.9
Other excises	31	60	9	7.4
Death and gift taxes	80	20	b	9.1
All other taxes	18	58	23	9.3

Source: U.S. Census Bureau, *Governmental Finances in 1976–77*, series GF77, no. 5 (U.S. Government Printing Office, 1978), p. 19. Figures are rounded.
a. Minor amount included in "individual income tax."
b. Minor amount included in "all other taxes."

government and forty-six states and the District of Columbia; death taxation was shared by the federal government and forty-nine states; and excises on gasoline, tobacco, and alcoholic beverages were widely used at all three levels of government.

In spite of these multiple usages, which have increased over time, the major tax sources have remained highly concentrated at one or another level of government (table 2-1). Almost all property tax receipts flowed into the hands of local governments in 1976–77; nearly 85 percent of income tax revenues went to the federal government; and the states collected the dominant share of motor vehicle, general sales, and motor fuel taxes. These, of course, are national patterns which conceal the great diversity that exists among states and local areas. Within this complex picture there is no doubt that vertical tax overlapping is important enough to warrant serious consideration.

Goals of Vertical Tax Coordination

Coordinating tax policy in a federal system of government is an extremely complicated business. It means preserving principles of economic efficiency and taxpayer equity while somehow maintaining the fiscal independence of state and local governments. One major source of conflict is the lack of any wide agreement over how personal and business income should best be defined for tax purposes. As a result, states may prefer to define their own tax bases rather than simply to conform to the federal base. Federal income tax law is further complicated by the use of numerous exceptions and exemptions, known as tax expenditures, that adjust the tax base so as to give special treatment to activities thought to serve various national goals.[2] Since some federal tax expenditures do little or nothing to serve the purposes of specific states or localities, while others may be positively inimical to their interests, there is good reason for state tax bases to be clearly differentiated from the federal. Moreover, the after-tax distribution of income resulting from federal policy may not be universally acceptable, and some state legislators may find it expedient to devise ways of modifying or even counteracting the effects of federal policy, depending on the tastes of their constituencies. Even those states that share the values and standards inherent in federal law can be expected to maintain full, separate control over the amount of their tax revenues.

There may be good and attractive reasons, then, for not coordinating state and local taxing activity in many situations, but this can seriously impair both fiscal equity and economic efficiency. Differing levels of taxation among jurisdictions may hamper interstate trade, create artificial incentives and disincentives for the location of businesses, and distort the allocation of national resources among different industries. A decentralized fiscal system also provides obvious incentives for states to discriminate against out-of-state individuals and businesses in the imposition of taxes. This tendency has been minimized, however, by a long series of Supreme Court decisions involving the privileges and immunities, the commerce, and the equal protection clauses of the U.S. Constitution, which have created a set of effective barriers to any significant amount of overtaxation of outsiders.[3] Undue diversity and complexity in state and local tax laws

2. The Congressional Budget Act of 1974 requires a listing of tax expenditures each year in the federal budget. See, for example, *Special Analyses, Budget of the United States Government, Fiscal Year 1980*, Special Analysis G, pp. 183–211.

3. Jerome R. Hellerstein, "State Tax Discrimination Against Out-of-Staters," *National Tax Journal*, vol. 30 (June 1977), pp. 113–33.

Table 2-2. Degree of State or Local Control of Taxation in Various Coordinated Taxing Schemes

Instrument	Tax administration	Choice of tax base	Choice of tax rate structure	Choice of tax rate levels	Determination of tax revenues
Coordinated tax administration	Full	Full	Full	Full	Full
Coordinated tax bases	Full	Partial or none	Full	Full	Partial
Tax supplements					
Own rates on higher level base	Full	Partial or none	Full	Full	Partial
Surcharge on higher level tax	Full	None	None	Full	Partial
Centralized tax administration					
Flexible	None	None	Full or none	Full	Partial
Tax sharing	None	None	None	None	None

create wasteful administrative and compliance costs which are especially burdensome to small interstate businesses. Uncertainty about possible changes in different state and local tax laws can make for too little business investment in some areas and too much elsewhere. And lack of coordination is quite likely to place inequitable burdens on different taxpayers.[4]

A number of difficult trade-offs must be considered, then, in the process of trying to achieve enough intergovernmental tax coordination to eliminate the worst effects of vertical tax overlapping. Table 2-2 lists a variety of alternatives and shows the degree of fiscal independence they allow state and local governments to exercise.

4. See the discussion of competing goals of federal legislation in the interstate taxation area in ACIR, *State and Local "Doing Business" Taxes on Out-of-State Financial Depositories,* report of a study under Public Law 93-100, Committee Print, Senate Committee on Banking, Housing and Urban Affairs, 94 Cong. 1 sess. (GPO, 1975), pp. 369–98.

Separation of Tax Sources

The most obvious solution to vertical overlapping is to divide the major tax sources among the different levels of government, granting each of them exclusive jurisdiction over its own type of tax. Suppose that tax collections in a given year were as follows:

	Federal	State
Tax A	80	10
Tax B	10	50

Under these circumstances, would it not be more efficient for the federal government to relinquish its share of tax B in return for state abandonment of tax A? With revenue maintenance, the tax structure would then be:

	Federal	State
Tax A	90	0
Tax B	0	60

But tax B might be such that it could not be effectively administered by the states acting alone, and the move would consequently be precluded on grounds of efficiency. Moreover, the shift might interfere unduly with the states' freedom to design their own tax structures. States that used tax A but not tax B might strongly prefer that pattern to the alternative. Finally, though the plan involved no change in national tax revenues, it would almost certainly have diverse effects among the states. Those that experienced a net increase in federal tax burdens would undoubtedly be less than enchanted with the reform. So would those that had relatively small portions of the B tax base.

Suppose alternatively that vertical tax overlapping never existed, that tax A was used only by the federal government and tax B exclusively by the state governments. If state governments should find themselves in need of additional revenue, they would face additional administrative and compliance costs that might well be less (or at least not significantly more) with tax A than with its principal competitors. If, in addition, tax A were judged high on equity grounds and relatively free of undesirable economic effects, the choice should go to it, even though its adoption increased the amount of vertical overlapping in the tax system.

Suffice to say that the drawbacks are such that tax separation has had only limited success in the United States and does not appear to be an important policy issue.[5] Some limited moves may be made toward separating tax bases, but most of the problems of tax coordination will need to be solved by other means.

Coordinated Tax Administration

One fairly obvious approach to tax coordination, especially attractive because it allows each government considerable freedom in designing and levying its own taxes, is cooperative or joint tax administration. In the income tax field, federal-state cooperation began as early as 1931, but for a long time its accomplishments were limited, partly for lack of appropriate economic incentives.[6] State officials could, and did, examine federal tax returns with profit to their governments. But the Internal Revenue Service was not reimbursed for the costs it incurred (state payments for audit abstracts and photostatic copies accrued to the U.S. Treasury's general fund) and thus did not seek to expand the cooperative arrangements. Again, in 1949, when a plan was developed for coordinating federal and state income tax audits, it was found that the states had little quid to offer for the federal quo.

The real breakthrough came in 1957, when the first of a series of federal "agreements on the coordination of tax administration" was signed with Minnesota (by 1976 forty-three income tax states and the District of Columbia had them). These agreements are distinguished by the breadth and flexibility of their terms. Exchange of information is not confined to income taxes, and there is a wide variety of useful data that the states can supply the IRS from their administrative files. The agreements form a mutually beneficial basis for federal-state coordinated tax administration. The IRS gains more than it spends on these agreements, and states can profit in several

5. James A. Maxwell and J. Richard Aronson have proposed partial or full federal withdrawal from excise taxation of tobacco and alcoholic beverages. "Federal Grants and Fiscal Balance: The Instrument and the Goal," *Public Policy*, vol. 20 (Fall 1972), pp. 579–93. The ACIR has considered, as a solution to the problems created by nonuniform state tax rates on cigarettes, a repeal of states' right to levy cigarette taxes. *Cigarette Bootlegging: A State AND Federal Responsibility*, Report A-65 (GPO, 1977), pp. 41–44.

6. ACIR, *Intergovernmental Cooperation in Tax Administration* (ACIR, 1961), pp. 2–7.

ways. Besides the direct revenue gains, which can be substantial,[7] there are prospects of improved taxpayer compliance with the law and the likelihood that, with federal technical assistance, the quality of state auditing will be greatly improved. Finally, there is the practicability, particularly as federal and state income tax laws are made more nearly alike, of setting up joint audit procedures, with savings to both governments.

Coordinated tax administration need not be confined to federal-state fiscal relations. States can help their local governments deal with both property and nonproperty taxes; counties can assist smaller jurisdictions within their boundaries; and adjoining units can cooperate to set up more efficient, pooled administration of their common taxes.[8]

Coordinated Tax Bases

The use of similar, or even identical, income tax bases by federal, state, and local governments can not only facilitate joint tax administration but also reduce the time and money spent by taxpayers in meeting their fiscal obligations. State and local individual income taxes are most closely coordinated with the federal tax in the three states (Nebraska, Rhode Island, and Vermont) that have made their tax a percentage of the federal tax. Next come the states that have adopted the federal individual income tax base (that is, federally defined taxable income) as their own, with minor modifications. To that base they apply their own separate tax rates.[9] Governments seeking greater independence have adopted federally defined adjusted gross income, with minor modifications; they use their own definitions of personal deductions and exemptions to compute the state or local tax base.[10] Governments with a coordinated base that allows substantial independence use their own tax base definitions or have adopted substantially modified versions of federally defined adjusted

7. Federation of Tax Administrators, "Federal-State Exchange of Tax Information," Research Report 48 (Chicago: FTA, 1962), pp. 15, 19.

8. For specific recommendations on state-local coordination, see ACIR, *State Legislative Program,* 10 vols. (GPO, 1975), especially vols. 2, 3.

9. In 1976 Alaska, Hawaii, Idaho, New Mexico, North Dakota, Oklahoma, Oregon, and Utah used this approach. ACIR, *Revenue and Debt,* p. 209, table 110. Modifications of federal taxable income usually included exemption of interest on federal notes and bonds and taxation of interest on the debt securities of other states.

10. In 1976 twenty-one states followed this intermediate approach. Ibid.

gross income.[11] A considerable degree of nonconformity also is found
in the definition of state corporate income tax bases. Many states
start with the federal definition of corporate taxable income, but they
add a great variety of modifications to it.[12]

The costs of income tax nonconformity depend very much on
which structural elements of the law are involved. Adding federally
exempt bond interest to the state base or including long-term capital
gains at full value, for example, creates little difficulty. Separate state
rules for depreciation or depletion deductions, on the other hand,
add accounting complexities that can be highly burdensome, especially for small firms.

Close conformity to federal income tax law is not without its costs
either. Structural changes in the federal base alter state tax revenues.
Countervailing state tax changes have to be promptly designed and
enacted to offset undesirable effects. If the equity and efficiency of
the federal base changes are not widely accepted in the state, questions arise about the virtues of continued conformity. And revenues
from a coordinated state income tax may be more difficult for budget
makers to predict. Whether federal legislators are more prone than
state legislators to change the tax structure seems very much an open
question, however. Conformity, in short, does introduce some uncertainty for states. This must be balanced against the clear benefits
of income tax coordination.[13]

Local income and retail sales taxes can also be closely coordinated
with the corresponding state tax base.[14] This is the general rule in
states that use local sales taxes. Among states with local income taxes,

11. Alabama, Arizona, Arkansas, California, Mississippi, New Jersey, North
Carolina, Pennsylvania, and South Carolina used this nonconforming approach in
1976. Ibid.

12. Thirty-three states start with the federal definition; thirteen define their own
independent tax bases. Ibid., p. 223. See also ACIR, *State and Local "Doing Business" Taxes*, pp. 262–71.

13. Whenever federal policy calls for changes in the individual income tax, the
selection of instruments to be used, ranked from best to worst in terms of intergovernmental tax coordination goals, is: an income tax surcharge or refundable tax
credit; a change in bracket tax rates; a change in personal deductions or personal
exemptions; a change in the definition of adjusted gross income.

14. For a discussion of the issues involved in coordination see Albert L. Warren,
"Integrating Local Non-Property Taxes Into the State Tax Structure," in National
Tax Association—Tax Institute of America, *Proceedings of the Sixty-Seventh Annual Conference on Taxation, 1974* (Columbus, Ohio: NTA-TIA, 1975), pp. 307–
13.

however, coordinated systems are less common.[15] The first city income tax, that enacted by Philadelphia in 1939, had to be restricted, because of state legal requirements, to wages and salaries and to the profits of sole proprietors and partners. Since then some states, such as Alabama, Delaware, Kentucky, Missouri, Ohio, and Pennsylvania, have chosen to use payrolls also while broad-based taxes have been adopted in such states as Indiana, Maryland, Michigan, and New York.

Tax Supplements

The ultimate in coordinated tax bases is provided by tax supplements. In Scandinavian countries this device is an important part of local finance.[16] It allows municipalities to vary their tax receipts each year in accordance with their financial needs since they either use the tax base defined by a higher level of government and apply their own rates to that base, or they levy a surcharge on the tax owed to the higher level of government. They need not have their own administrative staffs because the local tax is collected by the higher level of government, along with its own tax, and the proceeds are returned to the municipalities, which simply pay for the services provided to them by the collecting government. Taxpayers benefit also since they fill out only one tax form; in some cases they are probably unaware that they are paying taxes to two different governments.

In the United States, tax supplements have been most successfully used to integrate state and local sales taxes. Pioneered by Mississippi in 1950, the arrangement is now widely used. One coordination problem is created by the existence of overlying units of local government. If both counties and cities are authorized to levy a local sales (or income) tax, for example, city dwellers can find themselves subject to two levies instead of one. California, which allows counties and cities each to levy a 1 percent general-purpose local sales tax, solves this overlapping problem by requiring that counties give a credit for whatever tax (which can be less than 1 percent) the cities within their

15. ACIR, *Local Revenue Diversification: Income, Sales Taxes and User Charges*, Report A-47 (GPO, 1974), p. 55.

16. Harold M. Groves, "New Sources of Light on Intergovernmental Fiscal Relations," *National Tax Journal*, vol. 5 (September 1952), pp. 234–38; Martin Norr, Frank J. Duffy, and Harry Sterner, *Taxation in Sweden*, Harvard Law School, International Program in Taxation, World Tax Series (Little, Brown, 1959), pp. 519 ff.

boundaries choose to levy.[17] Colorado and Tennessee give counties the right to preempt the tax. In New York, cities and counties have equal prior rights; each level may claim up to one-half of the maximum permitted local sales tax rate.[18]

Local income tax supplements are used in Maryland, where counties are authorized to levy individual income taxes varying between 20 percent and 50 percent of the taxpayer's state tax liability.[19] All revenue goes to the county of residence regardless of where the taxpayer works, and cities within each county are allocated a specified share of the proceeds (except Baltimore which is a combined city-county). That precedent need not be followed in coordinated state-local income tax systems. At the cost of some additional administrative complexity, cities and counties could be allowed to apply their supplemental tax rates to a state base that included income earned within their jurisdictions by nonresidents. Overtaxation of commuters and interlocal businesses could be eliminated by a system of tax credits like that provided in the Federal-State Tax Collection Act of 1972.

State individual income tax supplements on the federal tax are precluded in their pure form by the intergovernmental immunity doctrine that is presumed to shield interest on government bonds from taxation by other governments. This hands-off policy has long been a target of tax reformers who advocate full taxation of bond interest of each level of government by the others on a nondiscriminatory basis. Federally defined adjusted gross income could then be used without modification for tax supplements by any state or local government choosing to do so. Strong state and local opposition to any such change, however, makes removal of this barrier unlikely.

A less serious barrier to state supplements on the federal income tax is the deductibility of state income taxes in the computation of the

17. California counties also receive a 0.25 percent local sales tax supplement which must be used for transportation purposes. See California State Board of Equalization, *Annual Report 1978–79, Fiscal Year Ended June 30, 1979,* Statistical Appendix, p. A-30.

18. ACIR, *Local Revenue Diversification,* pp. 46–47. Tax credits are used as a coordinating device in California, Washington, and Utah; the absence of either credits or prior rights in Alabama, Alaska, and Louisiana means that some overlapping of burdens can occur.

19. In 1979 eighteen counties and Baltimore City were using the maximum 50 percent rate, and the remaining five counties used rates of 20 percent, 35 percent, 40 percent, and 45 percent.

federal tax base. State supplements designed to avoid the anomaly of allowing deduction of their own tax could be applied only to a suitably modified federal tax base or tax liability. Similar adjustment problems exist for states that allow deduction of the federal income tax in determining the state base, as well as for any state not wishing to allow deductibility for local property or general sales taxes. None of these adjustments for federal tax deductions would be necessary, however, if the deductions were converted to tax credits.[20] Many reformers have supported such a federal tax change for some time.

Federal Tax Deductions and Tax Credits

Three different criteria for a well-designed, multiple-level tax system support the idea of federal deductibility for specific state and local taxes. Using the individual taxpayer's ability to pay taxes as a criterion for deductibility, the best measure from the federal government's point of view is one that excludes all state and local tax burdens that are not directly associated with commensurate state and local government benefits.[21] Accordingly, state and local individual income taxes should be deductible. Whether retail sales and general property taxes should also be deductible is less clear. Each has both benefits-received and ability-to-pay features that cannot readily be disentangled or measured. However, available evidence clearly indicates

20. A tax deduction reduces the size of the base to which the appropriate tax rates are applied in computing the taxpayer's final tax liability. A tax credit, in contrast, is subtracted directly from the tax liability. The value of a tax credit, therefore, is the same for everyone, while the value of a tax deduction increases with the marginal tax rate of the taxpayer.

21. If the distributional goals of government were allocated entirely to the federal level, so that state and local governments taxed only on a benefits-received basis, there would be no case, under this test, for federal deductibility of state and local taxes. The crucial element in making the case, in other words, is the presence of ability-to-pay elements in state and local tax systems. Conversely, if state governments wish to participate in the redistribution function, it might be argued that they should use ability-to-pay tax measures computed *net* of federal ability-to-pay tax burdens (notably the federal individual income tax) and gross of federal transfer payments. Federal deductibility alone, however, may well be a sufficient guarantee of tax equity in a federal system. See George F. Break, "Tax Principles in a Federal System," in Henry J. Aaron and Michael J. Boskin, eds., *The Economics of Taxation* (Brookings Institution, 1980); Richard A. Musgrave, *The Theory of Public Finance: A Study in Public Economy* (McGraw-Hill, 1959); Charles E. McLure, Jr., "Economic Aspects of Alternative Methods of Intergovernmental Financing," paper prepared for a symposium on Political Aspects of Intergovernmental Resource Allocation, Center for Adult Education, University of Maryland, May 12, 1970.

that they are widely regarded by the public as ability-to-pay taxes, and hence both they and state and local individual income taxes should be deductible by everyone in the computation of adjusted gross income rather than allowable only as personal deductions by itemizers. Under this logic, state and local tax deductions would no longer be a federal tax expenditure but rather an essential element in the computation of the proper federal income tax base.

The standard tests of a good tax system—equity, efficiency, and neutrality—also argue for deductibility. Uncoordinated multiple use of progressive income taxes could, in theory, result in a total marginal tax rate of 100 percent or more; federal deductibility of state and local individual income taxes is a simple means of precluding such confiscatory rates. Though in any well-run federal fiscal system such a device should not be needed to keep down tax rates, its presence in an imperfect world has obvious political appeal. In addition, deductibility may be a useful means of keeping total income tax rates below levels that impair economic incentives and thus create inefficiency.

The criterion of fiscal neutrality requires that when state and local individual income taxes are deductible, general sales and property levies should be deductible as well. If the federal government is not to bias state and local tax choices in favor of income taxes, states should be left free to determine the basic structure of their tax systems, and in particular to use income, sales, and property taxes on equal terms. There is a substantial body of opinion, however, that opposes this kind of tax neutrality on equity grounds. The total tax system is seen to be less progressive than it ought to be, and sales and property taxes are viewed as regressive levies whose use by state and local governments should be discouraged by the removal of federal deductibility. Opponents of this view either dispute both of the equity arguments on which it is based or argue that any likely equity gains would be far outweighed by the loss of state and local freedom of choice over the use of alternative ability-to-pay taxes.

The rationale for federal deductibility of state and local taxes that is of most direct interest here is that it provides a means both of strengthening state and local taxing powers and of moderating the locational distortions created by interjurisdictional differences in tax burdens. In a number of ways this is the weakest of the three rationales. Its goal is debatable, for there is no satisfactory evidence that state and local taxing powers are intrinsically inadequate, and opinions differ sharply over the importance of tax differentials as an inducement to locate in a particular area. But even if this goal does command wide public support, it is not clear that deductibility is the preferred policy instrument for achieving it.

Among tax instruments, the other main contender for accomplishing this aim would be a fractional tax credit for specified state and local taxes. On equity grounds, a tax credit is preferable because it confers the same tax advantage on everyone, while deductibility favors high- over lower-income taxpayers. On efficiency grounds, deductibility would be the better instrument if voter opposition to higher state and local taxes steadily rises with the income level of the taxpayer while tax credits would be the better choice if that opposition is independent of taxpayer income. Since household, rather than business, locational decisions are mainly at issue here, deductibility seems preferable.[22] Credits may have a more obvious effect in mitigating burdens for the average taxpayer than equal-yield personal tax deductions; but a deduction to be used in the computation of adjusted gross income might have as high a visibility as a tax credit. Tax credits, of course, may be more visible to state and local government officials, and hence more of a factor in their choice of alternative revenue sources. They may also be seen as a more coercive fiscal device since, unlike deductibility, they cannot be defended as an essential element in the computation of federal taxable income.

Regardless of the instrument chosen, individual income, general sales, and most household property taxes would qualify for federal assistance under a policy designed both to strengthen state and local taxing powers and reduce locational distortions. However, a distinction seems appropriate between property taxes paid on a taxpayer's principal residence and those paid on vacation or second homes. Only the former are likely to be important determinants of voter opposition to higher local property taxes; thus an efficient federal tax subsidy would be confined to primary-home property taxes.

All three rationales for federal deductions or credits support the logic which led to the repeal, in the Revenue Act of 1978, of federal

22. Business locational decisions are, to be sure, affected by differences in state and local business tax levels, and these differentials are significantly reduced by federal deductibility rules. Such deductibility, however, is an integral part of the computation of business net income and, as such, not a policy instrument usable to change the effectiveness of state and local taxing powers in a federal system.

deductibility of nonbusiness state and local gasoline taxes. There is a strong case for either a deduction or a credit for state and local individual income taxes. Deduction is an unambiguous requirement under an ability-to-pay rationale, a preferred instrument for achieving efficiency, equity, and neutrality, and one of several alternatives by which local taxing powers could be strengthened and locational distortions minimized. A tax credit is a possible instrument under the two latter rationales, but its choice should be based on systematic comparisons with all other available instruments, including those on the expenditure side of the budget.

The treatment of nonbusiness property and retail sales taxes should be closely related to that accorded state and local individual income taxes. Retention of deductibility for any one of this set creates a strong presumption favoring deductibility for all. All three can properly be regarded as ability-to-pay levies. Retention of income tax deductibility to further intergovernmental equity and efficiency goals would require retention of sales and property tax deductibility under the neutrality and efficiency rules. It is true that sales tax deductibility does create serious administrative problems, as the Carter administration stressed when it proposed in 1978 that this feature of federal law be repealed.[23] Compliance costs can be kept within acceptable bounds only by use of the standard sales tax tables, and these, of course, only specify average sales tax burdens for different-sized families at different levels of adjusted gross income. These sales tax tables, however, do serve some useful purposes. By informing consumers of the approximate magnitude of their sales tax burdens, which would otherwise be highly uncertain in most people's minds, the tables help place state and local spending and taxing decisions on a more informed basis. By reflecting the average impact of changes in the level and structure of sales tax burdens, the tables also maintain at least a rough degree of federal neutrality toward state and local choices among the main ability-to-pay taxes in the overall revenue system.

Full neutrality toward state and local revenue systems could be achieved only by denying deductibility or tax credit status to all state and local taxes. Only then would choices between user charges and public prices on the one hand and income, property, and sales taxes

---

23. U.S. Treasury Department, *The President's 1978 Tax Program: Detailed Descriptions and Supporting Analyses of the Proposals* (1978), pp. 51–54.

on the other be free of federal tax biases. Such a change, however, does not appear to have strong public appeal. Until it does, state and local benefit financing by means of user charges and fees will be discouraged to some degree by federal individual income tax policies.

Centralized Tax Administration

Centralized administration, which can take two main forms, is the ultimate in vertical tax coordination. Under the more flexible version a higher level government undertakes to administer the taxes imposed by lower level governments, all of which remain free to set their own tax rates and to vary them according to their own fiscal needs. Such a coordinated individual income tax system was defined and made available to states by the Federal-State Tax Collection Act of 1972.[24]

Under a second version of centralized tax administration—tax sharing—the higher level government imposes a uniform tax everywhere and then returns some portion of the tax yield obtained from each lower level jurisdiction to governmental units therein. The basis for sharing is, in short, the source of the tax revenue. Since tax rates are made uniform throughout the country, the dangers of interstate tax competition are avoided. While the arrangement may be both productive and efficient, it does reduce the flexibility of state tax systems. To alter their receipts from the centrally administered tax, states must first agree among themselves on what needs to be done and then have the desired changes made by the federal government.[25] This lack of lower level control and responsibility raises two broad questions about tax sharing. Why should the lower governments' shares be distributed on the basis of source rather than need or fiscal capacity, and why should those shares be tied to one specific tax of the higher level government rather than being funded from general revenues? By seeking the ultimate in intergovernmental tax coordination, in other words, tax sharing plans run into close competition with intergovernmental grants-in-aid and should be analyzed in that context.

INDIVIDUAL INCOME TAXES. The flexible form of centralized individual income tax administration proposed in the Federal-State Tax

24. Title 2 of Public Law 92-512, 86 Stat. 936. Title 1, the State and Local Fiscal Assistance Act of 1972, inaugurated general revenue sharing.

25. Canada's federal tax abatements, which apply to both individual and corporate income taxes, are a tax sharing arrangement. See ACIR, *In Search of Balance: Canada's Intergovernmental Experience* (GPO, 1971).

Collection Act of 1972, inviting states to enter into agreements with
the secretary of the treasury to have their taxes administered by the
federal government at no cost to them, would create substantial conformity between the tax bases of the two levels.[26] The plan gives states
an opportunity to reduce their administrative costs significantly[27] and
taxpayers a way to fulfill their state income tax obligations by com-
pleting a short additional schedule on their federal 1040 forms.[28] In
addition, it would give participating states a one-time revenue gain
as a result of putting the faster-operating federal withholding system
into operation.[29] (Those gains, however, presumably could be
achieved independently by any income tax state that made appropriate changes in its withholding system.)

The model federal-state collection system allows for three variations on the state tax treatment of income. The first permits a state to
apply its own rates to each resident's federal taxable income after
mandatory adjustments are made by subtracting any interest on federal debt securities and by adding deductions claimed for state or
local income taxes and also any interest on the bonds of other state
and local governments.[30] Optional adjustments can in addition be

26. Uncertainty about congressional intentions regarding payment of administrative costs was removed by the Tax Reform Act of 1976 (P.L. 94-455, section
2116) which states that no state will be charged, directly or indirectly, for federal
administration of its individual income tax.

27. Otto G. Stolz and George A. Purdy estimate that a typical state might save
at least half of its individual income tax administration costs through the elimination
of routine processing. "Tax Simplification and Efficiency Through Federal Collection," *Tax Notes,* June 13, 1977, p. 8.

28. Tax withholding could, however, become more complicated for employers
whose employees are residents of several contracting states. Jerome Kurtz, "Federal
Collection of State Individual Income Taxes," in NTA-TIA, *Proceedings, 1977,*
p. 15.

29. The gain for states with income taxes was estimated in 1972 at $1 billion at
fiscal 1970 income levels. Joint Committee on Internal Revenue Taxation, *General
Explanation of the State and Local Fiscal Assistance Act and the Federal-State Tax
Collection Act of 1972* (GPO, 1973), pp. 54, 71–72; Kurtz, "Federal Collection of
State Individual Income Taxes," p. 18. The costs of starting up the system were estimated in 1973 at $22.5 million if ten states chose to participate and at $33.3 million
if all states joined; incremental operating costs have been placed at $1.30 a return
with a total volume of 60 million returns.

30. Participating states may exempt interest on their own debt securities completely, or tax it completely, or tax only interest on new security issues. Joint Committee, *General Explanation,* p. 56.

made to allow for a state minimum income tax as well as credits for income taxes paid to other state and local governments, and a nonrefundable credit for state sales taxes (the latter provision added by the Tax Reform Act of 1976).[31] The second variation also applies to residents and makes their tax a percentage of the federal tax. The only mandatory adjustment in this tax supplement frees interest on federal debt securities from the state tax; the federal minimum tax is a built-in feature. States may, if they wish, use any of the other adjustments required or permitted under the preceding plan.

States using either of these methods of taxing residents' income may also apply a tax supplement plan to the income of any nonresidents who derive at least 25 percent of their wage and business income from sources within the taxing state. A basic guarantee is that nonresidents must not be taxed more heavily than residents.[32]

Like all tax supplement plans, this one gives states little choice over the fundamental structure of their individual income tax bases. They can, however, determine both the structure and level of their own tax rates. Changes for any given tax year can be made as late as November 1.[33]

Federal collection of state individual income taxes would mean lower compliance costs for taxpayers and might well reduce state administrative expenses more than it added to federal costs. Arrayed against these gains, however, are some important losses. Contracting states would sacrifice whatever advantages they see in having an income tax structure different from that of the federal government, and

31. The 1976 act eliminated the 1972 requirement that two states, with at least 5 percent of federal individual income tax returns, agree to participate before the piggybacking system could begin. Any state, regardless of size, may enter the system on its own.

32. For details of the law see ibid., pp. 51–72.

33. The terminal date allows the federal government time to prepare the state tax schedules to be mailed as part of taxpayers' federal income tax packets. Late-in-the-year congressional changes in federal individual income tax laws might be satisfactorily handled by the state delegating its rate-setting authority for income taxes to its executive branch (as Nebraska does) so that any required changes could be made quickly. Or protective provisions could be included in the state's agreement with the Treasury, so that any state tax shortfalls created by late congressional action could be covered, for example, by interest-free federal government advances repayable in the following year. See Stolz and Purdy, "Tax Simplification," p. 10.

whenever Congress enacted federal income tax reductions, state politicians would face two unpleasant options—either allowing state revenues to decline or raising state tax rates to counteract the federal changes.[34] States would have to rely entirely on federal auditing and enforcement, and those with strong auditing programs would find that inadequate (the Treasury Department's attempt to lay out rules for supplementary state audits contributed to a five-year delay in the issuance of implementing regulations for the 1972 act).[35] In any case, ACIR staff studies do show that significant progress was made between 1965 and 1976 toward the goal of bringing state and federal individual income tax law into conformity.[36]

CIGARETTE TAXES. Centralized federal administration for other taxes appears much less likely than for state individual income taxes. Recurrent complaints about large revenue losses from illegal interstate cigarette smuggling activities[37] should stimulate interest in a coordination plan proposed by the ACIR. It would replace the tax stamp system with a requirement that each cigarette manufacturer add to his invoice the amount of the tax imposed by the state to which the shipment was directed.[38] The federal government would then collect both its own and all state taxes and remit the latter to their respective jurisdictions. Since this would shift state cigarette tax collection from a large number of jobbers, wholesalers, and retailers to

34. One solution to this dilemma, which has been adopted in Canada, would be for the federal government to provide a revenue guarantee to all contracting states. However, as John Shannon has noted, such an arrangement could add a large unrestricted, source-oriented, federal grant program to the federal system. "State Income Taxes—Living With Complexity," *National Tax Journal*, vol. 30 (September 1977), p. 341.

35. Kurtz, "Federal Collection of State Individual Income Taxes," pp. 18–19.

36. Shannon, "State Income Taxes," p. 341.

37. The ACIR has estimated the revenue gains and losses from smuggling by comparing the existing state pattern of per capita cigarette sales with the pattern that would exist if there were no tax evasion. In 1975 total state losses came to $391 million, and the gains were only $54 million. Proportions of cigarette tax revenues lost ranged from highs of 19–20 percent in Washington and Connecticut to a low of 1 percent in South Dakota. The highest relative gainers were New Hampshire and Kentucky (47 percent and 35 percent of revenues, respectively) and the smallest were Maryland and Colorado (less than 1 percent of revenues). ACIR, *Cigarette Bootlegging*, pp. 63–66.

38. ACIR, *State-Federal Overlapping in Cigarette Taxes*, Report A-24 (GPO, 1964), pp. 53–62, and *Cigarette Bootlegging*, pp. 55–57.

only a few manufacturers, large savings in state administrative costs could be expected.[39] A similar arrangement might be applied to alcoholic beverage taxes.

DEATH TAXES. Federal administration of state death taxes, though attractive because of the administrative complexities inherent in this area, has elicited more discussion than action. Considerable diversity among state inheritance and estate taxes is probably the main factor inhibiting coordination.[40] In 1926, in an attempt to stimulate greater tax coordination and to moderate state competition for wealthy residents, the federal government enacted a 100 percent estate tax credit, subject to a proportional ceiling. State estate taxes could be fully offset against as much as 80 percent of the federal estate tax liability. This type of tax credit is a very crude instrument, for in effect it reduces the burden of state estate taxes to zero up to the federal ceiling, but makes no reduction at all for state taxes above that level. The result is an almost irresistible incentive to states to enact "pickup" taxes but no incentive to go beyond that point.[41] A fractional estate tax credit without a ceiling, in contrast, would avoid the credit's sharp cutoff point and provide a continuing incentive for states to increase their use of death taxes.

The significance of the federal estate tax credit as a coordinating instrument is greatly reduced because the ceiling is tied to federal liabilities computed at 1926 tax rates, which range only up to 16 percent. Conversion to current federal estate tax rates, of 18–70

39. The ACIR placed the average state cost of administering a stamp system at 4–5 percent of state revenues, compared with a cost of less than 0.03 percent of revenues for federal administration. *State-Federal Overlapping*, pp. 32–50. The 1975 revenue gain was estimated at about $87 million, or 2.5 percent of gross cigarette tax revenue. *Cigarette Bootlegging*, p. 56. In 1978 Congress took a different approach to the problem in order to support state cigarette tax enforcement. It enacted P.L. 95-575 which makes illegal the interstate shipment of 60,000 or more cigarettes to other than licensed dealers. The cigarettes are declared contraband and subject to seizure by the U.S. Bureau of Alcohol, Tobacco, and Firearms.

40. See ACIR, *Coordination of State and Federal Inheritance, Estate, and Gift Taxes* (GPO, 1961).

41. In 1976 one state (Nevada) had no death taxes; six had a federal pickup tax only; forty (including the District of Columbia) had a pickup tax combined with either an estate or an inheritance tax (or in two cases both); two had an estate tax only; and two had an inheritance tax only. See ACIR, *Revenue and Debt*, p. 231. At the beginning of the 1980s Nevada was still the only state without a death tax.

percent,[42] would reduce federal tax revenues considerably[43] and raise important questions about the desirability of this method of aiding state and local governments as compared to the available alternatives. A higher credit might well be used as a means of introducing more uniformity into the diverse set of state estate, inheritance, and gift taxes,[44] but if it reduced federal death tax revenues significantly it might eventually induce the federal government to vacate the death tax field completely, as happened in Canada in 1971.

The Canadian government before 1972 shared 75 percent of its estate tax revenues with the ten provinces, but only three of them (British Columbia, Ontario, and Quebec) had additional taxes of their own. At the end of 1971 Canada made capital gains accrued on assets passed at death subject to income taxation; concern about the additional burdens thereby placed on estates resulted in federal withdrawal from succession duties (the federal government received little net revenue from those duties, because of its tax sharing arrangements, and could withdraw with little revenue loss). Though six provinces reacted by passing uniform succession duty acts, use of death taxes has steadily declined since then, and by 1980 only one province (Quebec) still used them.[45] Given the high mobility of wealthy individuals, a set of uncoordinated and independent state or provincial death taxes seems unlikely to be an important source of revenue in any country.

CORPORATION INCOME TAXES. State and local taxes on corporate profits represent another area in which the efficiency gains from cen-

42. Joseph A. Pechman, *Federal Tax Policy,* 3d ed. (Brookings Institution, 1977), p. 313.

43. John W. Byrnes estimated that the 1926 credit of 80 percent was equivalent to a 10 percent credit in 1971. "Federal Action to Strengthen State and Local Revenue Capabilities," *National Tax Journal,* vol. 24 (September 1971), p. 368. Byrnes also estimated that his proposal of an 80 percent credit on the first $150,000 of taxable estate and 20 percent on the remainder would transfer over $1 billion to the states.

44. Pechman, *Federal Tax Policy,* pp. 266–68.

45. See the Canadian Tax Foundation's session on "Death Duty or Other Wealth Tax for Canada: Pros and Cons" in their *Report of the Proceedings of the Twenty-third Tax Conference, 1971* (Toronto: Canadian Tax Foundation, 1972), pp. 6–44; Wolfe D. Goodman, *The New Provincial Succession Duty System: An Examination of the Succession Duty Acts of the Atlantic Provinces, Manitoba and Saskatchewan,* Canadian Tax Paper 56 (Canadian Tax Foundation, 1972); George E. Carter, "Federal Abandonment of the Estate Tax: The Intergovernmental Fiscal Dimension," *Canadian Tax Journal,* vol. 21 (May–June 1973), pp. 232–46.

tralized federal administration, though potentially significant, appear to be insufficient to overbalance the benefits of independent state and local taxing powers. Adoption of the flexible version of centralized administration would require widespread agreement—which has been slow to develop—on both the conditions under which corporations become taxable within states and the manner in which interstate corporation income should be allocated among the competing claimants. Adoption of the inflexible version would promise valuable economic gains, but the political costs appear to be high. Establishing a uniform, nationwide corporate income tax that was shared in some way with state and local governments would eliminate one important source of fiscal distortion of businesses' locational decisions and simplify both state tax administration and corporate compliance responsibilities. It would also remove from state and local revenue systems a tax whose burden incidence, looked at from their point of view, is erratic, irrational, and largely irrelevant to either benefits-received or ability-to-pay financing goals.[46] Given the wide variation in state use of corporate profits taxation, however, it would be extremely difficult to devise a tax sharing formula that would leave no state worse off, avoid large windfall gains to others, and not cost the federal government a large amount of revenue.[47] Moreover, increases in corporation profits tax rates are widely accepted by the public at least as necessary accompaniments to increases in individual income tax rates, and the corporate tax is regarded by many as a relatively painless way of increasing government revenue.[48] State and local independence in setting individual income tax rates, therefore, is likely to imply similar independence in setting corporate tax rates.

SALES TAXES. If adoption of a federal sales tax should ever become

46. See Charles E. McLure, Jr., "Economic Aspects," pp. 30–32, and "The State Corporate Income Tax: Lambs in Wolves' Clothing," in Aaron and Boskin, *Economics of Taxation*. Of course, the real appeal of a state corporation income tax may not be the economist's ability-to-pay or benefits-received principles but rather the state taxpayer's "someone else will pay" test of a good tax.

47. In 1980 four states had no corporation income tax; one (South Dakota) reached banks and financial institutions only; and one (Michigan) had a single business tax on a value-added base.

48. This was one of the findings of a Roper poll taken in March 1976; *Wall Street Journal*, May 19, 1976. Whether this represents simply a "what you don't see can't hurt you" attitude or an informed judgment that the corporate tax is a desirable tax because its burdens fall mainly on high-income shareholders (or on consumers of corporate products) is an intriguing question for tax philosophers to study.

a serious possibility, a flexible type of centralized federal administration should be carefully considered. Interest in a federal sales tax has waxed and waned, not the least of the forces against it being the reluctance of state and local governments to admit another user to a tax area they have long enjoyed alone. However, if the federal levy took a retail-sales rather than a value-added form, substantial coordination with state sales taxes would be possible and would offer states at least some reward for relinquishing their monopoly of the sales tax.[49]

Horizontal Tax Overlapping

The problems that plague most taxes and complicate fiscal relationships among local as well as state governments are strikingly apparent in state taxation of interstate business income. In few other areas of taxation does the gap between the laws as written and the taxes as administered seem so great. After an intensive, three-year study of the problem, a House subcommittee concluded that

in broad areas the demands of the States upon interstate businesses are largely disregarded. For the unusually scrupulous, the very naive, or the simply unlucky, the legal rules may describe the system; for the great mass of interstate companies, practice bears little relationship to the law. . . . It is . . . a system in which the States are reaching farther and farther to impose smaller and smaller liabilities on more and more companies. It is . . . a system which calls upon tax administrators to enforce the unenforceable, and the taxpayer to comply with the uncompliable.[50]

Similar tax overlapping problems are created by the high mobility

49. John F. Due, "The Case for the Use of the Retail Form of Sales Tax in Preference to the Value-Added Tax," in Richard A. Musgrave, ed., *Broad-Based Taxes: New Options and Sources* (Johns Hopkins University Press, 1973), p. 207; also see Carl S. Shoup, "Factors Bearing on an Assumed Choice Between a Federal Retail-Sales Tax and a Federal Valued-Added Tax," and Charles E. McLure, Jr., "Economic Effects of Taxing Value Added," in ibid., pp. 215–26, 155–204; ACIR, *The Value-Added Tax and Alternative Sources of Federal Revenue*, Report M-78 (GPO, 1973); Charles E. McLure, Jr., and Norman B. Ture, *Value Added Tax: Two Views* (Washington: American Enterprise Institute for Public Policy Research, 1972); Charles E. McLure, Jr., "A Federal Tax on Valued Added: U.S. View," and comments by William F. Hellmuth, in NTA-TIA, *Proceedings, 1973*, pp. 96–108.

50. One of the conclusions of the Special Subcommittee on State Taxation of Interstate Commerce of the House Committee on the Judiciary, in *State Taxation of Interstate Commerce*, H. Rept. 1480, 88 Cong. 2 sess. (GPO, 1964), vol. 1, pp. 596, 598. (Known as the Willis Committee Report.)

of individual workers and consumers and by the constitutionally protected ease with which goods and services move across state and local boundaries. Minimizing horizontal tax inequities in such an environment is no small task.

Mobile Taxpayers

The metropolitan taxpayer who lives in one jurisdiction and works in another is a familiar figure in the modern world. How should the conflicting claims on his income from the government of residence and the government of employment be resolved? The economist bases his answer on the benefits-received theory of taxation,[51] though no precise solution can be obtained from it. There are a number of government programs, such as water supply systems or public parks, that generate only private benefits which can be allocated more or less accurately to specific individuals. If services of this type are financed, as the benefits-received doctrine says they should be, by user charges, fees, and prices, they will give rise to no allocation problems among local governments. Much the larger group of public programs, however, produces major social benefits that cannot be allocated to specific persons. These are public services, in the technical sense of the word, whose benefits accrue as a whole to each individual within the jurisdiction of the government that provides them. Satisfactory as this proposition may be for the person who never moves outside a single jurisdiction, it is not very helpful in identifying the benefits enjoyed by a person who does move. These benefits are clearly some function of the benefits generated by the different governments with which he has some contact. But what is the form of that function?

One relevant consideration, presumably, is the amount of time that an income earner and his family spend in each jurisdiction. Taxable income might be divided among competing governments by first excluding all governments with which the family has only minimal contact—for example, jurisdictions where they vacation or occasionally shop—and then allocating the right to tax their income among the remaining governments in rough proportion to the time spent working and living in each. In practice, this rule should restrict consideration to two governmental units, those of residence and employment.

51. The courts have also made use of the benefits-received doctrine to justify local income taxes on commuters. See ACIR, *The Commuter and the Municipal Income Tax,* Background Paper (ACIR, 1970), p. 6.

Of these the former should normally have the greater claim, since most city workers, and certainly their families, probably spend more time in their home suburbs than in the city.

A second relevant consideration is the pattern of local government expenditures. Among these, education ranks supreme, and this fact, too, favors the claim of the government of residence. While public schools do create social benefits that are broadly disseminated throughout the economy, localized social and private benefits are also important and are normally provided by the government of residence. Local welfare expenditures, in contrast, generate social benefits that are mainly nonlocal in nature. In principle, therefore, welfare financing should be removed from local responsibility and shifted to higher levels of government. But where local welfare financing is important, there is strong justification for a central city tax source that reaches nonresidents as well as residents.

The nature of the local income tax that is levied is also important because investment income is ordinarily taxed only by jurisdictions of residence, whereas wage and business income can be reached either where it is earned or where it is received. A broad-based local income tax, therefore, will provide some revenue to bedroom communities even if all wage income is allocated to jurisdictions of employment.

In the presence of conflicting considerations of this sort there is much to be said for simplicity when it comes to deciding on jurisdictional priorities under a local income tax. When used to finance school services, a local income tax should be completely residence-oriented.[52] When used to finance city or county services, it should be allocated in part on the basis of origin. This could readily be done either by allocating wage and business income equally to jurisdictions of origin and residence, or by requiring jurisdictions of residence to grant a tax credit for local income taxes paid elsewhere. The first favors jurisdictions of residence more than the second and would be particularly appropriate in states where there is little or no local responsibility for welfare financing.[53]

52. This is the rule used for school districts in Kentucky and Pennsylvania. ACIR, *Local Revenue Diversification*, p. 53.

53. With state help it is comparatively easy to make local income taxes equitable for taxpayers, but doing this so as to achieve equity among local governments is a more difficult problem. Wide differences in their expenditure responsibilities and needs and in their other revenue options must be taken into account in any equitable intergovernmental division of local income tax revenues.

Tax overlapping is also a problem in state individual income taxes, most of which allow a credit for income taxes paid to states of non-residence, some a credit for taxes paid to a state of residence, some both, and some neither.[54] Not only do the credits for taxes paid to states of nonresidence frequently depend on the nature of the reciprocity arrangements worked out between states, but state definitions of residence often conflict with one another. As a result, mobile taxpayers can find their incomes subject to taxation in more than one state. Some consistent and uniform solution to these problems of overlapping is clearly needed. It could be one of the valuable by-products of wide adoption of the centralized administration opportunities provided by the Federal-State Tax Collection Act of 1972.

Interstate Sales

The inequitable taxation of interstate sales is widely regarded as the most important problem created by state sales and use taxes. The problem can be attacked by assigning interstate sales either to the state of destination or to the state of origin, but neither solution is entirely satisfactory.

The destination principle rests on an ability-to-pay rationale that views the retail sales tax as a levy on consumers in proportion to their purchases of taxable commodities. That such purchases are one important measure of economic affluence, and hence of the taxpaying ability of individual households, is the basic justification for most national and state general sales taxes. Consistent with this view, the destination principle is the one normally applied to both international and interstate transactions. It assumes, in accordance with popular opinion and most professional views, that state sales tax burdens are fully shifted forward to consumers.[55] From this it follows that a sales tax state must exempt its exports to keep them from being at a competitive disadvantage in states without a sales tax and must tax its

54. ACIR, *Revenue and Debt,* pp. 206–07.
55. The classic presentations of the view that sales taxes are not shifted forward to consumers are Harry G. Brown, "The Incidence of a General Output or a General Sales Tax," *Journal of Political Economy,* vol. 47 (April 1939), pp. 254–62; Earl R. Rolph, *The Theory of Fiscal Economics* (University of California Press, 1954), chaps. 6, 7. See also Musgrave, *Theory of Public Finance,* chaps. 15, 16; Richard A. Musgrave and Peggy B. Musgrave, *Public Finance in Theory and Practice,* 2d ed. (McGraw-Hill, 1976), chap. 20. Skepticism about the sales tax burden on consumers is also expressed by Richard E. Wagner in *The Public Economy* (Markham, 1973), pp. 195–98.

imports to prevent them from entering at a competitive advantage over local products. To do this effectively, as the Fiscal and Financial (Neumark) Committee of the European Economic Community noted with regret,[56] requires fiscal frontiers at which all interstate shipments can be intercepted and controlled. Fortunately there are no such frontiers in the United States, so states have combined their sales taxes with use taxes. Collecting use taxes directly from the consumer is a losing game except on goods, such as automobiles, that must be registered in the state. Many consumers, however, can be reached indirectly by requiring out-of-state sellers to collect and remit use taxes on their behalf.[57] Sales tax states have pursued these opportunities with vigor and, in the process, have generated an interesting series of U.S. Supreme Court cases concerning the constitutionality of such tax-collecting arrangements. Some connection between the out-of-state business and the taxing state is required, and the critical question is how substantial it must be and what specific forms it may or may not take.[58] From this game of hide and seek a considerable amount of undertaxation presumably results. At the same time, perhaps under the pressure of proposed restrictive federal legislation, states have removed some of the most objectionable interstate features of their sales tax laws. Most states, for example, have now adopted a credit for sales taxes paid to other states, thereby greatly reducing the danger of overtaxation of interstate sales.

The administrative problems involved in applying the destination principle to interstate sales can be reduced but not eliminated. Over-the-counter purchases that people bring back to a higher tax state are "an inevitable leakage,"[59] and mail order purchases and sales may prove equally elusive. On the other hand, a number of improvements in practice await only the cooperative zeal needed to implement

56. *Tax Harmonization in the Common Market,* comp. and trans. by the editors of Commerce Clearing House Common Market Reports (Chicago: CCH, 1963), pp. 78–83.

57. In-state firms that buy goods subject to use tax can readily be assessed for those taxes if they are also registered vendors for sales tax purposes.

58. John F. Due, "Nexus for Use Taxes and National Geographic," *National Tax Journal,* vol. 30 (June 1977), pp. 213–17; Oliver Oldman and Ferdinand P. Schoettle, *State and Local Taxes and Finance: Text, Problems and Cases,* University Casebook Series (Foundation Press, 1974), pp. 522–36.

59. John F. Due, "State Sales Taxation and Interstate Transactions," in NTA-TIA, *Proceedings, 1973,* p. 432.

them.[60] A uniform rule could be adopted for identifying out-of-state vendors who are required to collect and remit a taxing state's use tax levies. While in principle the rule would cover all such sellers, political reality and administrative and compliance costs may limit the firms covered to those with some tangible business connection with the taxing state; they would be registered with the state's sales and use tax authorities.[61] Nonregistered out-of-state sellers could be required to collect and remit either the use tax of the destination state or the sales tax of the state of origin; auditing responsibilities, established by interstate agreements, would be most efficiently handled by states of origin. Federal sanction of all interstate agreements dealing with the exchange of sales tax information and auditing and collection procedures would insure their operation; such agreements that have been established, particularly in the Midwest, are hampered by their lack of legal status.[62]

The origin principle for taxing retail sales would place a levy on all goods sold to final consumers by businesses operating within the taxing state, regardless of the location of those final consumers. There would be no use taxes, since imports would already have been taxed in the state of origin. Such a tax system can be justified either on a benefits-received basis, where gross receipts from sales are used as the best measure of the value of government services provided to business firms, or on an ability-to-pay basis that assumes most sales tax burdens would be borne by factors of production located in the taxing state. But even economists who believe in backward shifting of sales taxes are likely to question the proposition that most such burdens remain within the boundaries of the taxing state. A benefits-received justification for sales taxation, on the other hand, makes

60. An important deterrent to the development of such zeal is the existence of four divergent interest groups: interstate businesses that wish to minimize both their tax burdens and their compliance costs, state tax authorities who wish to maximize their share of taxable interstate transactions and to minimize administration costs, in-state businesses that wish to minimize competitive disadvantages with regard to out-of-state vendors, and the federal government which, as representative of the general taxpayer, presumably wishes to improve the equity and efficiency of state and local tax systems. See ibid., p. 425.

61. For a discussion of Canadian registration procedures, and particularly of Quebec's attempt to register firms that only solicit business through catalogues, see J. A. Johnson, "The Treatment of Interprovincial Transactions Under the Sales Tax," in NTA-TIA, *Proceedings, 1973,* p. 443.

62. Due, "State Sales Taxation," p. 433.

sense only for local government levies used to finance police and
fire protection, streets, and similar services, and then the important
question is whether gross receipts are a better measure of benefits
than other available alternatives. A state-authorized local sales tax
with a uniform rate, such as that operating in California, could raise
other difficulties. If the tax rate is set well above benefits-received
levels, local communities will have a strong incentive to compete with
one another for shopping centers and other businesses generating
large volumes of taxable sales. Unless there are countervailing pressures from retail businesses to secure sufficient property tax reductions to keep their total local tax liabilities in line with the local costs
of the services they receive, fiscal disparities between communities
are likely to be exacerbated by the use of local sales taxes.[63] While a
uniform local sales tax does nothing to create, or strengthen, those
countervailing pressures, an independently determined nonuniform
system would.

The origin principle, then, has both theoretical support and operational potentialities when applied to local sales taxes, provided each
governmental unit has freedom of choice over its rates. A source-
oriented uniform local sales tax not only lacks these appeals but also
distributes statewide monies on a highly questionable basis. Applied
to state sales taxes, the origin principle has mainly a pragmatic appeal.
Administrative and compliance problems would be notably less than
those created by adherence to the destination principle—these advantages have been attractive enough to induce the European Community to move toward origin as the basis for its sales taxes. However, the origin principle lacks any strong economic justification
when applied to state sales taxes, and its political appeal is weakened
by the need to pass federal legislation circumventing constitutional
barriers to state taxation of interstate sales. In addition, businessmen
in high-tax states might question their ability to compete with out-of-
state firms subject to lower tax rates. Competitive fears of a different

63. Local sales tax revenues in Los Angeles County in fiscal 1978, for example,
ranged from less than $1 per capita in Bradbury to almost $8,000 in Industry and
over $15,000 in Vernon. California State Board of Equalization, *Annual Report
1977–78*, pp. A-27–A-28; California State Controller, *Annual Report of Financial
Transactions Concerning Cities of California, Fiscal Year 1977–78*, pp. 5–6.

nature, however, are also possible under a nonuniform sales tax system based on destination.[64] Which represents the greater distortion of economic markets will depend on the particular circumstances in each case, though some fiscal experts regard the origin principle as the greater risk.[65] A further problem concerns the divergent interests of the market states, whose imports exceed their exports, and the production states for whom the opposite relation prevails. If they were to tap their strongest sources of taxing power, the market states would concentrate on destination-based sales taxes and residence-based income taxes while the production states would prefer to use origin-based sales and income taxes. Some compromise being necessary, an appealing solution would be to stress one basis for sales taxation and the other for income taxation. The fact that state and local individual income taxes are mostly origin-oriented provides another argument for applying the destination principle to state sales taxes. State corporation income taxes could use either an origin or a mixed basis.

Taxation of interjurisdictional sales creates problems that cannot be handled completely satisfactorily. All things considered, the destination principle seems to be the better choice for state sales taxes and the origin principle for local sales taxes whose rates are independently determined by the taxing governments. Certainly improvments can be made in the application of these two principles to existing state and local sales tax systems. Such systems are not, however, the ideal way of taxing the consumption aspect of individual and family abilities to pay. Radical tax reform in that area would call for the establishment at the federal level of a progressive tax on personal spendings, or consumer expenditure. Whether this is an idea whose time is about to come is not clear, but it received considerable pro-

64. In 1978 forty-six states and the District of Columbia had general sales taxes, with rates ranging from 2 percent in Oklahoma to 7 percent in Connecticut. Local sales taxes were authorized in thirty states, the rates ranging from 0.5 percent in Nevada to 5 percent in Alaska (Alaska has no state sales tax). John F. Due, "Changes in State, Provincial and Local Sales Taxation in the Last Decade," *Canadian Tax Journal*, vol. 27 (January–February 1979), pp. 36–45. See also John F. Due, *State and Local Sales Taxation: Structure and Administration* (Chicago: Public Administration Service, 1971), chaps. 3, 4; reports of the Committee on State Sales and Use Taxation, in NTA-TIA, *Proceedings, 1973*, pp. 314–53, and *Proceedings, 1974*, pp. 456–78.

65. See, for example, Due, "State Sales Taxation," pp. 427, 431.

fessional attention in the 1970s.[66] Were such a tax ever adopted, an attractive intergovernmental accompaniment would be a law, similar to the Federal-State Tax Collection Act of 1972, offering centralized administration for suitably designed state and local spendings tax supplements. If these were to replace retail sales taxes, the nation would then have as part of its tax system a rational and coordinated segment based on one important aspect of taxpayer abilities to pay. Such possibilities, however, may be little more than gleams in the eyes of some tax reformers.

Interstate Business Income

The multistate corporation has probably been second only to the multinational as a source of tax headaches. The fundamental questions at issue are when a business should be taxable in a given state, and what should be that state's fair share of the taxable corporation's total interstate income.[67] Working out answers to these questions has involved an intricate blending of court decisions, federal legislation and threats of legislation, fitful cooperative efforts among states, and

66. See, for example, ACIR, *The Expenditure Tax: Concept, Administration and Possible Applications* (GPO, 1974); William D. Andrews, "A Consumption-Type or Cash Flow Personal Income Tax," and Alvin C. Warren, Jr., "Fairness and a Consumption-Type or Cash Flow Personal Income Tax," *Harvard Law Review*, vol. 87 (April 1974), pp. 1113–88, and vol. 88 (March 1975), pp. 931–58; Patrick L. Kelley, "Is an Expenditure Tax Feasible?" *National Tax Journal*, vol. 23 (September 1970), pp. 237–53; Richard E. Slitor, "Administrative Aspects of Expenditures Taxation," in Musgrave, *Broad-Based Taxes*, pp. 227–63; U.S. Treasury Department, *Blueprints for Basic Tax Reform* (GPO, 1977); Sven-Olof Lodin, *Progressive Expenditure Tax—An Alternative?* A Report of the 1972 Government Commission on Taxation (Stockholm: LiberFörlag, 1978); Institute for Fiscal Studies, *The Structure and Reform of Direct Taxation: Report of a Committee Chaired by Professor J. E. Meade* (London: Allen and Unwin, 1978); Joseph A. Pechman, ed., *What Should Be Taxed: Income or Expenditure?* (Brookings Institution, 1980).

67. A detailed analysis is given in Charles E. McLure, Jr., "State Income Taxation of Multistate Corporations in the United States of America," in United Nations, Economic and Social Affairs Department, *The Impact of Multinational Corporations on Development and on International Relations*, Technical Papers: Taxation, UN Doc. ST/ESA/11 (1974), pp. 58–111, and "Taxation of Multijurisdictional Corporate Income: Lessons of the U.S. Experience," in Wallace E. Oates, ed., *The Political Economy of Fiscal Federalism* (Lexington Books, 1977), pp. 241–59. For a discussion of the Canadian experience see Ernest H. Smith, "Allocating to Provinces the Taxable Income of Corporations: How the Federal-Provincial Allocation Rules Evolved," *Canadian Tax Journal*, vol. 24 (September–October 1976), pp. 543–71.

detailed legislative studies.[68] An important milestone was the U.S. Supreme Court's 1959 decision upholding a state's right to tax a corporation's net income that was derived solely from operations in interstate commerce.[69] The connection with the taxing state in that instance was a leased office used by employee-salesmen. The *Northwestern States* decision contributed to a growing business alarm about expanding state taxing powers, and Congress reacted by passing Public Law 86-272 in September 1959. This law established a minimum-jurisdiction standard that prohibited a state's taxing of income derived from sales within its borders when the only business activity in the state was the solicitation of orders to be sent outside the state for approval and shipment. The law also commissioned a detailed study of interstate taxation of business income aimed at the development of recommendations for federal legislative action. The resulting Willis Committee Report,[70] published in four volumes in 1964 and 1965, contains information on such important aspects of the tax treatment of interstate business as the great diversity in state laws, the widespread noncompliance by business and nonenforcement by states, the wide incidence of over- and under-taxation, and the disturbing tendency of the system to favor local over out-of-state firms and big businesses over smaller ones. The report includes a volume of recommendations for reform that are well worth serious consideration.[71]

The states themselves were not inactive in seeking solutions. After considerable study, the National Conference of Commissioners on Uniform State Laws adopted in 1957 the Uniform Division of Income for Tax Purposes Act (UDITPA), and by mid-1976 twenty-five of the forty-six states with corporation income taxes adhered to the main provisions of the conference's model law.[72] Cooperative policies were also developed by a group of participating states and when these

68. See Oldman and Schoettle, *State and Local Taxes*, pp. 550–665; ACIR, *State and Local "Doing Business" Taxes*, pp. 325–68.

69. *Northwestern States Portland Cement Co.* v. *Minnesota*, 358 U.S. 450 (1959).

70. *State Taxation*, H. Rept. 1480. Emanuel Celler, chairman of the House Judiciary Committee, called the report "a landmark in our constitutional history." Ibid., vol. 1, p. III.

71. *State Taxation of Interstate Commerce*, H. Rept. 952, 89 Cong. 1 sess., vol. 4 (GPO, 1965). See also the ACIR recommendations adopted in 1966 in response to the Willis Committee Report, reproduced in ACIR, *State and Local "Doing Business" Taxes*, pp. 1031–37.

72. ACIR, *Revenue and Debt*, p. 223.

were approved by the required minimum number of seven states, the Multistate Tax Compact came into existence in August 1967. A Multistate Tax Commission was created to develop uniform regulations governing the taxation of interstate business; its 1976–77 report listed nineteen member states and twelve associates.[73] Such voluntary agreements lack the effectiveness they could have if they could secure federal sanction through congressional approval. Nonetheless, even without that approval the Multistate Tax Commission cooperated so successfully with several states in the conducting of joint audits as to produce enough additional business tax revenue to induce U.S. Steel Corporation and other large companies to challenge its legality in the courts. In 1976 the U.S. District Court in New York unanimously ruled in favor of the commission, holding that congressional approval is not required by the U.S. Constitution to establish its legality because the commission's activities neither increase states' powers nor diminish the U.S. government's.[74]

Interstate business tax problems were a topic of intensive study by a Senate subcommittee in 1973, following which Congress passed the State Taxation of Depositories Act which directed the ACIR to make a study and recommend legislation pertaining to the application of state doing-business taxes to out-of-state banks and other depository financial institutions.[75]

CONSIDERATION OF BENEFITS RECEIVED. Which states should have the right to tax the income of a multistate business and how that income should be fairly apportioned among them are closely related questions that basically rest on benefits-received considerations. As expressed in a 1977 Supreme Court decision, the fundamental constitutional requirements for a tax on the privilege of doing business in a given state are that the tax not discriminate against interstate com-

73. Multistate Tax Commission, *Tenth Annual Report for the Fiscal Year Ending June 30, 1977.* Associate members are states that have not adopted the Multistate Tax Compact and thus have no voting rights but do participate in the commission's discussions and activities.

74. The case was appealed to the U.S. Supreme Court, which upheld the lower court's decision in February 1978. *United States Steel Corp.* v. *Multistate Tax Commission,* 434 U.S. 452 (1978).

75. P.L. 93-100, sec. 7, signed August 16, 1973. See John F. Rolph III, "Summary of Current Legislative, Administrative and Judicial Developments Affecting the Taxation of Commercial Banks," in NTA-TIA, *Proceedings, 1974,* pp. 480–86. The ACIR report, *State and Local "Doing Business" Taxes,* was submitted to Congress in May and September 1975, but no federal legislation ensued.

merce, that it be both fairly related to the services provided by the state to the business and properly apportioned to activities within the taxing state, and that it be based on sufficient nexus between the state and the taxed activities.[76] The implicit assumption, then, is that the benefits from state intermediate services to business are closely related to the volume of productive activities carried out by the business in that state. The measure of such activities is value added (its use in designing local tax systems is discussed in chapter 5).

While in principle any beneficial influence, however nebulous, that a state government may have on business operations is sufficient to establish a taxable nexus, in practice it may be desirable, for reasons of tax simplicity and certainty, to restrict taxing jurisdiction to those states with which the business has some substantial connection. A common interpretation of that general rule, recommended by both the Willis Committee and the ACIR report on out-of-state financial depositories, is the ownership or use of tangible property or the employment of persons in the taxing state. Such a taxable nexus rule would be consistent with Public Law 86-272, and its operation should entail acceptably low administrative and compliance costs. Much would depend on the exact wording and interpretation of the rule and on the ease with which it could be integrated with division-of-income rules. Until some uniform nexus rule is widely adopted, the taxability of interstate business is likely to remain as chaotic and unsatisfactory as the Willis Committee found it.[77]

SEPARATE ACCOUNTING. Multistate business income can be divided up among the prospective claimants by separate accounting, by specific allocation, or by formula apportionment. Separate accounting involves the cracking apart of a single corporate enterprise for tax purposes. For example, if two separate divisions of a corporation, one in each of two states, buy their inputs and sell their output independently of each other, tax officials (particularly those in the state with the more profitable of the two divisions) may be tempted to treat them as if they were separate enterprises. Economists, however, object to this procedure because it ignores important economies of scale—in management, advertising, and fund raising—that the two

76. See Donald P. Simet and Arthur D. Lynn, Jr., "Interstate Commerce Must Pay Its Way: The Demise of Spector," *National Tax Journal*, vol. 31 (March 1978), p. 53.
77. *State Taxation*, H. Rept. 1480, vol. 1, pp. 141–52.

divisions could not realize if they did operate separately. Nevertheless, state tax officials may find it difficult to view a diversified corporation stressing decentralized management in the same way as a
corporation engaged in one integrated set of operations; they may
be willing, therefore, to incur some additional administrative costs
in order to treat the two types differently.[78]

SPECIFIC ALLOCATION. Tax officials frequently attempt to distinguish between a multistate corporation's mainstream income,
which cannot be claimed exclusively by any one state, and various
kinds of subsidiary income, which can.[79] The exclusive right to tax
the income derived from renting space to other businesses in a corporation's headquarters building in New York City, for example,
could be claimed by either the city or the state of New York, or both.[80]
Such specific allocation of income is most difficult when applied to
intangible assets. Dividend and interest income, for example, has
traditionally been allocated to the state of residence of the recipient,
but claims to corporate residence may be entered by both the state
in which the business is incorporated and any state that views itself
as the corporation's commercial domicile.[81] Nor is net dividend or

78. For a discussion of the problems involved see Arthur B. Barber, "State Income Tax Uniformity Concerning Taxable Units," *National Tax Journal*, vol. 16
(December 1963), pp. 354–64; *State Taxation*, H. Rept. 1480, vol. 1, pp. 160–67.

79. In mid-1974 twenty-two states applied specific allocation to nonbusiness
income generally; twenty-one applied it to specified kinds of income; one used it
only for foreign corporations; and three had no provision for specific allocation. For
further details see ACIR, *State and Local "Doing Business" Taxes*, pp. 823–47.

80. Other states, of course, might seek to combine the rental income with the
corporation's other income which would be then apportioned by formula among all
the states in which the corporation carried out business operations. For an analysis
of the problem see Arthur B. Barber, " 'Nonapportionable Income' Under a Uniform
State Net Income Tax Law Imposed by Congress," *National Tax Journal*, vol. 16
(June 1963), pp. 147–58.

81. In addition, nonresidence states may seek to include dividends and interest
in the total taxable income subject to interstate apportionment. In 1980 the U.S.
Supreme Court in fact upheld a state supreme court's decision that Vermont could
constitutionally apply its apportionment formula to a taxable income measure for
New York-based Mobil Corporation that included foreign dividends. At least for
that type of income, the case raised the basic issue of whether both specific allocation
and formula apportionment are allowed by the Constitution, and if not which one
should be given precedence. The Court noted in its decision that Mobil's operations
in Vermont appeared to be part of one unitary business. *Mobil Oil Corporation* v.
Commissioner of Taxation of Vermont, no. 78-1201.

interest income easy to measure since, in obtaining it, a corporation may incur costs that are difficult to segregate from its other expenses.[82] The gains from specific income allocation may not be worth the costs involved.

THE UNITARY BUSINESS CONCEPT. Whatever the role assigned to specific allocation of income, a difficult choice must be made between integrated business operations producing income that cannot be divided up in any nonarbitrary way and those interrelated business operations that can more realistically be separated into their component parts, the income from which can then be allocated to different tax claimants. The latter choice is the one applied by different countries to the taxation of multinational corporations, but difficult problems arise over the proper prices to be placed on goods and services transferred between corporate affiliates. Since these are not arms-length transactions between independent enterprises, there is an obvious incentive for the corporations to manipulate the prices in question in order to minimize tax burdens. State tax authorities, when dealing with such corporations, must decide whether to accept the distinction between foreign source and domestic income that is shown either in the corporations' accounts or in their federal tax returns; doing so means restricting the state's tax reach to a domestic income base that may or may not be realistically measured. In particular, it may be understated by manipulated pricing practices that the IRS has been unable to challenge or by the overallocation of corporate management and research expenses to domestic operations. Rejecting the distinction, on the other hand, requires either the administratively costly application of the state's own separate accounting rules and regulations to corporations with foreign operations or the adoption

---

82. Dividend income is also susceptible to double taxation, since dividends, like other transfers, can be counted as income to the receiver or to the payer, but not to both. Including dividends in the income of corporate recipients introduces a destination element into state tax systems, treats dividend and interest income in the same way, but puts the responsibility for avoidance of overtaxation on states of origin, which should then allow deduction of such dividends from their own tax bases. Excluding intercorporate dividends from state income tax bases avoids these problems but at the cost of introducing an economically unjustified distinction between the treatments accorded dividend and interest income.

of the controversial concept of unitary income pioneered by California.[83]

In essence the unitary business approach attempts to look beyond legal accounting conventions in order to define the true boundaries of the full range of integrated business activities carried out by any business operating in a given state. Unconventional results of two opposite kinds may thereby be obtained. On the one hand, a corporation accustomed to the use of consolidated accounts for its different parts may find them separated for tax purposes; and on the other hand, a group of affiliated corporations using separate accounts may find them combined for tax purposes. When this combination requires the inclusion of the income of foreign corporations on state tax returns, there is likely to be both surprise and consternation in corporate board rooms. Economic realities, however, have been known to produce such reactions before.

The unitary business approach cannot be faulted on theoretical grounds. The income of a truly integrated set of business operations, no matter how spread out geographically or how finely divided among different business units, is itself a single entity. If the affiliation of a group of corporations has a significant impact on the corporate profits of the group, it can be considered a unitary business enterprise whose total income must be apportioned for tax purposes on the basis of some more or less arbitrary formula. If their affiliation has little or no impact on profits, separate accounting is the appropriate tax treatment. Making a reliable estimate of the economic effects of affiliation is no easy task, however. In the eyes of some authorities its accomplishment is probably inconsistent with efficient tax administration and may have to be abandoned.[84] But, if most multinational corporations are really integrated business operations, universal application of the unitary approach using a standard apportionment formula is an attractive goal for international, as well as interstate,

83. Discussions of this concept may be found in Tax Foundation, *Taxation of Interstate Business,* Proceedings, Tax Foundation Seminar (New York: Tax Foundation, 1970); Thomas P. Kerester, "Pros and Cons of State Taxation of Foreign Source Income," in NTA-TIA, *Proceedings, 1974,* pp. 274–80; Peggy B. Musgrave, "The U.K. Treaty Debate: Some Lessons for the Future," *Tax Notes,* July 10, 1978, pp. 27–29.

84. See, for example, Peter Miller, "State Income Taxation of Multiple Corporations, and Multiple Businesses," in Tax Foundation, *Taxation of Interstate Business,* pp. 77, 81.

tax policy. And states should be able to realize important administrative gains if they adopt the unitary method wherever possible to replace independent application of their own separate accounting rules to multinational business.[85] In any case, it is clear that use by some states of the unitary income concept and by others of separate accounting procedures increases the inequities and inefficiencies that tax coordination policy is designed to minimize.[86]

APPORTIONMENT BY FORMULA. Diversity and controversy are also the chief characteristics of current practices dealing with the apportionment by formula of the unitary, or mainstream, income of an integrated interstate corporation. A three-factor formula based on property, payroll, and sales has become widely accepted,[87] but many experts have been highly critical of including sales.[88] As the Willis Committee put it, "of all the steps involved in the process of dividing income for tax purposes, the attribution of sales presents more problems than any other."[89]

85. Application of the unitary income approach to multinational corporations has been criticized for including income from foreign sources in state tax bases. Inclusion of foreign source income in the computations used to derive state tax bases, however, does not imply improper inclusion in those bases. If the unitary concept is properly applied and if the income apportionment formula is reasonable, the result is simply a better definition of taxable domestic source income than could be obtained by separate accounting.

86. Though the Treasury Department has not directly taken any substantive position on the proper allocation of state taxes on interstate business, it did so indirectly in a tax treaty negotiated with the United Kingdom that would have denied states the right to apply the unitary business doctrine to any subsidiary of a U.K.-controlled corporation. The U.S. Senate ratified the treaty only after a protocol was added incorporating the Senate's reservation that preserved the right of states to apply the unitary rule to multinational corporations. See Ferdinand P. Schoettle, "The U.K. Treaty and the State Taxation of Corporate Income," *Tax Notes*, April 4, 1977, pp. 3–8; "Senate Reserves Article 9(4) in U.K. Treaty Ratification," *Tax Notes*, July 3, 1978, p. 6; *Congressional Record*, daily edition (July 9, 1979), p. 58814. The treaty was subsequently ratified by the United Kingdom with the Senate protocol intact.

87. By mid-1974 the formula was used by 45 of the 47 states prescribing division-of-base procedures for corporate taxation. See *State Taxation*, H. Rept. 1480, vol. 1, p. 119; ACIR, *State and Local "Doing Business" Taxes*, pp. 291–94.

88. Arthur B. Barber, "A Suggested Shot at a Gordian Knot of Income Apportionment," *National Tax Journal*, vol. 13 (September 1960), pp. 243–51; Charles E. Ratliff, Jr., *Interstate Apportionment of Business Income for State Income Tax Purposes* (University of North Carolina Press, 1962); Paul Studenski, "The Need for Federal Curbs on State Taxes on Interstate Commerce: An Economist's Viewpoint," *Virginia Law Review*, vol. 46 (October 1960), pp. 1121–49.

89. *State Taxation*, H. Rept. 1480, vol. 1, p. 181.

The most popular procedure, which has become increasingly so in recent years, is to allocate sales on a destination basis to the state of the consumer.[90] Unfortunately, this appears to be the most troublesome of all the available standards, for it greatly expands the number of companies that are, potentially at least, subject to taxation in more than one state. In the Willis Committee's sample of interstate companies, for example, 66 percent of the manufacturing and 74 percent of the mercantile companies had places of business in only one state.[91] Under a rule that allocated sales by origin (as well as under an income-apportionment formula based only on property and payroll), most of these companies would be taxable in one state only. The saving to them from complying with an origin rather than a destination rule could be substantial.[92]

The destination sales factor also is criticized for allocating income to many states that lack sufficient nexus, or jurisdictional connection, to tax it. While in some cases a throwback rule is used to reallocate that income to its state of origin,[93] in others interstate corporations simply go undertaxed, compared to home corporations with like amounts of income.[94] Among thirteen undertaxed multistate companies studied by the Willis Committee, two were taxed on less than

90. The ultimate in destination-sales usage is Iowa's unique single-factor apportionment formula for taxable corporate income. This practice was challenged in the courts by an Illinois feed manufacturer selling to farmers in Iowa, but the constitutionality of a sales-only apportionment formula was upheld by the U.S. Supreme Court in 1978. *Moorman Manufacturing Co.* v. *Bair,* 437 U.S. 267 (1978). See also Lindley H. Clark, Jr., *Wall Street Journal,* July 11, 1978.

91. *State Taxation,* H. Rept. 1480, vol. 1, pp. 77–78.

92. Ibid., pp. 508–13.

93. The UDITPA rules include a throwback provision; in mid-1974, 26 of the 41 states using a destination sales factor had a throwback rule. ACIR, *State and Local "Doing Business" Taxes,* pp. 860–79.

94. Among interstate companies themselves the effects of a throwback rule can be exceedingly complicated. If all states levied a corporation income tax at the same rate and used a three-factor, destination-sales apportionment formula, the absence of a throwback rule would result in undertaxation of some multistate companies and the collection of too little revenue in some states. General use of a throwback rule, on the other hand, would equalize the tax treatment of all interstate corporations but would provide too much revenue to some states and too little to others. These attractions of a throwback rule are considerably weakened, and may be reversed, in a system where some states have no corporate tax and others levy it at widely differing rates. For these and other reasons some experts oppose the use of the throwback rules. See C. R. Cahoon and William R. Brown, "The Interstate Tax Dilemma—A Proposed Solution," *National Tax Journal,* vol. 26 (June 1973), pp. 192–93.

half their incomes and the rest on amounts varying from 52.6 percent to 98.5 percent.[95] Undertaxation, of course, is by no means a fortuitous phenomenon. States have frequently adopted a destination sales factor mainly to attract new business by offering it a "favorable tax climate."[96] The practice is basically a kind of window dressing designed to combine the appearance of high business tax rates with low tax burdens on companies with a large export component. As McLure has noted, a shift from an origin- toward a destination-based tax is equivalent to currency devaluation for the state in question and has the same attractions as that policy has for national governments. On the other hand, from the taxing state's point of view a destination sales factor is equivalent in its economic effects to the imposition of a retail sales tax and hence counter to the goals usually sought by imposing, or increasing, a state corporate income tax.[97] Ainsworth has shown that either a high or a low tax state that wishes to minimize the tax burden on home-based business will find it advantageous to move from origin sales to destination sales; having made that change, however, neither state can improve its position by returning to an origin basis.[98] It seems unlikely, therefore, that the states will give up their destination sales factors voluntarily. If they do not, state taxation of corporate income is likely to remain in an unsettled state of partial recapture and partial escape of intended tax burdens until some major overhaul of jurisdictional and apportionment rules is agreed upon.

Some experts believe that such an overhaul would involve the complete elimination of the sales factor from income apportionment formulas. They argue that income should be apportioned according to the location of the land, labor, and capital goods that produce it. Sales thus would be entitled to consideration only to the extent that the company's own labor and property were involved in the transactions; otherwise the value added in selling should be attributed to other businesses and their incomes taxed accordingly. To some, then, logic calls for a two-factor income apportionment formula based on tangible property and payrolls—an argument reinforced by practical

95. *State Taxation*, H. Rept. 1480, vol. 1, p. 395.

96. Ibid., pp. 122–27.

97. McLure, "State Income Taxation of Multistate Corporations," pp. 68–69, and "State Corporate Income Tax."

98. Kenneth G. Ainsworth, "Apportionment and Industry Shares of State Corporate Income Tax Liabilities," in NTA-TIA, *Proceedings, 1974*, pp. 245–57.

considerations. Not only would nexus problems be greatly simplified, but administrative and compliance costs would be reduced as well.[99]

The problem, of course, is to persuade the nonindustrial states that a production-oriented apportionment formula would not unduly compromise their interests. The Willis Committee's detailed, quantitative comparison of the revenue effects of the three leading types of formulas—property and payrolls only; property, payrolls, and a destination sales factor; and property, payrolls, and an origin sales factor—indicated that the revenue importance of the choice of formula was not great in 1963 and could be expected to become even less so in the future. Nevertheless some states would lose,[100] and compromises would be needed to sell them the two-factor formula as a uniform standard for apportioning income. One means of offsetting the losses, for example, would be federal legislation requiring interstate sellers to collect and remit sales and use taxes to destination states.

Controversy over the choice of a two-factor or three-factor formula is but the tip of the iceberg that interstate tax reformers must circumvent. The weights to be assigned to the apportionment factors must be chosen, and the precise quantitative dimensions of the factors must be specified. Each is a fertile source of interstate diversity and confusion. The most common, but least logical, weighting system used is one assigning equal importance to the factors included in the apportionment formula.[101] Property and payroll do not contribute equally to productive activity. However, to adjust the weights in line with the relative importance of property income and labor income in total value added by each interstate business would greatly complicate income apportionment formulas.[102] In a three-factor formula, total value of sales and total value of production, which are simply two ways of measuring the same economic activity, should

99. *State Taxation,* H. Rept. 1480, vol. 1, pp. 521–63.
100. Ibid., pp. 554–57.
101. ACIR, *State and Local "Doing Business" Taxes,* pp. 294–95, 848–59.
102. If the two states in which a given corporation did business each had one-quarter of the one factor and three-quarters of the other, for example, an equal-weight, two-factor apportionment formula would assign one-half of the total profits of the business to each. If payroll were 80 percent and profits 20 percent of total value added, however, the state with three-quarters of the payroll would have 65 percent of the value added and the state with three-quarters of the property would have only 35 percent.

each have equal weight. Property and payroll, in other words, should together have the same weight as sales.[103]

Perhaps the most obscure source of nonuniformity in the taxation of interstate income is the slippery final step of assigning specific factors between home and other states and placing money values on them. Treatment of properties that are rented, in transit, or under construction may differ from state to state. Property valuations may be based on depreciated original cost, on depreciated replacement cost, or on estimated market value. Payrolls may include or exclude fringe benefits, and attribution may be determined by where the services are performed, where the employee is based, or where the employee is registered for unemployment insurance (the UDITPA rule).[104]

All of these administrative diversities are troublesome, but the inefficiencies and inequities created by them may well be less important than the economic distortions resulting from state taxation of corporation income in the first place. McLure has demonstrated that such a tax system, when analyzed from the point of view of the states, produces mainly an irrational, discriminatory set of taxes on payrolls, property, and sales (assuming allocation of corporate profits by the standard three-factor formula) rather than the desired levy on corporate income.[105] While a move toward uniformity in state corporate tax rates, perhaps under the auspices of the Multistate Tax Commission, would be helpful, the best solution, in McLure's view, would be a separation of tax sources that denied states any use of corporate income taxes. Reimbursement could then be made through the federal grant system. Attractive as such a radical reform may be to economists in principle, it is fraught with so many political and practical difficulties that improving the existing system of interstate business income taxation seems a more realistic option.

RESOLVING CORPORATE TAX PROBLEMS. Realism, then, calls for a pragmatic solution that would pay considerable attention to existing practice and would sacrifice some elements of the ideal—whatever that may be—to obtain an early agreement by the states on uniform

103. Such a property-payroll-sales formula (weighted 25-25-50) is used by Florida, Massachusetts, and New York and is provided as one choice for the taxpayer in Wisconsin.

104. See *State Taxation*, H. Rept. 1480, vol. 1, pp. 171–79.

105. "State Corporate Income Tax."

jurisdictional and income-allocation rules. The range of possibilities is, of course, large, but certain policy options deserve consideration.

Since elimination of the corporation income tax as a source of state or local revenue seems so far to have had little political or popular appeal, policymakers might as well adapt their policies to that reality. From a national point of view, the more uniform state corporation income tax rates are the better. From a state point of view, the minimization of administrative and compliance costs may be the best policy goal. Tightening the nexus rules that determine the taxability of business income in different jurisdictions is one way of achieving that goal. Some physical presence in the state, measured by property and payroll, would be the most attractive option. If reality dictates the inclusion of sales as well, some minimum requirement below which no taxable nexus exists, as recommended by the Willis Committee in 1965, would be the next-best choice.

The desirable goal of a single, universally used apportionment formula for multistate business income could be best implemented by adoption of a two-factor, property and payroll, formula. However, if use of a three-factor formula that includes sales on a destination basis is too entrenched to be dislodged, tax reform should be concentrated on ways and means of making the usage of that kind of formula as uniform as possible. Specific allocations of particular kinds of income have little to recommend them. An attractive policy goal, in other words, would be the use of a uniform formula in the apportionment of the total income of all closely integrated multistate and multinational corporations. The choice between such a unitary treatment of total corporation income and separate accounting for the component parts of a decentralized corporate enterprise is a difficult one that may well be best left to the parties involved to resolve, subject to appeal by either side to the courts. What is and what is not a closely integrated corporation is an empirical question which cannot readily be determined by any set of rules, however complicated.

A more closely coordinated national tax system promises a strengthening both of the economy and of the revenue-raising powers of state and local governments. These important benefits could be realized without any undue sacrifice of state and local fiscal independence. Skillfully coordinated tax policies alone, however, will not produce a problem-free federal fiscal system. Other instruments must also be carefully honed for service in that important task.

CHAPTER THREE

The Economics of
Intergovernmental Grants

GROWTH and diversification have been the hallmarks of intergovernmental grants-in-aid in the United States in recent years. Between 1954 and 1977, for example, federal government aid rose from 11 percent to 33 percent of state and local general revenue from own sources, and state grants increased from 42 percent to 60 percent of local government general revenue from own sources.[1] This impressive growth record was accompanied by the development of new forms of aid at the federal level and by a heightened interest in the reform of school financing systems at the state level (see chapters 4 and 5).

Grants-in-aid may be classified in numerous ways.[2] The classifica-

1. U.S. Advisory Commission on Intergovernmental Relations, *Significant Features of Fiscal Federalism, 1978–79 Edition* (U.S. Government Printing Office, 1979), pp. 78, 81. Primary data on intergovernmental grants are published by the U.S. Census Bureau, in the national income accounts, and in the Special Analyses of the Budget of the United States Government. For differences in the three sources, see *Special Analyses, Budget of the United States Government, Fiscal Year 1978*, pp. 273–75.

2. See, for example, Jesse Burkhead and Jerry Miner, *Public Expenditure* (Aldine, 1971), p. 285; ACIR, *Federal Grants, Their Effects on State-Local Expenditures, Employment Levels, Wage Rates: The Intergovernmental Grant System: An Assessment and Proposed Policies*, Report A-61 (GPO, 1977), pp. 25–29.

Table 3-1. The Many Dimensions of Intergovernmental Grants

1. *How funds are used by recipient*
   a. Unrestricted
   b. General, with limited restrictions
   c. Block, within broad program areas
   d. Categorical or functional, within narrow program areas

2. *How funds are allocated to recipient*
   a. Formula, unrestricted
   b. Formula, subject to limited restrictions
   c. Formula, with administrative checks
   d. Competitive applications by grantees (project grants)

3. *Degree of participation by grantor*
   a. None (beyond provision of grant funds)
   b. Administrative oversight
   c. Technical services; cooperative management
   d. Grantee matching requirements up to the limit of grantor funds (closed-end matching grants)
   e. Grantee matching requirements with unlimited grantor funds (open-ended matching grants)

tion in table 3-1 highlights both the flexibility of grants as a fiscal instrument and the diversity that complicates the assessment of the effects of different grant programs. Four basic types of grant are widely used.

Categorical grants of the open-ended matching variety (3e) have the economic effect of stimulating state and local expenditure in designated functional areas (1d) by lowering the price at which grantees can acquire the program benefits; grantees are free to buy as much as they like at that lower price. The grants are allocated by formula with administrative checks on their use (2c). Federal grants for public assistance and medicaid, which accounted for about 18 percent of total federal grant expenditures in fiscal 1978, fall in this category. State matching grants of any kind are rare.

Unconditional general grants allocated by formula fall at the opposite end of the economic spectrum. Their effect is to increase the money income of recipient governments but not to change the prices at which they can purchase goods and services for their citizens. Though there are no examples of a completely unrestricted federal general grant (1a, 2a, 3a) in the United States, general revenue sharing (1b, 2b, 3b) comes close.[3] About 10 percent of state grant funds goes for general support of local government.

Fixed-amount grants for specified purposes are the most popular type of grant in the United States, accounting for 88 percent of federal grant expenditures in fiscal 1978 and over 85 percent of state grant expenditures in fiscal 1972. This category includes the traditional federal categorical matching closed-end grant (1d, 2c, 3cd), federal block grants (1c, 2bc, 3b), and most state grants for education and highways.[4] Though messy in the eyes of many economists because they combine income and price effects in ways that are difficult to disentangle, these fixed-sum special-purpose grants have numerous attractions. Not the least of these may be their ability to conciliate appearance and reality, seeming to support some function close to the heart of the grantor while in reality allowing the grantee to use the funds for any local purpose desired. Closed-end grants have the further advantage of greatly simplifying the budgetary and administrative problems of the grantor. Open-ended grants, in contrast, create budgetary uncertainties by committing the grantor to the provision of whatever funds grantees choose to match. And if the aided activities are not tightly defined, recipients may exert explosive pressures on spending levels by diverting open-ended grant funds to programs the grantor had neither intended nor wished to support.[5]

Project grants are distinguished by the requirement that donees compete for the available funds by submitting detailed plans concerning their use (2d). Some potential recipients may choose not to compete, either because they lack the technical expertise needed to prepare the required plans or because they regard the risks of failure as too high to justify the costs of applying. For the grantor, on the other

3. In Canada, federal-provincial tax equalization grants fall in the completely unrestricted category. Australia also uses unconditional financial assistance grants. See ACIR, *In Search of Balance: Canada's Intergovernmental Experience* (GPO, 1971); David B. Perry, "Federal-Provincial Fiscal Relations: The Last Six Years and the Next Five," *Canadian Tax Journal,* vol. 20 (July–August 1972), pp. 349–60; James A. Maxwell, "Revenue-Sharing in Canada and Australia: Some Implications for the United States," *National Tax Journal,* vol. 24 (June 1971), pp. 251–65.

4. In states with separate school districts, education grants looked at from the point of view of the state government are grants restricted to one function; but from the point of view of the school district, they are general-purpose grants unless their use is restricted to particular education programs.

5. Martha Derthick, *Uncontrollable Spending for Social Services Grants* (Brookings Institution, 1975).

hand, project grants provide welcome opportunities to reject low-priority proposals and to adjust the terms of support for others so as to maximize the public benefits to be obtained from the funds expended. In fiscal 1972, project grants accounted for 21 percent of federal grant expenditures but less than 2 percent of state grant spending.

The greater importance of project grants in the federal grant system suggests that the relationship between the two parties to a transaction may have a significant impact on grant design. The degree and type of controls exercised by grantors might well be different on grants between two independent powers than on grants between superior and subordinate powers or grants involving a mixture of independent and subordinate powers.

The Case for and against Intergovernmental Grants

Though the reasons for using intergovernmental grants in federal fiscal systems have been widely discussed and are generally understood to be compelling, the case for grants is by no means a solid and unshakable one. It rests to a large degree on second-best, rather than first-best, considerations—better alternatives may exist in principle, but grants appear to be the best feasible means of attaining various fiscal and economic goals. In a changing world, however, grants may not always remain so, and it is thus important to understand both their weaknesses and their strengths relative to alternative fiscal instruments.

The economic rationale for intergovernmental grants arises from three well-known deficiencies of most modern federal fiscal systems: the existence of program benefits that spill over from one governmental jurisdiction to another, fiscal imbalances of various kinds, and unmet needs of lower income people. The decentralization of political power, the encouragement of merit goods, and the promotion of innovation and experimentation are other aspects of the basic rationale.[6] Other objectives, such as stabilization of the economy, may not be particularly well served by grant programs on their own, but may

6. For other discussions of grant program objectives see, for example, Edward R. Fried and others, *Setting National Priorities: The 1974 Budget* (Brookings Institution, 1973), chap. 5; Richard A. Musgrave and Peggy B. Musgrave, *Public Finance in Theory and Practice*, 2d ed. (McGraw-Hill, 1976), pp. 625–30; Charles L. Schultze, "Sorting Out the Social Grant Programs: An Economist's Criteria," *American Economic Review*, vol. 64 (May 1974, *Papers and Proceedings, 1973*), pp. 183–86.

be promoted through timely additions to existing programs. The antirecession fiscal assistance program, added to general revenue sharing in 1976, is one such example.

Benefit Spillouts

Whenever the benefits of a particular state or local government program accrue both to insiders who pay for the program and to outsiders who, though able to pay for it, receive it free, inequities arise. Economic inefficiencies exist if those who pay for the program expand it only to the point where their own marginal benefits equal their marginal tax costs, rather than to the socially optimal point where total marginal benefits equal total marginal costs. Without counteracting forces, then, programs with benefit spillouts are likely to be given less support than they merit, as compared to programs without spillouts or to goods sold in the marketplace, thus producing an inefficient diversion of resources from superior to inferior uses.

To avoid these distortions, governmental jurisdictions might be reorganized and extended so that governments' boundaries coincided more or less with the benefit areas of the programs they administer and finance. This solution might be helpful in specific instances, but governmental reorganizations are notoriously difficult to bring about, and interstate spillovers would be particularly hard to deal with. Even more important, to try to contain the benefit spillovers of all existing major programs would call for increasing the already numerous special-purpose local governments and would be costly and time-consuming for voters.

A properly designed intergovernmental grant appears, therefore, to be the preferred policy instrument for dealing with government programs with benefit spillovers. Since the problem arises from tax costs that produce only partial program benefits, the goal would be to reduce the costs to insiders until they come into line with the benefits enjoyed by those groups. For a local government spillout program this could be done by a federal or state open-ended matching grant, with the grantor's share of total costs set equal to the outsider share of total program benefits. In economic terms such a grant would reduce the price at which insiders could purchase the program's total benefits. If that price were set correctly, the local government would choose to operate the program at the socially optimal level, and there would be no free-rider groups.

In such an instance intergovernmental grants offer a first-best solution to a fiscal problem. Deciding on when that solution should be adopted and exactly how it should be implemented, however, is no small problem. Some critics question the importance of benefit spillovers. Others stress the possibility that countervailing forces may automatically eliminate the distortions they cause and note that voluntary, cooperative action by state and local governments can deal with any remaining problems. Some argue, in short, that there is no need for grants to counteract spillovers, while others, less sanguine, argue that the idea of solution by grants is fine in principle but impossible in practice.[7] How damaging to the case for open-ended, matching grants are these criticisms?

In the financing of public schools, for example, those who believe that local schools generate mainly private, and few public, benefits see no justification for any government grants.[8] Others who believe that schools offer important public benefits may so value their contribution to society as a whole that they are willing to support good schools even though their benefits mainly accrue elsewhere (since educational effects are not localized when students are free to move away).[9] For such voters, benefit spillovers do not distort school financing choices, and there is no need for compensatory grants. There is, however, no empirical evidence to support this hypothesis rather than the alternative one that voters are more willing to finance the good, well-educated society at home than in regions where they do not live.[10]

Still another possibility is that the burdens of local school taxes are partly shifted to outsiders. If this shifting should exactly equal the flow of benefits to outsiders, local voters who react only to their own benefits and burdens would choose to operate their schools at the

7. See, for example, Selma J. Mushkin and John F. Cotton, *Functional Federalism: Grants-in-Aid and PPB Systems* (George Washington University, State-Local Finances Project, 1968), pp. 43–47.

8. See, for example, Yoram Barzel, "Private Schools and Public School Finance," *Journal of Political Economy,* vol. 81 (January–February 1973), pp. 174–76.

9. See, for example, Donald J. Curran and Raymond J. Krasniewski, "State Aid to Local Governments—What Form Should It Take?" National Tax Association— Tax Institute of America, *Proceedings of the Sixty-Seventh Annual Conference on Taxation, 1974* (Columbus, Ohio: NTA-TIA, 1975), pp. 220–22.

10. Charles T. Clotfelter, however, presents some evidence that states with higher rates of out-migration of graduates give less support to student-related higher education expenditures; "Public Spending for Higher Education; An Empirical Test of Two Hypotheses," *Public Finance,* vol. 31, no. 2 (1976), pp. 177–95.

same level as would voters who take total benefits and costs into account. The result would be the socially optimal amount of local school services, and any misguided use of grants to compensate for spillovers would simply make matters worse. Nor are tax burden (cost) spillouts the only potential countervailing force. Budgetary choices that generate benefit spillouts may also generate equally important benefit spillins. Taxpayers may be quite willing to finance good schools if they believe that such schools attract good citizens and help make for a good local society. This willingness need not be diminished by the fear that some of the young people being educated will leave the area as long as there is reason to assume that well-educated parents will be induced to move in. Unfortunately for policymakers, the answer to whether countervailing cost and benefit spillovers do in fact tend to achieve such nice, socially optimal, balances is unknown.[11]

Other critics of matching grants concede that the countervailing effects may frequently be too small to eliminate the distortions caused by benefit spillouts but argue that bargaining and cooperative action among the affected state or local governments can be relied on to produce socially optimal results.[12] Grant proponents, on the other hand, stress the many hurdles that successful intergovernmental bargaining of this sort would have to overcome, particularly when the number of affected parties is large.[13] Whether people can solve their problems without government intervention, in this case by the use of intergovernmental grants, is a long-standing issue not likely to be soon resolved.

The spillover theory of intergovernmental grants suffers from the fact that state and local program benefits cannot even be identified clearly in many cases, let alone be measured quantitatively. In the absence of reliable measurements it is impossible to say whether the

11. See Werner Z. Hirsch, Elbert W. Segelhorst, and Morton J. Marcus, *Spillover of Public Education Costs and Benefits* (University of California—Los Angeles, Institute of Government and Public Affairs, 1964); Burton A. Weisbrod, *External Benefits of Public Education: An Economic Analysis* (Industrial Relations Section, Princeton University, 1964).

12. For the basic theoretical analysis of these issues see R. H. Coase, "The Problem of Social Cost," *Journal of Law and Economics*, vol. 3 (October 1960), pp. 1–44; James M. Buchanan and William Craig Stubblebine, "Externality," *Economica*, vol. 29 (November 1962), pp. 371–84.

13. See Musgrave and Musgrave, *Public Finance*, pp. 626–27.

outsider share of total program benefits, and hence the appropriate matching share for the grantor, is 10 percent, or 90 percent, or any other number. This being the case, it is not surprising to find, as Charles Schultze has stressed, that most federal categorical grants are not in fact designed with benefit spillovers in mind.[14] Nevertheless, if distorting spillouts exist, however uncertain their true dimensions may be, their presence cannot be ignored by the designers of intergovernmental grants. Benefit spillovers can create serious economic inefficiencies and inequities, and intergovernmental grants, designed with those effects in mind, may well be the preferred fiscal instrument for combatting them.

Vertical Fiscal Imbalance

Federal systems of government are likely to be characterized by chronic fiscal imbalance among the different levels of government. Whereas tax revenues can be most equitably and efficiently raised by the higher levels of government, proponents of intergovernmental grants argue, the proceeds can often be spent most effectively at the lower levels of government. On the tax side, the generally progressive federal tax system is commonly contrasted with the regressive structure of many state and local taxes, and taxpayer mobility, real or imagined, is seen as holding state and local spending below widely desired levels. Critics see a risk of overcentralizing political power by adding to the federal government's dominance in raising revenue. On the expenditure side, on the other hand, the arguments favoring tax sharing stress the decentralization of governmental activities— namely, the superior ability of lower level governments to satisfy geographical diversity in the taste and need for public services and to experiment with new methods of production and delivery of those services. Taken together, these considerations create a case for balancing grants from higher to lower levels of government, distributed without strings or controls to the jurisdictions from which the revenues being distributed were obtained—that is, for some kind of tax sharing arrangement.

The case for tax sharing as a means of correcting fiscal imbalances has been attacked on the grounds that rather than being endemic to federal systems of government these imbalances result simply from

14. "Sorting Out the Social Grant Programs," p. 182.

fiscal mismanagement. A more pragmatic criticism accepts the basic premise of chronic fiscal imbalances but argues that they are best dealt with not by tax sharing but by other grant designs.

The mismanagement critics maintain that an equitable distribution of income and wealth in the nation as a whole is an important governmental goal that can be brought about by the operation of the federal government's tax and transfer programs. A second goal, whose feasibility depends on the achievement of the first, is the benefits-received financing of all state and local government programs. Given the proper use of ability-to-pay taxation (both positive and negative) and in-kind subsidies by the national government, the argument goes, there would be no need for redistributive policies at lower levels of government. Allocation of state and local tax burdens on a benefits-received basis would then be both equitable and efficient. State and local taxpayers would pay for the specific benefits they enjoy, would vote for spending changes according to their individual tastes, and would find no reason to move from one jurisdiction to another because of disparities in tax burdens and public service benefits.[15] In such a world there would be no fiscal imbalances to justify equilibrating intergovernmental grants.

The real world, however, is something else again. It may be true that some of the federal government's evident failure to achieve a widely accepted national distribution of income and wealth is attributable to mismanagement of the relevant tax, transfer, and subsidy programs; but that will be regarded by many as the normal state

15. For further discussion of the redistributive and allocative functions of government and of the potential roles of ability-to-pay and benefits-received financing see Richard A. Musgrave, *The Theory of Public Finance: A Study in Public Economy* (McGraw-Hill, 1959), chaps. 1, 4, 5. The uncertain extent to which benefits-received financing of state and local government services would eliminate any fiscal distortion of household and business decisions to locate in different areas is discussed by Richard A. Musgrave, "Approaches to a Fiscal Theory of Political Federalism," and James M. Buchanan, "Comments," in *Public Finances: Needs, Sources and Utilization,* A Conference of the Universities—National Bureau Committee for Economic Research, National Bureau of Economic Research (Princeton University Press, 1961), pp. 117–29. This interchange was a continuation of an extensive debate concerning grants and fiscal equity begun by James M. Buchanan in "Federalism and Fiscal Equity," *American Economic Review,* vol. 40 (September 1950), pp. 583–99, reprinted in Richard A. Musgrave and Carl S. Shoup, ed., *Readings in the Economics of Taxation* (Irwin for American Economic Association, 1959), pp. 93–109. Other contributors to the debate are cited in Musgrave and Buchanan, *Public Finances.*

of affairs, not subject to much improvement. More fundamentally, it may be argued that differences between regions in tastes preclude the achievement of any national consensus on redistributive programs and require the introduction of ability-to-pay elements into state and local tax systems. Diversity in individual tastes for income redistribution could thereby be more fully satisfied, those with like preferences in that regard tending to live and work in the same taxing jurisdictions. As long as those preferring low degrees of fiscal redistribution were not all rich and those favoring high degrees were not all poor, the system could function efficiently to achieve its diverse equity goals. Beyond some hard-to-define point, however, attempts by any one state or local government to make any significant move away from the norm are likely to be counterproductive.

There are, then, strong reasons for having some ability-to-pay elements in most state and local tax systems; for whatever reason, they certainly exist now. The result is a set of vertical fiscal imbalances, whose dimensions are hard to measure, that creates a presumptive need for intergovernmental balancing grants.

The fiscal imbalances are not necessarily permanent fixtures, however. The country's attitude toward redistributive goals may change; significant reforms may be achieved in the federal tax and welfare programs; and state and local governments, spurred by tax and expenditure limitation movements, may introduce more benefits-received elements into their revenue systems.[16] The designers of intergovernmental grants should watch closely for such developments as well as for any changes that economic growth may make in the fiscal imbalances that justify intergovernmental aid programs.

In the early 1960s it was fashionable, and realistic, to base the case for unconditional federal grants on a mismatch of fiscal growth elasticities between the federal and the state and local levels of government. Federal revenues tended to grow more rapidly than both full-employment national income and the federal government's need for new programs, thereby creating a fiscal drag inimical to the achievement of high levels of national employment.[17] State and local

16. Richard M. Bird, *Charging for Public Services: A New Look at an Old Idea,* Canadian Tax Paper 59 (Toronto: Canadian Tax Foundation, 1976).

17. On this point see *Economic Report of the President, January 1962,* pp. 78–82; Walter W. Heller, *New Dimensions of Political Economy* (Harvard University Press, 1966), chap. 2.

tax revenues, in contrast, tended to grow more slowly than both national income and state and local demands for public services, thereby creating recurrent fiscal crises, undue reliance on regressive taxes, or unmet public needs. What more logical solution than to distribute some of the surplus federal revenues to hard-pressed state and local governments?[18] By the 1970s, however, there were few federal budget surpluses to distribute to anyone.[19] Fortunately, state and local fiscal problems had, on the average, eased considerably, mainly because the cost of maintaining current levels of service began to rise less rapidly than the revenues from current state and local tax systems.[20] Encouraging as these trends may be for the country as a whole, it does not, of course, mean that all state and local governments will be free from fiscal crises.

However uncertain future needs for balancing intergovernmental grants may be, their present attractions seem indisputable. If so, the important question concerns the form that the grants should take. In theory, vertical fiscal imbalances call for some form of tax sharing arrangement. But such free money transfers may be destructive of incentives of donors to give generously and of recipients to spend the

18. Heller, *New Dimensions,* chap. 3; Joseph A. Pechman, "Financing State and Local Government," *Proceedings of a Symposium on Federal Taxation* (American Bankers Association, 1965), pp. 71–84 (Brookings Reprint 103); Walter W. Heller and Joseph A. Pechman, "Questions and Answers on Revenue Sharing," in *Revenue Sharing and Its Alternatives: What Future for Fiscal Federalism?* Hearings before the Subcommittee on Fiscal Policy of the Joint Economic Committee, 90 Cong. 1 sess. (GPO, 1967), pp. 111–17 (Brookings Reprint 135).

19. In the Brookings Institution's evaluation of the president's 1980 budget, Joseph A. Pechman and Robert W. Hartman projected that by fiscal 1982–84 "there will be some room for additional outlays and tax cuts." "The 1980 Budget and the Budget Outlook," in Joseph A. Pechman, ed., *Setting National Priorities: The 1980 Budget* (Brookings Institution, 1979), p. 55. The size of these discretionary margins, however, is dwarfed by the demands likely to be made on them. Longer run projections for the federal government have also been made by Charles L. Schultze. Assuming the continuation of all 1977 tax and spending programs, Schultze's estimates indicate that nonrecession revenues would rise from 20 percent of full employment GNP in fiscal 1977 to 21 percent in 1981 and nearly 23 percent in 1986, while nonrecession constant-quality program expenditures, also equal to 20 percent of 1977 full employment GNP, would fall to 19 percent of nonrecession GNP in 1981 and to 18 percent in 1986. The result would be an opportunity for discretionary spending increases or tax reductions of significant amounts. See Charles L. Schultze, "Federal Spending: Past, Present, and Future," in Henry Owen and Charles L. Schultze, eds., *Setting National Priorities: The Next Ten Years* (Brookings Institution, 1976), pp. 351–54.

20. Emil M. Sunley, Jr., "State and Local Governments," in ibid., p. 408.

proceeds carefully and efficiently. This argument does not demolish the case for balancing grants, but it does suggest that there are limits to the importance they can safely be allowed to attain if both parties to the contract are to behave responsibly.

By their very nature, federally collected individual income tax revenues that are returned to their source provide more money for rich than for poor districts. The more progressive that federal tax is, the more this is true. Federal income tax sharing, in short, would deal with vertical, and not horizontal, fiscal imbalances. If disparities in fiscal needs and capacities create a compelling case for federal grants, as many believe, some type of redistributive grant should be given priority. Since equalizing grants would contribute to the solution of vertical imbalances, the need for tax sharing arrangements, it is argued, should be evaluated after such grants have been placed in operation. Unfortunately, this is much more easily said than done.

Horizontal Fiscal Disparities and Imbalance

The case for intergovernmental grants whose primary purpose is to aid state and local governments with relatively low fiscal abilities, or relatively high fiscal needs, or both is, on the surface at least, highly attractive. Why should wealthy communities be able to buy public goods of high quality at low tax rates while poor ones struggle to achieve minimum levels of service by taxing themselves at very high rates? This nagging question, brought dramatically to public attention by the Serrano and Rodriguez court cases attacking the equity of local school finance systems,[21] lies at the heart of the issue of redistributive grants. Many assume without question an urgent need to mitigate or eliminate horizontal fiscal disparities among both states and local communities and press strongly for redistributive grant programs of one kind or another. Their aim, of course, is to establish a more equitable fiscal system that compensates for the economic inefficiencies created whenever businesses and households reject location choices based on economic realities because of inter-community tax and expenditure differentials. Unfortunately, it is far from clear exactly how these desired results can best be brought about.

For some the answer involves the simultaneous improvement of

21. *Serrano v. Priest*, 5 C. 3d 584, 487 P.2d 1241 (1971); *San Antonio Independent School District v. Rodriguez*, 411 U.S. 1 (1973).

federal income redistribution programs and shift of state and local revenue systems to a benefits-received basis. In a world with no significant vertical or horizontal fiscal imbalances, the fact that good schools cost a higher percentage of family income in poor than in rich communities would no more be a cause for government intervention than the fact that a television set, say, costs a higher percentage of a low-income family budget than of a high-income one. There would, in short, be no need for intergovernmental redistributive grants.

Others take a quite different route, maintaining that market reactions to fiscal disparities between communities will normally provide all, or most, of the adjustments needed. The key proposition here is that land, buildings, and local public services are all purchased jointly, in one package, by households and businesses, and that in well-behaved real estate markets, land prices will tend to reflect any disparities that exist long enough to matter. Communities with a high tax cost for a given quality of government services will have relatively low land prices, other things equal, and localities with high-quality services for a given tax cost will have high land values. This happens because well-informed buyers and sellers can be expected to capitalize future expected intercommunity tax and government benefit differentials and to incorporate these fiscal capital costs or values in the total price set on a given real estate package.[22] As a result, economic reality can only be discerned by looking at the total land-building-governmental package with its combined locational, operational, and public service benefits and costs. Its fiscal components alone are meaningless because they are closely related to other components, and to base an intergovernmental grant program on them would create inequities rather than alleviating them.

These interactions between land prices and intercommunity dis-

22. Suppose that two adjacent communities offer identical public services but that in A the effective property tax rate is 3 percent of market value while in B it is 4 percent. The annual property tax in A on a $60,000 house is therefore $1,800. If the relevant interest rate for home buyers is, say, 10 percent, what would be the market value of an identical house located in community B? If most people saw the fiscal disparity between the two communities as a very temporary phenomenon, the value would be only a little less than $60,000. But if the disparity were expected to continue indefinitely, the market value of the house in B would differ by the capitalized value of the difference in the annual property tax liability on the two houses—$4,286, which is simply the amount required, at an interest rate of 10 percent, to pay the excess tax of $428.56. An informed buyer would, in theory, be indifferent between identical houses selling for $60,000 in A and for $55,714 in B.

parities are an important, though often neglected, element in the public policy arena. This is not to argue that the process of fiscal capitalization operates well enough everywhere to eliminate all need for redistribution grants. Few would attribute that degree of perfection to real estate markets. Information is incomplete and expensive, various kinds of barriers to mobility exist, and competitive forces are sometimes weak. Even so, capitalization effects do exist in varying degrees, and neither the need for, nor the best design of, redistribution grants can be determined without taking them into account. Fiscal disparities alone, in other words, do not create the inequitable and inefficient imbalances that justify government intervention.

In summary, as long as state and local tax systems retain their strong ability-to-pay orientation, and as long as real estate markets operate imperfectly, both vertical and horizontal imbalances can be expected to exist. One way to deal with these inequities and inefficiencies is by the use of federal unrestricted, redistributive grants. The redistributive features of the grants should apply more strongly to state and regional than to local governments because ability-to-pay financing is more important at the higher levels of government, and offsetting capitalization effects are weaker. In other words, the incidence of fiscal imbalances is likely to be highest at the state level and lowest at the local level. In grants to local governments, precedence should be given to communities with relatively high numbers of low-income families because those families are typically less mobile than others and their communities are consequently more likely to exhibit significant fiscal imbalances. It is an inherent characteristic of these unrestricted grants, however, that their funds accrue to the benefit of the whole community rather than to specific families or groups within it. Their purpose is to moderate fiscal imbalances for all households and not just for those with low incomes.

Unmet Needs of Low-Income Groups

There seems little doubt that one of the strongest forces behind the rapid growth in intergovernmental grants has been a desire to assist low-income families. Yet the obvious instruments for this purpose are direct government transfers and in-kind subsidies to the people in question. Is there, then, any need to consider grants for this purpose at all? Grants may, of course, seem reasonable simply because direct transfers and subsidies are seen to be inadequate and because most grants do provide some aid, however inefficiently, to low-income groups. A stronger, though controversial, case for grants can be based on the proposition that certain local government programs are merit goods deserving some element of government support, particularly for low-income groups.[23] If this view of local government services (other than schools) were taken, for example, the federal government could use a straight matching grant as an incentive to expand provision of the services in question, or it could seek to favor low-income beneficiaries by varying the matching ratio according to the number of low-income families in each recipient jurisdiction. The latter type of program might make some communities more receptive to low-income newcomers because of the increased grant aid their presence would attract but not help much in jurisdictions where they lacked political power. A better instrument would then be a categorical or block grant restricted to state and local programs that benefit mainly low-income groups.

Fiscal Partnerships

Whatever the reasons for intergovernmental grant programs, the result is the creation of a fiscal partnership between two (or more) levels of government. Looking at grants in this way makes it easier to understand both what the roles of the two parties actually are and what they should be.[24]

Broadly, fiscal partnerships may be described as either joint ventures or uneasy alliances. When the two parties share common goals which are better pursued together than separately, their joint venture clearly can operate most efficiently if each contributes according to its own comparative advantage. In general this is likely to mean that the higher level of government, the donor, should provide a major share of the funds, since it can raise them more effectively, and also those specialized resources, such as highly skilled professional expertise, that are not readily available to small governments. The donee, on the other hand, can bring to the venture its own specialized

23. See Lester C. Thurow, "Cash Versus In-Kind Transfers," *American Economic Review*, vol. 64 (May 1974, *Papers and Proceedings, 1973*), pp. 190–95.

24. See Burkhead and Miner, *Public Expenditure*, pp. 278–82.

knowledge of local tastes and other idiosyncracies[25] and an ability to experiment with alternative instruments and procedures at acceptably low costs.

Uneasy alliances, in contrast, are made between partners who have different goals but nevertheless find it mutually profitable to work together. The result is likely to be an activity distinguished by unstable compromises of conflicting interests and by a high degree of political negotiating and bargaining.[26] Donors will typically attempt to direct donees' activities in the desired direction, to restrict their freedom in various ways, and to do all this with the least expenditure of donor funds. Donees, on the other hand, will try to convert restricted funds into fungible resources, by directing as much of the donors' money as possible into activities that would have been undertaken anyway, and to make the donors' effective matching rates as high as possible, by shifting activities from low- to high-matching programs or from no-matching to matching categories. In such grant programs there may be a large gap between appearance, as seen in the authorizing legislation and implementing regulations, and reality, as determined by the actual behavior of the two parties. Economic researchers are only just beginning to analyze grant programs in such a context.

The uneasy alliance concept may also be useful in the broader context of all the parties with an interest in specific intergovernmental programs. In addition to the top government officials who administer a program and constitute the fiscal partnership in its narrow sense, there are the clients who enjoy the benefits of the program, the government workers who operate it, the general taxpayers who finance it, and the elected politicians who direct it. Each of these groups has its own particular goals which it pursues subject to the general constraint that all other parties must be at least reasonably satisfied with the achievement of their own goals.[27] Since these group goals are mutually conflicting in various ways, the whole operation is an uneasy

25. The arrangement is similar to that between the national weather forecasting service, with its skilled scientists and expensive equipment, and local forecasters who know, from long experience, how different weather patterns are likely to be altered by the special topographical characteristics of their own areas.

26. Helen Ingram, "Policy Implementation Through Bargaining: The Case of Federal Grants-in-Aid," *Public Policy,* vol. 25 (Fall 1977), pp. 499–526.

27. For an analysis of the budgetary process based on self-interested behavior of the different participant groups see Douglas G. Hartle, *A Theory of the Expenditure Budgetary Process,* Ontario Economic Council Research Study 5 (University of Toronto Press for the Ontario Economic Council, 1976).

alliance. Moreover, its characteristics will shift from time to time in any given place, and they will also differ from place to place at any given time. The critical importance of these shifts and differences is that they determine the nature of the economic effects of specific grant programs.

This means that the analysis of intergovernmental grants must be based on a set of alternative theoretical models, each emphasizing the behavior of grant programs in an environment dominated by one of the participating groups, or by an alliance of cooperating groups. No one of these models can apply to all situations at all times, but each has something to contribute to the final answer. In some cases a single model will suffice because operation of the grant program is in fact dominated by one of the participating groups. In other cases, however, the outcome will be a more complex compromise of conflicting interests.

Theories of Intergovernmental Grants

Predicting the effects of different kinds of grant programs requires a relevant theory of economic, political, and bureaucratic behavior.[28] In general, people are assumed to behave so as to maximize the attainment of one or more goals within a set of constraints (such as income limits). Since each of the groups participating in a grant partnership has its own special goals, the way in which that program can be expected to operate will depend on which group or combination of groups dominates the decisionmaking process. Some theories deal only with the achievement of one particular group's goals, while others stress the conflicts and compromises that characterize situations in which several groups interact.

Economic Models

Economic models of intergovernmental grants stress the interests of voter-taxpayers who choose the level of expenditures on grant programs in much the same way that they choose expenditure levels for other government programs or for private goods and services.

28. See, for example, Dennis C. Mueller, "Public Choice: A Survey," *Journal of Economic Literature,* vol. 14 (June 1976), pp. 395–433; William Orzechowski, "Economic Models of Bureaucracy: Survey, Extensions, and Evidence," in Thomas E. Borcherding, ed., *Budgets and Bureaucrats: The Sources of Government Growth* (Duke University Press, 1977), pp. 229–59.

Their goal is maximization of the total utility, or pleasure, received from the allocation of a fixed budget to the purchase of private goods, the payment of taxes for government services, and personal saving.[29] While private consumption and saving items may be selected individually, according to taste, from all those available on the open market, public consumption must be provided collectively to all. There must therefore be some mechanism by which all the conflicting individual tastes and desires for government services are translated (compromised) into collective choices for government action. In some models this is done by an all-wise politician who accurately senses the will of his constituents, provides the correct bundle of goods and services, and is rewarded by reelection or by promotion to higher public office. Other models use a majority-vote choice mechanism in which the tastes of the median voter determine the amount and composition of the public budget.[30]

One weakness of these models, of course, is that they neglect the interests of all other participant groups.[31] This may clearly be seen by comparing two ways in which a given community would employ a specified sum of money, one given in lump sums to each voter, and the other in an unrestricted grant to the local government. Some eco-

29. A good example of the use of this kind of model to analyze federal grant programs is found in Edward M. Gramlich and Harvey Galper, "State and Local Fiscal Behavior and Federal Grant Policy," *Brookings Papers on Economic Activity,* *1:1973,* pp. 15–65. See also Wallace E. Oates, *Fiscal Federalism* (Harcourt Brace Jovanovich, 1972), chap. 3.

30. See James L. Barr and Otto A. Davis, "An Elementary Political and Economic Theory of the Expenditures of Local Governments," *Southern Economic Journal,* vol. 33 (October 1966), pp. 149–65; Howard R. Bowen, "The Interpretation of Voting in the Allocation of Economic Resources," *Quarterly Journal of Economics,* vol. 58 (November 1943), pp. 27–48, reprinted in Kenneth J. Arrow and Tibor Scitovsky, eds., *Readings in Welfare Economics* (Irwin for the American Economic Association, 1969), pp. 115–32; James M. Buchanan and Gordon Tullock, *The Calculus of Consent: Logical Foundations of Constitutional Democracy* (University of Michigan Press, 1962); William S. Comanor, "The Median Voter Rule and the Theory of Political Choice," *Journal of Public Economics,* vol. 5 (January–February 1976), pp. 169–77; Anthony Downs, *An Economic Theory of Democracy* (Harper and Brothers, 1957).

31. Another criticism of economic models is that they try to extend economic behavior principles beyond the private market, where their relevance is reasonably clear, to the public sector, where it is not. Utility maximization may well be the main motivating force behind private decisions about consumption, but it need not be so for choices of governmental expenditures where consideration of the general public good may weigh importantly with many voters and other participants.

nomic models predict that the two kinds of allocation would produce exactly the same increases in private and public spending, the transfers through a small increase in taxes and government spending and the grant through a large reduction in taxes.[32] The local government, in other words, is seen as a well-run club, so highly responsive to the relatively homogeneous tastes of its members that it doesn't matter whether an outside gift comes to the club itself or to the members separately.[33]

This view of the decisionmaking process, however, is unduly narrow. Local taxpayer-voters are also taxpayers and voters at the state and federal levels, and they may find themselves in the frustrating position of desiring higher local government spending but fearing the adverse effects of higher local taxes. Under such circumstances they would favor federal or state grants over federal or state tax cuts. The use of all grant funds to increase local spending, in other words, is not necessarily inconsistent with such an extended version of the median voter model. However, if a high-spending coalition dominated government at the federal level and a low-spending one at the local level, an economic model would still predict that most of the grant money would be used to reduce local taxes.

Bureaucratic Models

Quite another picture of the two different ways of allocating outside money is given by bureaucratic theories of local government behavior. Their standard prediction is that whereas transfers of lump sums to taxpayers would induce very little increase in government taxes and spending, unrestricted government grants would raise public spending greatly and private spending very little. The money, in short, tends to stick in whichever sector, public or private, it is first

32. See David F. Bradford and Wallace E. Oates, "The Analysis of Revenue Sharing in a New Approach to Collective Fiscal Decisions," *Quarterly Journal of Economics*, vol. 85 (August 1971), pp. 416–39, and "Towards a Predictive Theory of Intergovernmental Grants," *American Economic Review*, vol. 61 (May 1971, *Papers and Proceedings, 1970*), pp. 440–48.

33. Similarly, imposing higher state or federal taxes on the residents of a given community and distributing the proceeds to their local government as an unrestricted grant would have no effect on either total private consumption or local government spending. The classic analysis of clubs is by James M. Buchanan, "An Economic Theory of Clubs," *Economica*, vol. 32 (February 1965), pp. 1–14.

received. These "flypaper effects"[34] result from the fact that bureaucratic models stress government officials' and workers' pursuit of their own utility goals, rather than those of taxpayer-voters, in the choice and operation of government programs. One possible result, emphasized by the budget-maximizing models, is a larger government sector than that desired by most voters.[35] Another result, emphasized by the X-efficiency and neoclassical firm models, is the provision of public output at costs well above the minimum levels attainable.[36] In neither case do taxpayers receive full value for their money. They

34. This term was apparently coined by Arthur Okun. See Edward M. Gramlich, "Intergovernmental Grants: A Review of the Empirical Literature," in Wallace E. Oates, ed., *The Political Economy of Fiscal Federalism* (Lexington Books, 1977).

35. These models hypothesize that bureaucrats maximize the size of their budgets within a total-funds-available constraint. See C. Northcote Parkinson, *Parkinson's Law and Other Studies in Administration* (Houghton Mifflin, Riverside Press, 1957); Gordon Tullock, *The Politics of Bureaucracy* (Washington: Public Affairs Press, 1965); William A. Niskanen, Jr., "The Peculiar Economics of Bureaucracy," *American Economic Review,* vol. 58 (May 1968, *Papers and Proceedings, 1967*), pp. 293–305, *Bureaucracy and Representative Government* (Aldine-Atherton, 1971), and "Bureaucrats and Politicians," in Economic Analysis of Political Behavior, Proceedings of a Conference, Universities-National Bureau Conference Series no. 29, *Journal of Law and Economics,* vol. 18 (December 1975), pp. 617–43; Martin McGuire, "Notes on Grants-in-Aid and Economic Interactions Among Governments," *Canadian Journal of Economics,* vol. 6 (May 1973), pp. 207–21.

36. In essence, costs are high because bureaucrats and workers maximize their own utility functions and there are not sufficient controls and constraints to force them to work toward minimum costs. Harvey Leibenstein views this kind of situation, which he terms "X-inefficiency," as offering a much more promising source of increased output from given resources than economists' more familiar allocative inefficiency (the use of resources in activities with low rather than high rates of return). See "Allocative Efficiency vs. 'X-Efficiency,'" *American Economic Review,* vol. 56 (June 1966), pp. 392–415, and "Competition and *X*-Efficiency: A Reply," *Journal of Political Economy,* vol. 81 (May–June 1973), pp. 765–77; George J. Stigler, "The Xistence of X-Efficiency," *American Economic Review,* vol. 66 (March 1976), pp. 213–16; Albert Breton, *The Economic Theory of Representative Government* (Aldine, 1974); Albert Breton and Ronald Weintrobe, "The Equilibrium Size of a Budget-maximizing Bureau: A Note on Niskanen's Theory of Bureaucracy," *Journal of Political Economy,* vol. 83 (February 1975), pp. 195–207. Models of the neoclassical firm, in which the separation of ownership and management permits managers to pursue their own goals subject only to some minimum-profit constraint, stress production at above-minimum costs. See William J. Baumol, *Business Behavior, Value and Growth* (Macmillan, 1959); Robin Marris, *The Economic Theory of 'Managerial' Capitalism* (Free Press of Glencoe, 1964); Oliver E. Williamson, *The Economics of Discretionary Behavior: Managerial Objectives in a Theory of the Firm* (Markham, 1967).

are thereby led either to give elected officials more effective means of controlling self-seeking bureaucratic behavior or to devise rules and other arrangements that set strict limits on bureaucratic freedom.[37] Whenever the net outcome of all these conflicting maneuvers is government behavior dominated by organizational concerns rather than citizen preferences, intergovernmental grants are likely to generate flypaper and other effects not predicted by many economic models.

Interactive Models

The most eclectic of the theoretical models are the interactive models, whose main concern is with the conflicts and compromises that characterize the operation of government programs. They focus on the nature of the relationships that develop among different participating groups. No single group dominates, there are numerous goals and instruments to be considered, and decisions must be made in spite of a high degree of uncertainty about the effects of different policy actions. One reaction is the adoption of very simple decision rules, usually involving incremental budgeting that stresses internal rather than external group values and goals.[38] Another is the design of sequential decisionmaking procedures that encourage experimentation and information gathering and allow the participating parties to modify their behavior accordingly.[39]

By applying theories of information, organizational structure, strategic behavior, and decisionmaking under uncertainty,[40] interactive models of public choice produce a number of distinctive hy-

37. These institutional arrangements include taxes that are relatively insensitive to economic growth and to inflation, taxes whose burdens are relatively certain and clear to taxpayers, fragmented rather than centralized local government structures, restrictions on the use of debt financing, and zero-based rather than incremental budgeting.

38. See John P. Crecine, *Government Problem Solving: A Computer Simulation of Municipal Budgeting* (Rand McNally, 1969); Patrick D. Larkey, "Process Models and Program Evaluation: The Impact of General Revenue Sharing on Municipal Fiscal Behavior—A Summary," in NTA-TIA, *Proceedings, 1976,* pp. 167–78.

39. See, for example, the analysis of administered contracts by Victor P. Goldberg, "Toward an Expanded Economic Theory of Contract," *Journal of Economic Issues,* vol. 10 (March 1976), pp. 45–61, and "Regulation and Administered Contracts," *Bell Journal of Economics,* vol. 7 (Autumn 1976), pp. 426–48.

40. See, for example, Oliver E. Williamson, *Markets and Hierarchies—Analysis and Antitrust Implications: A Study in the Economics of Internal Organization* (Free Press, 1975); John Von Neumann and Oskar Morgenstern, *Theory of Games and Economic Behavior,* 3d ed. (Princeton University Press, 1953).

potheses about the effects of intergovernmental grants. One is that
outcomes will vary considerably from one kind of institutional and
organizational structure to another. A second is that the true values
of certain key policy parameters may differ significantly from what
they appear to be in the authorizing law or implementing regulations.
If effective matching rates for grants differ materially from the statutory levels, for example, analysis that does not probe deeply into the
practical operation of the fiscal partnership in question will yield
seriously misleading results. A third hypothesis is that many kinds of
grants may usefully be looked at as the purchase of a desired benefit
or service by the grantor. The grant is made to buy something that
grantees are presumably better able to provide than the grantors
themselves are.[41] Interactive theories can be more productively applied to some kinds of grant programs than to others. The program of
aid to families with dependent children, for example, provides a fertile
field for interactive modeling because of its ambiguously defined
goals, uncertain lines of intergovernmental authority, and strong reliance on bargaining and negotiated settlements.[42] Other grant programs may be most profitably handled by either economic or bureaucratic models.

Economic and Political Effects of Grants

Intergovernmental grants have many varied effects. Most are economic in nature—price effects reflecting reductions in the cost to
grantees of providing the funded services or benefits, income effects
reflecting the additional funds available for aided programs, and

41. John T. Rowntree, Jr., "The Efficiency of Intergovernmental Grants" (Ph.D.
dissertation, University of California—Berkeley, 1966). Applying this interpretation
of an exchange relationship to Comprehensive Employment and Training Act
(CETA) grants, Katz and Wiseman argue that in its programs of subsidized employment in the public sector the federal government is basically trying to buy a
number of jobs for workers with particular characteristics. Harry Katz and Michael
Wiseman, "An Essay on Subsidized Employment in the Public Sector," in National
Commission for Manpower Policy, *Job Creation Through Public Service Employment,* vol. 3: *Commissioned Papers* (Washington: National Commission for Manpower Policy, 1978), pp. 151–234.

42. Irene Lurie, "Estimates of Tax Rates in the AFDC Program," and Bradley R.
Schiller, "AFDC Tax Rates: Some Further Evidence," *National Tax Journal,* vol. 27
(March 1974), pp. 93–111, and vol. 30 (March 1977), pp. 93–94; Frederick C.
Doolittle, "Intergovernmental Relations in Federal Grant Programs: The Case of
Aid for Families With Dependent Children" (Ph.D. dissertation, University of Cali-
fornia—Berkeley, 1977).

indirect effects on other programs and governmental units and on government borrowing activities.[43] The political effects of grant programs reflect changes in governmental processes, or structures.[44] Each kind of effect has both a narrow scope, focusing only on governmental behavior, and a broad scope, extending the picture to include all groups, regions, and activities affected by government.

PRICE EFFECTS. An open-ended, matching grant under which the grantor provides, say, $1 for every $2 spent by the grantee for the program from its own funds (a grantor matching ratio of 50 percent) creates an effective price reduction of 33 percent. This happens because the grantee can buy $1 of program benefits for 67 cents of its own funds, compared to a full $1 before the grant agreement was enacted.[45] Reactions to this kind of price reduction will be of the three main kinds long distinguished in consumer demand theory.

The grantee's response would be fiscally neutral if program activities increase by a percentage equal to the percentage reduction in price. In technical terms this represents a grantee price elasticity of demand equal to unity. In fiscal terms it means that the grantee would spend exactly the same amount of its own funds on the program with

43. Theoretical economic analyses of grants include Jon Harford, "Optimizing Intergovernmental Grants With Three Levels of Government," *Public Finance Quarterly*, vol. 5 (January 1977), pp. 99–116; Louis J. James, "The Stimulation and Substitution Effects of Grants-in-Aid: A General Equilibrium Analysis," *National Tax Journal*, vol. 26 (June 1973), pp. 251–65; Eytan Sheshinski, "The Supply of Communal Goods and Revenue Sharing," in Martin S. Feldstein and Robert P. Inman, eds., *The Economics of Public Services*, Proceedings of a Conference Held by the International Economic Association (London: Macmillan, 1977), pp. 253–73; Ronald K. Teeples, "A Model of a Matching Grant-in-Aid Program with External Tax Effects," *National Tax Journal*, vol. 22 (December 1969), pp. 486–95; Charles Waldauer, "Grant Structures and Their Effects on Aided Government Expenditures: An Indifference Curve Analysis," *Public Finance*, vol. 28, no. 2 (1973), pp. 212–26; James A. Wilde, "The Expenditure Effects of Grant-in-Aid Programs" and "Grants-in-Aid: The Analytics of Design and Response," *National Tax Journal*, vol. 21 (September 1968), pp. 340–48, and vol. 24 (June 1971), pp. 143–55.

44. See, for example, L. L. Ecker-Racz, *The Politics and Economics of State-Local Finance* (Prentice-Hall, 1970); Phillip Monypenny, "Federal Grants-in-Aid to State Governments; A Political Analysis," *National Tax Journal*, vol. 13 (March 1960), pp. 1–16; Richard E. Wagner, *The Fiscal Organization of American Federalism: Description, Analysis, Reform* (Markham, 1971), and *The Public Economy* (Markham, 1973); Deil S. Wright, *Federal Grants-in-Aid: Perspectives and Alternatives* (Washington: American Enterprise Institute for Public Policy Research, 1968).

45. In general, if the grantor's share of program costs is m and the grantee's share is $1 - m$, the grantor's matching ratio is $m/1 - m$, the effective price to the grantee is $1 - m$, and the grant-created reduction in price is m percent.

the grant in operation as in the absence of the grant. For the grantor there is then the satisfaction of knowing that the total expenditures on the aided program will be higher by the full amount of the grant. For the grantee there is the budgetary convenience of not having to find more money to spend on the aided program, and there are no released program funds to be allocated to other activities or to tax reduction. If there are no cross-price elasticity effects, the matching grant will have no spillover effects on the rest of the grantee's budget and hence may be said to be fiscally neutral.

The other two price effects are more complicated. If the grantee reacts by spending less of its own money on the grant-aided program than before (a price elasticity of demand of less than unity), funds will be released for use elsewhere, and to that extent the grant may be said to have failed to accomplish its presumed purpose.[46] Such substitution effects are a critical element in the design of intergovernmental grants. The grantee may, on the other hand, react by spending more of its own funds than before on the aided program (a price elasticity of demand greater than unity). In this case the grant stimulates more support for the program than the grant monies themselves provide, and grantees will need to make suitable budgetary adjustments elsewhere to be able to come up with that extra support.[47]

46. Whether the grantor's purpose may really be presumed to be the narrow one of expanding program expenditures by the exact amount of the grant, rather than the general one of moving expenditures up toward some predetermined goal, is, of course, an open question. The narrow presumed goal, in other words, is not necessarily the proper one, nor indeed the one that grantors typically have in mind.

47. See Edward M. Gramlich, "The Effect of Federal Grants on State-Local Expenditures," in NTA-TIA, *Proceedings, 1969,* pp. 572–73. Gramlich subdivides stimulative grant reactions by defining "perfect matching"—achieved when total expenditures on grant-aided programs are higher than they otherwise would be by both the amount of the grant and the required matching share of recipients. In terms of the definitions in footnote 45, this means that $E_1 = E_0 + G + (1 - m)G/m$, where E_0 is the expenditures in the absence of any grant, E_1 the expenditures in the presence of a matching grant, G the amount of grant funds, and $(1 - m)G/m$ the grantee funds legally required to match the grant funds G. In this case $E_1 = E_0 + G/m$ and the change in program expenditures resulting from a unit change in grant funds is $1/m$ (which Gramlich calls the legal matching ratio, g). He estimates that over the 1955–70 period this ratio was about 1.4, which in turn means that the average federal share of aided program expenditures (m) was 0.71 and the average state and local share ($1 - m$) was 0.29. Having defined perfect matching in this way, Gramlich divides the effects of a change in the total program resulting from a unit change in grant funds ($\Delta E/\Delta G$) into three groups—limited stimulation ($1 < \Delta E/\Delta G < g$), perfect matching ($\Delta E/\Delta G = g$), and complementary ($\Delta E/\Delta G > g$).

Determining the price effects of different kinds of matching grants is a complex empirical task. Not all matching grants generate such effects. Open-ended functional grants do but at the federal level are confined mainly to the welfare and medicaid areas. Much more numerous and important are closed-end functional matching grants and matching project grants, which may or may not create price effects. Even a nine-to-one matching grant will not do so if the limit on grantor funds is, say, $90 million, and those funds flow to grantees who are already spending more than $100 million on the program. Such grantees will behave in the same way whether the $90 million comes in without strings or as a categorical matching closed-end grant. In effect, the grant, however high its matching ratio or restricted its prescribed use, would act exactly like a completely unrestricted, nonmatching grant. In other cases, of course, matching closed-end functional or project grants may have both income and price effects.

Measurements of the price effects of intergovernmental grants differ depending on which theoretical model of grantee behavior is used. Whereas in economic models the price reactions of voter-taxpayers are the same as those of local government officials, in bureaucratic models this is not the case. Moreover, as the interactive models stress, the true matching ratio, and hence the grantee's effective price, may differ significantly from the statutory matching ratio. All of this means that econometric studies of intergovernmental grants, of which there are many,[48] must be used with care. Only if they use the correct matching ratio (price variable) and relate it to the behavior of the group that is effectively in charge of the recipient government's decisionmaking can empirical studies provide the information needed for the optimal design of intergovernmental grants.[49]

---

48. For summaries of these studies see Richard M. Bird, *The Growth of Government Spending in Canada,* Canadian Tax Paper 51 (Toronto: Canadian Tax Foundation, 1970) (appendix B reviews U.S. studies of the determinants of state and local expenditures); John Eric Fredland, *Determinants of State and Local Expenditures: An Annotated Bibliography* (Washington: Urban Institute, 1974); Gramlich, "Effect of Federal Grants," and "Intergovernmental Grants," pp. 219–39; Robert P. Inman, *The Political Economy of Local Fiscal Behavior: An Interpretative Review,* Discussion Paper 49 (University of Pennsylvania, Fels Center of Government, 1974).

49. In addition, of course, the studies must be judged by the usual technical econometric and statistical standards.

INCOME EFFECTS. A completely unrestricted grant increases the funds available to recipient governments, thereby providing additional income that may or may not be spent in the same way that other revenues have been spent. In the first instance the income effects of such grants can be readily predicted and evaluated. Reactions of the second kind to unconditional grants are far more difficult to deal with, however, since the marginal propensity of such grantees to consume differs from their average propensity. Predicting the effects of income grants in these cases must be done on the basis of significant, observable relationships between grantee characteristics and their choice of ways to spend additional grant income. Theoretically, of course, the basic purpose of unrestricted grants is to increase grantees' buying powers without limiting their freedom of choice, and their actual uses for the funds in question should be irrelevant to any evaluation of the grants. In practice, however, such disinterestedness on the part of grantors is likely to be a rare quality, except perhaps for tax-sharing programs. When grantors do care how their money is spent, they may either prefer other kinds of grant design, or they may find it possible to vary allocation formulas for unrestricted grants so as to encourage the expenditure patterns they prefer.

Another important income effect comes from the allocation of funds between the private and public sectors. Economic models frequently predict that an increase in grantor taxes used to raise grantee government incomes will leave the size of government unchanged, while bureaucratic models predict an increase. Empirical evidence clearly indicates that such financial transfers do increase the size of the public sector significantly. Whereas a $1 increase in per capita private incomes tends to raise state and local government spending by $0.05 to $0.10, a similar increase in state and local government income tends to raise public spending by $0.25 to $1.[50] Though the stimulative effects of income grants thus appear to be highly variable,

50. For a summary of the evidence see Gramlich, "Intergovernmental Grants." Gramlich and Galper estimated that general revenue sharing grants would raise spending by recipients by 25–43 percent of the funds involved in the long run, while private income increases would raise government spending by only 10 percent. "State and Local Fiscal Behavior," pp. 30–46. Applying a quite different theoretical model to state grants, Martin C. McGuire found the marginal propensities to spend on local government programs to be only 0.09 from private incomes but 0.85 from state grants. "A Method for Estimating the Effect of a Subsidy on the Receiver's Resource Constraint: With an Application to US Local Governments 1964–1971," *Journal of Public Economics,* vol. 10 (August 1978), pp. 25–44.

they are in all cases considerably larger than private individuals' propensities to spend on government services. The flypaper hypothesis, in short, is confirmed.

Income effects can also be generated by grants that are restricted in one way or another. Recipients will always try to divert grant funds from their intended uses to any higher priority programs of their own, and there are numerous circumstances under which such diversions are entirely possible. An obvious case would be a nonmatching grant of $100 million, nominally restricted to a particular state or local program, X, given to grantees who are already spending $100 million a year or more on X. Less obvious would be the grantee who is already spending $75 million on X but whose propensity to spend additional income on X is 0.25 or greater. Fixed-sum, restricted grants can become increasingly fungible over time as greater affluence leads grantees to wish to spend more and more on the aided program in any case. For the same reasons, grants that provide funds only to grantees who maintain the pregrant levels of locally financed spending on aided programs·will also become increasingly subject to diversion.[51]

INDIRECT EFFECTS. If grant aid is given to independent school districts, one direct effect may be lower school property taxes than otherwise would exist. For cities, counties, and special districts using the same tax base this in turn would mean expanded opportunities to increase their own tax rates. An indirect effect of school grants, therefore, could be higher expenditures on the part of other local government units. Grants may also stimulate, or even necessitate, increases in other expenditures that are complementary to the aided categories. Still other indirect effects, sometimes intended by donors and anticipated by donees and sometimes not, occur when grant programs are terminated. The services in question being difficult to cut off, grant aid may have to be replaced more or less fully by the donees' own funds.

Nor are all indirect effects confined to the public sector. Some very

51. In his study of state-aided local school spending over the 1964–71 period, McGuire found that, on the average, 70 percent of the restricted funds were successfully converted into fungible resources. The percentage showed a distinct tendency to rise over the period, from a range of 45–55 percent at the beginning to 59–79 percent at the end. Ibid., pp. 42–43. Another example of significant diversion is provided by Edward Miller, "The Economics of Matching Grants: The ABC Highway Program," *National Tax Journal,* vol. 27 (June 1974), pp. 221–29.

important ones occur gradually as the initial impact of grant programs is transmitted to the private sector, creating changes that feed back to both donor and donee governments whose reactions begin the same process all over again. These interactive effects are likely to be particularly important when grant programs affect the individual communities in a large urban area differently. Land values, household and business location choices and investment decisions, shopping patterns and traffic flows will all change to some degree. When this multiple round of effects has settled into a new equilibrium, the final impact of the grants on donee budgets may differ significantly from the initial impact. For policymakers the important questions are how rapidly all of this happens and how different the impact and final effects are likely to be. Only if all interactions are small, or very slow in developing their full force, can planners act safely on the basis of initial impacts alone. A study of the effects of grant aid in the New York metropolitan area using a general equilibrium regional fiscal and economic model concluded that the impact effects exceeded the long-run effects by 20–60 percent and that about 90 percent of the long-run dampening had occurred by the end of five years.[52] If similarly important differences between short-run and long-run effects show up in other empirical studies, policymakers will do well to shift their attention from the well-established impact effects of grant programs to their more obscure and complex indirect effects.

PROCESS EFFECTS. Equally subtle and complicated are the changes brought about by grant programs in the processes by which government decisions are made and carried out. A major aim of grant partnerships, of course, has been to improve operating procedures in the public sector, particularly at the state and local level; these gains in intergovernmental cooperation have been accruing, albeit unevenly, for some time. Nor are they by any means confined to grant-aided programs.[53] Unfortunately, the effects of changes in process, by their very nature, are exceedingly difficult to quantify. Moreover, the extent to which grant instruments alone, rather than other forces, have created them is often impossible to determine.

52. Robert P. Inman, "Micro-Fiscal Planning in the Regional Economy: A General Equilibrium Approach," *Journal of Public Economics*, vol. 7 (April 1977), pp. 251–54.

53. See, for example, Daniel J. Elazar, *The American Partnership: Intergovernmental Co-operation in the Nineteenth-Century United States* (University of Chicago Press, 1962).

Detailed case studies are the most promising way of identifying the specific results of particular grant programs. As a result of her analysis of public assistance in Massachusetts between 1936 and 1967, for example, Martha Derthick concluded that the process effects accompanying the development of that program were highly significant. Though they also resulted from strictly local factors, they were nevertheless "accelerated and in important ways shaped by federal action."[54]

In principle, the benefits of changes in processes flow both ways, each party to the grant contract standing to gain from the other's special knowledge and abilities. In practice, however, the superior financial powers of donors give them a significant advantage as initiators. Even so-called unrestricted grants of money can be accompanied by more or less constraining rules about how grant-supported programs are to be chosen and operated. General revenue sharing provides an interesting example of this kind of manipulation of process.

Guidelines for Grant Design

Analysis of the reasons for and effects of grants provides policymakers with a number of useful guidelines for the design of new and better programs.[55] In principle, designers should begin by identifying a number of clearly defined public-sector goals to which grants can make some contribution. For each goal the alternative instruments should then be evaluated and ranked. When an appropriately designed grant program emerges from this test as best instrument, it should be pursued; in all other cases, nongrant programs should be chosen. In practice, of course, there will be many departures from such clear-cut standards. Government goals are frequently vague and ambiguous; grant programs may be imprecisely designed and highly uncertain in their effects; it may be impossible to rank alternative instruments objectively; instruments that are clearly superior to grants may for one reason or another not be utilized; and there may

54. *The Influence of Federal Grants: Public Assistance in Massachusetts* (Harvard University Press, 1970), p. 194.
55. See Mushkin and Cotton, *Functional Federalism*, chap. 3. That close attention to the many details of grant design is important for policymakers was one of the findings of the ACIR's empirical analysis of grant effects. See *Federal Grants*, p. 63.

be more goals for which grants are proposed than there are separate
grant instruments to pursue them.[56]

The results of all these difficulties are not hard to foresee. Grant
programs will be used when better means of achieving the same ends
exist. Moreover, those grant programs that are used will be designed
to move the public sector short distances toward several goals rather
than a longer distance toward one goal. Whether this situation is
seen as "a disgrace to the human race," as was the federal tax system
by Jimmy Carter during his 1976 campaign for the presidency, or
as a tribute to political ingenuity and compromise, it clearly provides
a happy hunting ground for all policy analysts and fiscal reformers.
It certainly underscores the importance of periodic zero-based
budgeting for grant programs whose priorities may have been eroded
by other governmental programs or by changing economic conditions.

Policy Guidelines for Pure Price Subsidy Grants

Open-ended matching grants are an appropriate instrument for
the support of programs in which there is both a strong national or
state concern and a demonstrated lack of sufficient state or local
support. Benefit spillouts are a necessary, though not sufficient, justification for these grants. A prima facie case exists for the use of price
subsidy grants whenever the spillouts that inhibit adequate local support of the program are not offset by countervailing forces. Programs
receiving this form of aid should be those for which potential grantees
exhibit a high price elasticity of demand. Low price elasticities suggest the absence of significant benefit spillouts and make it likely
that open-ended matching grants would be diverted to other uses; in
such cases, income grants become an attractive alternative.

Programs for which this instrument is chosen should be tightly
defined and carefully distinguished from those with less important
benefit spillouts or no spillouts at all. Experience with social service
grants in the early 1970s provides a vivid illustration of the budgetary
excesses and unintended substitution effects likely to accompany
vaguely defined price-subsidy grant programs.[57] While distinctions

56. For an analysis of grants in a goals-instruments framework see Robert P.
Inman, *Efficiency, Equity and the Design of Regional Grants-in-Aid,* Fels Discussion
Paper 14 (University of Pennsylvania: Fels Center of Government, n.d.).

57. Derthick, *Uncontrollable Spending.*

based on the degree of grantor interest in benefit spillouts may be difficult to make, they are essential criteria in the justification and design of open-ended matching grants. Among aided programs, matching ratios should vary directly with the strength of grantor interest and inversely with the degree of grantee support. In the absence of evidence as to these differentials, matching ratios should be equal. Admittedly, these rules work better in theory than in practice, making the choice of matching ratios usually a trial and error procedure based largely on observed donee behavior. Such inexactitude in a process carried out over time by a large number of independent grantor policymaking agencies can only result in an uncoordinated, haphazard set of differential matching ratios. It is essential, therefore, that periodic evaluations of the reasons for these differentials be built into the budgetary framework of grant programs.

Though pure price subsidy grants are not a widely used instrument in the United States, they make a significant difference in a number of important areas of policy. In the redesign of federal-state-local welfare programs, even if the long-run goal is widespread federalization, the question of how state and local governments will react to the removal of existing federal matching grants is a major consideration. A detailed econometric study of the program of aid to families with dependent children, over the 1963–72 period, found that only the price variable exerted a significant influence on the behavior of state and local governments.[58] Pure price subsidies, then, have apparently been an effective grant instrument in this area. One policy implication, as Orr noted, is that enactment of a federally financed AFDC benefit floor, set to hold the average federal share of total benefits constant, would reduce benefit levels by as much as 16 percent if it were accompanied by removal of federal matching at the margin.[59]

Another policy area in which matching grants are likely to play an important role is the reform of local school finance. Even if the setting of school-aid matching ratios on the basis of benefit spillouts is rejected as impractical, price subsidy grants may be an effective

58. Larry L. Orr, "Income Transfers as a Public Good: An Application to AFDC," *American Economic Review,* vol. 66 (June 1976), pp. 359–71. See also Frank A. Sloan, "A Model of State Income Maintenance Decisions," *Public Finance Quarterly,* vol. 5 (April 1977), pp. 139–73.
59. "Income Transfers," p. 370.

way of breaking the link between local district wealth and school spending that court decisions have found to be unconstitutional. This would be especially true if the wealth elasticity of local school districts' demands for educational services were relatively low and their price elasticity of demand relatively high. Under such circumstances a mild degree of price discrimination on the part of state school aid programs, reflected in matching ratios that varied inversely with school district wealth, would be able to neutralize the effects of disparities in wealth on school spending.[60] More generally, the aim would be to set the local tax price of education high enough in wealthy districts (by low, or even negative, matching ratios) to counteract exactly any propensities they have to spend more on education simply because they are wealthy, and to do the reverse in poor districts. There are, of course, many facets to the design of reforms that would improve the equity and efficiency of school finance, but matching grants of one kind or another are likely to be an important ingredient.[61]

Finally, intergovernmental price subsidies are sometimes an implicit part of programs and policies adopted for other reasons. The personal deduction for residential property taxes under the federal individual income tax, for example, is a matching grant to all taxpayers who itemize their deductions, with the federal ratio equal to the taxpayer's marginal tax rate. State-authorized circuit breakers to lighten property tax burdens can also be variable-rate matching grants for those households that qualify for such fiscal assistance. In communities where residents perceive the tax burdens on certain

60. Martin S. Feldstein came to this conclusion in his pioneering study of school finance in Massachusetts, and it led him to criticize the district power equalizing (DPE) formula for school grants. According to his estimates, DPE grants would be an overkill policy that would create a strong negative relationship between district wealth and school spending. "Wealth Neutrality and Local Choice in Public Education," *American Economic Review,* vol. 65 (March 1975), pp. 75–89.

61. See, for example, the reform plans analyzed in James F. Gatti and Leonard J. Tashman, "Equalizing Matching Grants and the Allocative and Distributive Objectives of Public School Financing," *National Tax Journal,* vol. 29 (December 1976), pp. 461–76; Robert P. Inman, "Optimal Fiscal Reform of Metropolitan Schools: Some Simulation Results," *American Economic Review,* vol. 68 (March 1978), pp. 107–28, and "Grants in a Metropolitan Economy—A Framework for Policy," in *Financing the New Federalism: Revenue Sharing, Conditional Grants, and Taxation,* Papers by Inman and others, The Governance of Metropolitan Regions no. 5, Wallace E. Oates, ed. (Johns Hopkins University Press for Resources for the Future, 1975), pp. 88–114.

business property to be totally or partially shifted to other jurisdictions and the burdens on other kinds of property to remain on themselves, a property tax increase will, from the residents' point of view, automatically generate an open-ended matching grant-in-aid. In this case the ratio may be as high as the proportion of business property in the taxable property of the community. The distinguishing characteristic of all three kinds of implicit grant effects is that they are felt directly by taxpayers rather than by local governments. Nevertheless, their presence may well influence the behavior of local governments in important ways.

Policy Guidelines for Pure Income Grants

The critical choice in the design of unrestricted general grants is the allocation formula by which the untied funds are to be distributed to different recipients. The commonly accepted general principle is that these allocations should vary inversely with the grantee government's fiscal capacity and directly with its fiscal needs.[62] Giving specific content to these guidelines, however, is no task for the novice or for the fainthearted.

The first great difficulty, and one that is shared by all public redistributive programs, is to distinguish fiscal disparities that exist quite independently of the subsidy recipients' behavior from those that do not. Only the former are presumably deserving of assistance financed by the general taxpayer.[63] A clear example of the undeserving poor is the community where unusually high costs of local services are the direct result of the citizens' deliberate choice to live in an unfavorable physical environment. Somewhat less clear is the city that chooses or is forced to pay unionized employees in the public sector higher wage rates than prevail elsewhere. Clear in principle but difficult to measure in practice are high costs that result from inefficient management of the public sector or unmet needs that exist because local residents refuse to tax themselves sufficiently. Perhaps the best testimony as to the great difficulty of making any of these distinctions

62. For a detailed analysis of alternative allocative formulas see Musgrave, "Approaches to a Fiscal Theory of Political Federalism," pp. 97–122.

63. For an analysis of unrestricted grants that stresses this distinction see Julian Le Grand, "Fiscal Equity and Central Government Grants to Local Authorities," *Economic Journal,* vol. 85 (September 1975), pp. 531–47.

is that they are usually ignored in the design of intergovernmental grants.

Equally complex and controversial, but impossible to ignore, are the disparities arising from unusually high fiscal needs or low fiscal capacities. If unrestricted redistributive grant programs are to be designed, these disparities must be measured and the allocation of grant funds related in some equitable fashion to those measures.

Measures of Fiscal Capacity

The formidable task of measuring state and local governments' fiscal capacities, an essential part of any equitable allocation of unrestricted grants, can be approached from the angle either of weighing the capacity of each governmental unit's residents to bear tax burdens as indicated by community income and wealth levels or of judging the ability of different governmental units to finance their operations by using some standard revenue system. If all state and local tax systems were destination-based, the two approaches would be the same, and no great problem would be encountered in choosing a general framework for measuring fiscal capacity. State and local tax systems, however, are significantly origin-oriented now and are likely to continue to be so. This means that communities with mainly low-income families, and hence a low ability to bear tax burdens, can have high revenue-raising capabilities if they have enough multi-jurisdictional business property, income, or sales. Conversely, high-income residential communities may rank below average in their taxing abilities because of their lack of business property.

The problem of choosing between these two general concepts of fiscal capacity is similar to that involved in measuring the incidence of state and local tax burdens. Studies aimed at allocating the burdens of state and local tax increases resulting from forces that are nation-wide in scope, and hence general in impact, are best served by a theoretical framework that surveys comparable tax changes throughout the country. This broad purview has become known as the Wisconsin approach because of its use in a 1959 study of that state's tax burdens.[64] If the purpose, on the other hand, is to pinpoint the burdens of a tax increase resulting from factors special to a given state

64. University of Wisconsin Tax Study Committee, *Wisconsin's State and Local Tax Burden: Impact, Incidence and Tax Revision Alternatives* (University of Wisconsin, 1959), chap. 2.

or locality, the correct model is one that ignores the effects of any tax changes occurring elsewhere. This is known as the Michigan approach.[65] The choice of method for studying tax burdens depends on the purpose to be served. In measuring fiscal capacity, however, the choice is more complicated. Suitability to the purpose to be served —namely, the concentration of intergovernmental grant monies in the hands of the most deserving and needy recipients—is one important consideration, to be sure. But there are also others, such as the ready availability of the required data and a wide public understanding of, and support for, the measure chosen. All would be well, of course, if the alternative indexes of capacity all gave approximately the same results. Unfortunately, that is not the case.

The difference in results is amply demonstrated by a plethora of systematic comparisons of alternative fiscal capacity measures.[66] A look at the menu of such devices indicates the great variety of choice that is available.

INCOME. Perhaps the best-known yardstick for state fiscal capacities is per capita personal income, a series that is computed quarterly by the Bureau of Economic Analysis (BEA) for the national income accounts. Public familiarity and ready availability make this gauge of ability to bear tax burdens a prime candidate for use in grant design. There are superior measures of ability to pay, as any income tax expert will testify, but none possesses the pragmatic qualifications of BEA's personal income series.[67] No doubt the BEA standard could be improved, but the case remains to be made for an alternative that is sufficiently better in conception and different in its geographical incidence to be worth the cost of developing it.

Being a determination of income received by the residents of a

65. The Michigan model was used in a 1958 study of the state's tax burdens; see Richard A. Musgrave and Darwin W. Daicoff, "Who Pays the Michigan Taxes?" in *Michigan Tax Study: Staff Papers* (Lansing, Michigan, 1958), pp. 131–83. For a discussion of the Michigan and Wisconsin approaches see Charles E. McLure, Jr., "The Interstate Exporting of State and Local Taxes: Estimates for 1962," *National Tax Journal*, vol. 20 (March 1967), pp. 51–52 (*Tax Exporting in the United States: Estimates for 1962*, Brookings Reprint 132).

66. See, in particular, Robert D. Reischauer, "Rich Governments—Poor Governments: Determining the Fiscal Capacity and Revenue Requirements of State and Local Government" (Brookings Institution, December 1974).

67. For a wide-ranging discussion of alternative income concepts as measures of ability to pay taxes see Joseph A. Pechman, ed., *Comprehensive Income Taxation* (Brookings Institution, 1977).

given area, BEA personal income is a destination-based measure of tax capacity. An origin-based gauge, in contrast, would show the total income produced in each area. No such comprehensive series is available, but three other measurement options offer some means of assessing regional abilities to raise government revenues.[68]

IDEAL REVENUE SYSTEM. The yield of some ideal revenue or tax system has obvious attractions as an index of state and local fiscal capacities. It would allow grant recipients to use whatever nonideal system they wished, but they would not be free to claim low fiscal capacities as a result of their choice. The problem with this type of measure, of course, is that there are about as many different ideal revenue systems as there are designers thereof.[69] In the absence of a broad consensus on this question, there can be no agreement on specific fiscal capacity measures of this type.

TYPICAL REVENUE SYSTEM. Failure to agree on what *should be* greatly strengthens the appeal of a typical or average revenue system as a measure of fiscal capacity. The ACIR's representative tax or revenue system, for example, delineates the typical form of twenty-three kinds of different state and local taxes.[70] It computes a national

68. The BEA measures of personal income do show labor and entrepreneurial income by both place of residence and place of work, but no attempt is made to allocate property income to the areas in which it was generated because of substantial conceptual and statistical difficulties. "Local Area Personal Income," *Survey of Current Business*, vol. 54 (May 1974), pt. 2, pp. 1–5. See also "County and Metropolitan Area Personal Income," *Survey of Current Business*, vol. 59 (April 1979), pp. 25–47, where estimates for standard metropolitan statistical areas and counties are given on a residence basis only.

69. For an early attempt to define an ideal system, see "Preliminary Report of the Committee Appointed by The National Tax Association to Prepare a Plan of a Model System of State and Local Taxation," in National Tax Association, *Proceedings of the Twelfth Annual Conference on Taxation, 1919* (New York: NTA, 1920), pp. 426–70. For more recent suggestions see John Shannon, "State-Local Tax Systems: Proposals and Objectives," *National Civic Review*, vol. 61 (April 1972), pp. 170–79.

70. This total includes four different categories of taxable property. In addition, state individual income taxes are subdivided into seven adjusted gross income classes, for each of which a separate national average tax rate is estimated. See ACIR, *Measures of State and Local Fiscal Capacity and Tax Effort*, Report M-16 (GPO, 1962), and *Measuring the Fiscal Capacity and Effort of State and Local Areas*, Information Report (GPO, 1971). The first study pioneered the determination of representative tax system yields for states as a whole, while the second extended the methodology to include nontax revenue sources and borrowing and then applied those measures to substate areas.

average rate for each tax by dividing the actual revenue raised by state and local governments from that source by the nationwide value of the base, and then derives the tax capacity of each state by multiplying the national average tax rates by the amounts of the corresponding tax bases in that state and adding up the results. Similar procedures can also be applied to nontax revenues. Fiscal capacity, in other words, is measured by the revenue that could be raised in a given area if the government there employed all of the standard sources at the nationwide average intensity of use. The measure may also be viewed as a multidimensional aggregate converted to an average by weighting each part by the national average tax rate applicable to it.

The concept of a representative revenue system is criticized because it is based on the use of a single average in a world in which tastes in taxation may differ significantly.[71] Diversity is clearly greater among states than among local governments in a given state, but it is still an open question whether interstate differentials are so large that they invalidate any use of average fiscal capacity measures. Many different handles for taxation may be seized upon in different places, but in the final analysis the ability to tax rests either on income received or income produced, or both. The critical question, then, is the extent to which any given area can effectively reach either of these bases, given the constraints imposed on access to them by common tax practice in the country as a whole. Judged on this basis, the ACIR representative revenue system seems reasonable enough to place the burden of proof on those who would propose a better measure.

A more fundamental criticism of the concept of an average tax system is that market adjustments can create an inverse relationship between tax rates imposed on given bases and the sizes of those bases. This is likely to be particularly evident among independent jurisdictions in a large urban area, as the discussion of tax capitalization makes clear. A community, in other words, may appear to have a low fiscal capacity simply because it imposes unusually high tax rates, other things equal. This means, in general, that measures based

71. See John S. Akin, "Fiscal Capacity and the Estimation Method of the Advisory Commission on Intergovernmental Relations," *National Tax Journal*, vol. 26 (June 1973), pp. 275–91; Allen D. Manvel, "Tax Capacity versus Tax Performance: A Comment," *National Tax Journal*, vol. 26 (June 1973), pp. 293–94.

on a representative tax system would underestimate the fiscal capacity of jurisdictions with high tax rates and overestimate that of areas with low tax rates. Though the direction of these biases may be clear, their quantitative importance is largely unknown. Again the unwelcome task arises of having to distinguish between those low (or high) fiscal capacities that are created by a citizenry's voluntary actions and those that are not.

Whatever the advantages and disadvantages of the ACIR's representative revenue system, this approach clearly does give a measure of fiscal capacity that differs from that based on per capita personal income. In general, mining states such as Louisiana, Montana, and Texas, tourist states such as Nevada and Florida, and agricultural states such as North Dakota and Wyoming exhibit a higher fiscal capacity under the ACIR measure. Smaller, though sometimes significant, differences show up when the ACIR tax capacity measure is compared with a broader index that includes nontax revenue sources.[72] Still another extension would add the rate of change in fiscal capacity over some past period to the level existing in the current year to derive a two-dimensional measure. Defining fiscal pressure as the ratio of own-source tax collections to a fiscal capacity measure, and comparing indexes of the level of fiscal pressure in 1975 and of the average annual rate of change in fiscal pressure between 1964 and 1975, John Ross and John Shannon found sharp contrasts between states in which pressures were high and rising (New York and Massachusetts) and states where they were low and falling (New Hampshire and Oklahoma).[73] Their two-dimensional approach makes it possible to identify states with similar fiscal pressures in a single year but considerably different trends. Minnesota, Rhode Island, and Wisconsin, for example, all had 1975 fiscal pres-

72. ACIR, *Measuring the Fiscal Capacity and Effort of State and Local Areas,* pp. 10–12. Two states may have similar fiscal capacities because they have similar mineral resource endowments, for example, but if one imposes severance taxes while the other collects mineral rents and royalties, only a broad revenue capacity index will rank them correctly. Extending the representative financing system to substate (county) regions is hampered by the difficulties of obtaining data for local governments, particularly when they overlap with one another in complex ways.

73. ACIR, *Measuring the Fiscal "Blood Pressure" of the States—1964–1975,* Information Paper M-111 (GPO, 1977). Ross and Shannon used both per capita personal income and the yields of the ACIR representative tax system as measures of fiscal capacity.

sures close to 25 percent above the national average when measured by the ACIR representative tax method, but in Minnesota these pressures rose at a rate 73 percent above the national average for 1964–75, while in Wisconsin they rose at a rate that was 71 percent below the national average.

BEHAVIORAL MODELS. If an ideal revenue system appears to be too subjective and a representative revenue system too arbitrary an approach for measuring fiscal capacity, an analytic behavioral approach may have appeal. It conceives of government expenditures as being determined in part by fiscal capacities and in part by a host of other factors affecting community needs and tastes for public services. If the latter factors can be fully identified and their effects on spending levels successfully measured, differences in fiscal capacity could then be isolated by this approach.

Take the question of how different kinds of taxable property should be treated in measuring the fiscal capacity of local governments. To weight them equally would be to adopt the dubious assumption either that there is no exporting of local property tax burdens or that whatever exporting occurs is the same for each kind of property. Many economists reject this proposition, but few are able to say exactly what proportion of the tax burdens placed on different kinds of property is in fact exported. For voter choices of local taxing levels, of course, it is the perceived, not the actual, degree of exporting that matters, and the only way of quantifying these perceptions is by systematic analyses of all of the determinants of local government spending behavior.

In a study of the determinants of local school expenditures in Massachusetts in 1970, Helen F. Ladd investigates the effects of different kinds of property in that context.[74] Her econometric expenditure model—which hypothesizes that two communities have equal fiscal capacities if, apart from different tastes or needs for spending, they provide the same level of school services—includes tax capacity,

74. "Local Education Expenditures, Fiscal Capacity, and the Composition of the Property Tax Base," *National Tax Journal*, vol. 28 (June 1975), pp. 145–58. See also Akin, "Fiscal Capacity"; Harvey E. Brazer and others, *Fiscal Needs and Resources: A Report to the New York State Commission on the Quality, Cost and Financing of Elementary and Secondary Education* (draft) (November 1971), chap. 4; W. Douglas Morgan, "An Alternative Measure of Fiscal Capacity," *National Tax Journal*, vol. 27 (June 1974), pp. 361–65.

intergovernmental aid, and voter preference and need variables. Tax capacity is a function of median family income and the separate market values of residential, commercial, and industrial property. Her analysis shows that different kinds of property do make different average contributions to a community's willingness to finance its schools.[75] In particular, when residential property is used as the standard of reference with a weight of 1, the estimated weights for commercial and industrial property are 1.26 and 0.55, respectively.[76] Ladd's behavioral measure produces different rankings of local fiscal capacity than the standard measure that omits family income and weights all components of the property tax base equally. In general, it produces lower rankings for communities with low median family income, high proportions of low-income families, and high degrees of industrialization.

The problem with behavioral measures of fiscal capacity, of course, is the great difficulty analysts encounter in specifying their estimating equations. Measuring levels of local or state government service accurately and determining the effects on those levels of all important determining factors other than fiscal capacity is a very big task indeed. It is unsettling, for example, that none of the taste variables produced strongly significant statistical estimates in the Massachusetts study. Another difficult empirical question is whether business property provides communities with clear gains in their level of well-being or generates fiscal gains at the cost of environmental degradation of one kind or another. Arguing that these gains and losses will tend to be equated in urban areas where competition for business is active and hence that business property does not add to community capacities to finance public services, William Fox concludes from

75. A given community's fiscal capacity is measured by estimating what it would spend on schools if its tastes and needs for education were average for the sample of communities studied. This involves setting all of the independent variables in the regression equation, other than the fiscal capacity measures, at their arithmetic means for the sample as a whole and then estimating school expenditures for each community.

76. The implications are that Massachusetts voters do perceive a partial, but not a full, shifting of business property tax burdens to outsiders, and that commercial property provides greater opportunities to export burdens than does industrial property. This may be because industrial property is typically more mobile and hence more likely to respond negatively to increases in tax rates.

his study of forty-four Ohio cities in 1970 that business property should be omitted completely from measures of local capacity.[77]

Clearly, the behavioral approach has yet to produce definitive capacity measures,[78] and until it does, some standard revenue measure is needed to provide a basis for rewarding government units with relatively low abilities to finance their ordinary and necessary public services. As long as state and local revenue systems contain significant origin-based elements, a measure based on ability to raise revenue will be superior to one based on ability to bear tax burdens such as per capita personal income.[79] While the latter measure is the more readily available of the alternatives, data do exist from which annual estimates for a measure of a representative tax system for states could be derived.[80]

77. William F. Fox, "Fiscal Capacity or Resource Capacity?" in NTA-TIA, *Proceedings of the Seventieth Annual Conference on Taxation, 1977* (1978), pp. 389–96. Fox proposes resource capacity, which includes all means of providing for public services, as superior to fiscal capacity as a measure for distributing intergovernmental grants. In his opinion, then, business property adds to fiscal, but not to resource, capacity. A similar view is part of a detailed model of local government behavior developed and tested by William A. Fischel, "Fiscal and Environmental Considerations in the Location of Firms in Suburban Communities," in Edwin S. Mills and Wallace E. Oates, eds., *Fiscal Zoning and Land Use Controls: The Economic Issues* (Lexington Books, 1975), pp. 119–73. Ladd's findings ("Local Education Expenditures") suggest that industrial property may fit the Fischel-Fox hypothesis better than does commercial property.

78. Another behavioral approach, still in an early stage of development, involves estimating empirically the maximum level of aggregate utility attainable in each state or locality, given its total available resources, and then using those utility levels as measures of fiscal capacity. John S. Akin, "Estimates of State Resource Constraints Derived from a Specific Utility Function: An Alternative Measure of Fiscal Capacity," *National Tax Journal*, vol. 32 (March 1979), pp. 61–71.

79. This is not to say that per capita personal income lacks for supporters. Thomas Pogue, for example, has concluded that it is at least as good as the ACIR representative tax system measure. "Tax Exporting and the Measurement of Fiscal Capacity," in NTA-TIA, *Proceedings, 1976*, pp. 79–89. However, Pogue's conclusion is implicit in his distinctive definition of fiscal capacity, which contains two highly questionable elements—the measurement of fiscal capacity with reference to a standard level of per capita disposable income that implies a zero income elasticity of demand for private goods, and the inclusion in his capacity measure of imported tax burdens, which appear to be mainly independent of local taxing decisions and thus not relevant to the measurement of local abilities to raise tax revenues.

80. Richard P. Nathan, Allen D. Manvel, and Susannah E. Calkins, *Monitoring Revenue Sharing* (Brookings Institution, 1975), p. 140.

Measures of Fiscal Need

The other major component of a formula for allocating redistributive grants is a measure of fiscal need. For many of the same reasons, it is just as difficult to define and derive as is a measure of fiscal capacity.[81] Indeed, alternative need measures may be classified into the same categories as are measures of the ability to raise government revenues.

Ideal measures of fiscal need usually reflect the opinions of experts in each functional area about minimum service standards. But they are often derived with little regard either to opportunity costs or consumer preferences. Average measures, by contrast, define need as "the cost of supplying average performance levels for the existing mix of state-local programs."[82] The difficulties involved in this approach to measuring fiscal need are much the same as those encountered in using a representative tax system to measure fiscal capacity. They include defining the standard service mix and average performance levels in a world of differing tastes, determining the costs of those performance levels in areas with different input prices and different kinds of client populations to be served, and eliminating those need differentials that result from community choice rather than from unavoidable circumstances. Other questions concern the extent to which the determinants of need, once they have been incorporated in distribution formulas, may be manipulated by potential grant recipients to their own advantage.

Economists who are dissatisfied with the subjective and arbitrary nature of both ideal and average measures of fiscal need have derived behavioral measures based on state and local expenditures, which are viewed as responding to fiscal capacities and voter tastes on the one hand and to community needs on the other. Voter tastes in turn are determined by a complex set of socioeconomic factors. In measuring need the analyst sets the fiscal capacity and taste variables at their

81. A comprehensive analysis of different dimensions of urban need is given in Peggy L. Cuciti, *City Need and the Responsiveness of Federal Grants Programs,* prepared for the Subcommittee on the City of the House Committee on Banking, Finance, and Urban Affairs, Subcommittee Print, 95 Cong. 2 sess. (GPO, 1978).

82. Richard A. Musgrave and A. Mitchell Polinsky, "Revenue Sharing—A Critical View," in *Financing State and Local Governments,* Proceedings of the Monetary Conference, June 1970. (Federal Reserve Bank of Boston, 1970), p. 29.

mean levels and then estimates expenditures for each community.[83] This equates need with what each community would actually spend if all were of average fiscal capacity and had average tastes for government services. The approach has the great advantage of deriving the needs measure from the actual behavior of the group under study rather than basing it on outside judgment. Its chief disadvantage of course lies in the great difficulty of establishing a satisfactory equation to explain spending on different state and local government programs.[84]

Policy Guidelines

Precision in the design of pure income grants is not a virtue. To be sure, the return of some portion of national income tax revenues to the jurisdictions of source could be administratively simple and precise, the shared portion of the tax revenue being allocated to the governmental units in which the federal tax returns were filed. Such an allocation, however, would not have a close economic relationship to source since it would ignore all of the complexities created by taxpayers with multiple residences and multiple jurisdictions of work and productive activity. Moreover, it is not simply a sharing of tax revenues that most advocates of pure income grants seek to achieve. The prime goal of these grants is intergovernmental redistribution of purchasing power. Though neither fiscal capacity nor fiscal need can be defined precisely, let alone measured accurately, some general guidelines for the design of pure income grants can be offered.

Since free-market adjustments cannot be counted on to bring the tax cost of state and local services closely in line with the benefits received from those services, income grants should be designed to deal with chronic fiscal disparities. Stress should be given to interregional and interstate redistribution since the market is more likely to eliminate fiscal disparities within large urban areas than between

83. A good example of the use of this approach is Brazer, *Fiscal Needs and Resources,* chap. 5.
84. Other suggested measures of fiscal need are the level of property tax rates in local communities—high rates being regarded as a good indicator of above-average needs—and the effects of income grants on property taxes—grant-induced tax increases being regarded as more desirable in high-income than in low-income communities. See Robert P. Strauss, "The Impact of Block Grants on Local Expenditures and Property Tax Rates," *Journal of Public Economics,* vol. 3 (August 1974), pp. 269–84.

regions or states. Aid should be targeted toward communities with high concentrations of relatively immobile people because until the disadvantages brought on by immobility are eliminated by economic developments or other government programs, intergovernmental grant aid can provide important interim assistance.

Since there is no one ideal redistributive grant formula, experimental use of several different ones has much to recommend it. The effects of alternative grant programs on the most important state and local fiscal problems could be compared so as to determine which programs should be retained and expanded. Block grants provide an opportunity for such experimentation at the federal level.

As long as state and local tax systems retain their strong degree of origin orientation, measures of fiscal capacity used for allocating grants should be based on the ability of different governmental units to raise tax revenues rather than on their ability to bear tax burdens. This requires a shift of emphasis from such readily available measures as resident personal income to the development and use of ability-to-tax measures such as personal income by area of origin, the ACIR's representative revenue system indexes, or behavioral measures that take due account of such pertinent factors as the exporting of tax burdens and trade-offs between business property and environmental quality.

Policy Guidelines for Closed-End Functional or Block Grants

Closed-end functional grants, either matching or nonmatching, are likely to be preferred by grantor governments to either price subsidy or income grants. Unlike open-ended matching grants they give grantors both budgetary control and less uncertainty about funding requirements, and unlike unrestricted income grants they allow grantors to imprint their own priorities on intergovernmental aid programs. Nevertheless there is considerable risk that the grantors' intentions will not be realized. Grant monies that appear to be restricted to particular programs may be convertible into fungible resources that recipients can use in any way they choose. Matching requirements intended to function as price subsidies may fail to do so. Both possibilities should be kept in mind by grant designers.

If closed-end functional grants are efficiently to further grantor objectives, they should either be confined to programs that grantee governments do not typically support from their own funds or be designed to require some maintenance of effort on the grantees' part. Of course, neither strategy is foolproof. Programs once unattractive to state and local governments may become so, and gaps may open between support levels required of grantees and those that they would provide in any case. Yet they are more likely to reflect grantor objectives than are grants directed at established state and local programs without maintenance-of-effort features.

If closed-end functional grants are widely diverted to recipients' general use, there is a strong, albeit debatable, case for either converting them into pure income grants or eliminating them entirely. This case rests on the far from solid assumption that better choices and decisions will be made in the public sector when people know what is really going on than when they do not. Fungible closed-end grants give the appearance that grantor priorities are being furthered when in fact they are not. Their conversion to unrestricted grants, on the one hand, would keep grantees' programs intact and eliminate the distorted picture presented to grantors. Their replacement by direct spending programs of the grantor government, on the other hand, would reallocate funds from unintended, low-priority uses to higher valued ones. Many would regard either of these alternatives as distinct governmental improvements.

Because of their broader scope, closed-end block grants are in general more likely to generate substitution effects than are narrow categorical grants. Consequently grant designers and reformers should watch carefully for this. Nevertheless, even if block grants are found to be highly fungible, their different allocation formulas provide useful variations on the pattern by which general-aid funds are distributed to state and local governments. There are so many uncertainties involved in calculating disparities in fiscal capacities and needs that the use of several different redistributive formulas is likely to be better than reliance on only one. Politically, this may be more readily accomplished by a combination of general revenue sharing and block grant programs than by a single unrestricted grant program using different formulas to parcel out its funds.

There is considerable risk and uncertainty in the use of matching requirements with closed-end grants. If these requirements are seen as price subsidies, the risks are twofold—the grantor's funds may be quite ineffective as price incentives, or they may actually distort the budgetary choices of recipient governments. Whenever grantees spend more on aided programs than the sum of the grantor's aid and their own required matching portion, there is no price effect at the margin of choice where it counts. In jurisdictions where bureaucratic control over public decisionmaking processes is strong, bureaucrats may opt to do what consumer-voters might prefer not to do—that is, use up the full amount of the grant allocations available to their government. Even though the general citizenry were, in other words, to conclude that the effective tax price of the aided public good had not been reduced sufficiently to warrant spending enough of their own money to make full use of the matching funds, bureaucrats might have the tendency to use all free funds provided from outside regardless of the local matching costs.[85] In such circumstances full utilization of the matching grant allotments, looked at from the point of view of consumer-voters, would mean either excessive tax burdens or undersupport for programs not assisted by the grant.

The matching features of closed-end grants are also uncertain means of improving the operation of joint fiscal ventures. For this purpose, matching should perform not as a price incentive provided to independent agencies that operate the aided programs on their own, but rather as an efficiency incentive aimed at inducing each active partner to perform responsibly. How effectively it works is not clear. Joint funding arrangements, however, do have wide appeal, which may be reason enough not to do away with matching entirely. Not only does it provide an incentive for grantees to take the aided programs more seriously, but it is also a protection for them against excessive controls from outside.

Policy Guidelines for Project Grants

Perhaps the best kind of grant design, from the point of view of the grantor, is aid extended for the support of particular projects proposed by state or local governments. Because applications for such

85. Failure on the part of grantee governments to make full use of the matching offer has the effect of making closed-end matching grants act as pure price subsidy aids, since the closed end feature is then irrelevant. Unused allotments, therefore, are an indication that closed-end grants have price effects.

programs are competitive, funding agencies are able to reject low-priority projects, to induce improvements in the design of promising proposals, and to concentrate funds where the grantor's goals will best be served. Moreover, where administrative discretion in the setting of matching ratios is built into the design of programs, it may be used to foment a maximum amount of activity with a given amount of funds. This requires, in technical terms, that the grantor act as a discriminating monopolist, charging each local government a price that is inversely proportional to its elasticity of demand for the aided output. If the grantor has the information needed to estimate these demand elasticities, and the ability to vary effective matching ratios, then it may achieve the efficiency goal of maximizing the amount of desired program expenditures induced by each dollar of its outlay. Can and should these two qualities be incorporated in the design and operation of project grant programs?

Varied matching requirements are likely to be regarded as discriminatory, particularly by potential recipients of aid. Such variations, therefore, are not likely to be written explicitly into the law. Giving program administrators a high degree of discretionary authority, however, may in fact produce the same result by permitting them to bargain with grantees and vary their definitions of grantee expenditures eligible for different amounts of grantor aid. Between 1966 and 1971 the Department of Housing and Urban Development's basic water and sewer facilities program operated in that fashion.[86] Howard Chernick found that though the nominal local government matching ratio for that program was 50 percent, the average ratio at which successful projects were funded was 63 percent. The ratio, moreover, varied from project to project, and the amount of that variation, as measured by the standard deviation, increased from 0.07 in 1966 to 0.12 in 1970. Not only do these variations support the discriminating monopolist hypothesis, but their increase over time indicates that

86. Howard A. Chernick, "The Economics of Bureaucratic Behavior: An Application to the Allocation of Federal Project Grants" (Ph.D. dissertation, University of Pennsylvania, 1976), "Bureaucratic Behavior and the Allocation of Resources in a System of Fiscal Federalism," Working Paper, Office of Income Security Policy, Department of Health, Education, and Welfare (August 1978), and "An Economic Model of the Distribution of Project Grants," in Peter Mieszkowski and William H. Oakland, eds., *Fiscal Federalism and Grants-in-Aid,* COUPE Papers on Public Economics, vol. 1 (Washington: Urban Institute, 1979), pp. 81–103.

grant administrators systematically acquired more and more information about grantees' probable price elasticities of demand as the program matured.[87]

It does appear, then, that variable-matching programs can be designed and operated so as to increase the efficiency with which grantor funds are allocated for specific projects. How far this kind of design should be pushed is difficult to judge. It is necessary to know the costs of obtaining information about state and local demand curves and to have estimates of the potential gains to be obtained by price discrimination on the part of grantors. In any case, as Chernick stresses, project grants do provide a mechanism that can be used to induce state and local governments to reveal their true preferences concerning different kinds of public goods. Such information is clearly an important ingredient in the design of grant programs of all kinds.

Another important aspect of the design of project grants is the nature of the competitive application process. Where this is purely pro forma and virtually all applications are accepted, both time and paperwork can be saved simply by allocating the funds by formula subject to the usual audits before and after the project is undertaken. But where competition is intense and relatively few applications are approved, so that many worthy aspirants are turned down and still others discouraged from even applying, not only does the amount of funds available need to be increased, but a simpler application process that would be cheaper for the applicant needs to be devised.[88] Comparison of the characteristics of governments that apply for such grants and those that do not could provide useful guidance in the redesign of application rules and procedures. It could also give administrators a better basis for estimating grantees' demand elasticities and hence for establishing efficient variations in project matching ratios.

87. Chernick notes that such information can be derived from studies of the socioeconomic characteristics of different communities, from probable variations in the ratio of external to internal benefits (which should be positively related to grantee price elasticities of demand), and from differences in the need of grantees to meet the local match from additional government funds rather than shifting funds from other programs.

88. Grantor bureaus committed to growth have a strong incentive to lower quality standards for approved projects in order to keep pressure on the budgetary authorities for more and more funds. Independent evaluations are one way to keep these tendencies in check.

Project grants, by their very nature, provide designers with both opportunities and hazards. On the one hand, they are well suited to the encouragement of experimentation that may pay returns many times greater than the seed money involved. Apart from the high risks that innovative undertakings may fail, there is a distinct danger that project aid, because it supports only part of some activities and not others, may bias the choices of grantees and result in waste of resources. More generally, any grant program that is selective in its subsidies of different input expenditures will alter grantees' production techniques by changing relative input prices. Whether such changes are desirable or not will depend on whether private market forces are working badly or well. In the absence of firm evidence that grantee production choices are distorted and that no superior instruments exist for eliminating these distortions, all input expenditures should be aided equally.

One popular form of federal grant, because of its high visibility and its known and controllable budgetary impact, is aid for state and local construction projects. These grants have several notable effects. They shorten optimal economic lives and hence speed up the need for replacement expenditures; they shift production techniques away from labor and hence make them more capital intensive; and they reduce incentives to incur maintenance costs. In the absence of countervailing distortions, all of these effects are economically undesirable. William B. Tye in an analysis of capital grants for urban mass transportation, estimated that these subsidies, with their two-thirds federal matching ratio, cut the optimal lifetime of motor buses in half and wasted 22–23 percent of the grant funds distributed.[89]

A different kind of inefficiency is stressed by Jon Rasmussen, whose standard economic choice model showed that matching grants that discriminate among input expenditures by eligibility rules or differential matching rates will induce less spending by grantees than would equal amounts of unrestricted and uniform matching grants.[90] If the grantor's aim is to stimulate more output of certain kinds, in

89. "The Capital Grant as a Subsidy Device: The Case Study of Urban Mass Transportation," *The Economics of Federal Subsidy Programs*, A Compendium of Papers Submitted to the Subcommittee on Priorities and Economy in Government, Joint Economic Committee, 93 Cong. 1 sess. (GPO, 1973), pt. 6: *Transportation Subsidies*, pp. 796–826.

90. "The Allocative Effects of Grants-in-Aid: Some Extensions and Qualifications," *National Tax Journal*, vol. 29 (June 1976), pp. 211–19.

other words, the efficient instrument is a grant design that treats all inputs equally. Nevertheless, as both Tye and Rasmussen stress, restricted grants do have important political and budgetary advantages against which their economic inefficiencies must be balanced in the final analysis.

CHAPTER FOUR

The U.S. Grant System

ON THE EVE of the first renewal of the federal government's general revenue sharing program, John Shannon suggested that a well-rounded federal aid system should be divided into three parts: categorical grants for programs marked with some specific national interest, block grants where the national interest applies only to broad functional areas, and general-support grants to strengthen state and local spending powers and to reduce intergovernmental fiscal disparities.[1] Whether there is any special divinity to this triune classification remains to be seen. It is, in any case, the system that is used in the official tabulations of federal grants.[2] Not many years ago, categorical grants were the only kind made. Apart from some minor amounts of shared revenue, the first broad-based grant program, school aid in federally affected areas, was enacted in 1950; the first block grant

1. John Shannon, "Federal Revenue Sharing—Time for Renewal?" *National Tax Journal*, vol. 27 (December 1974), p. 496.
2. The budgetary definition of federal aid to state and local governments is the provision of resources to support some state or local government service to the public. It accordingly includes grants-in-aid, loans, and tax expenditures. In fiscal 1977 federal grants-in-aid were $68.4 billion; loan disbursements were $3.4 billion, but repayments reduced net outlays to only $0.1 billion. Two tax expenditures were classified as federal aid: deductibility of state and local nonbusiness taxes resulted in estimated revenue losses of $12.6 billion and exclusion of interest on state and local debt in losses of $4.8 billion. See *Special Analyses, Budget of the United States Government, Fiscal Year 1979*, pp. 158–60, 175–99.

Table 4-1. Federal Grants-in-Aid, by Form of Grant, Fiscal 1972, 1975, and 1978

Form of grant	1972	1975	1978
	Millions of dollars		
General purpose	516	7,008	9,603
General revenue sharing	...	6,130	6,823
Other	516	878	2,780
Broad based	2,903	4,654	11,462
Community development block grants	...	38	2,464
Comprehensive health grants	90	82	88
Criminal justice assistance	281	577	346
Employment and training aid	...	1,333	1,992
Local public works grants	...	...	3,057
School aid in federally affected areas	602	577	706
Social services grants	1,930	2,047	2,809
Other	30,953	38,170	56,824
Total	34,372	49,832	77,889
	Percent of total		
General purpose	1.5	14.1	12.3
Broad based	8.4	9.3	14.7
Other	90.1	76.6	73.0

Source: *Special Analyses, Budget of the United States Government, Fiscal Year 1980*, p. 230.

program, comprehensive health grants, was established in 1966; and general revenue sharing began in 1972. Between 1972 and 1978, as table 4-1 shows, broad-based and general-purpose grants grew rapidly, from less than a tenth to more than one-fourth of federal grant outlays.

Whatever their form or function, federal grants have been a major growth component of federal government operations.[3] Only 5 percent

3. In addition to the budget series used here, measures of federal aid are published regularly in the U.S. Census Bureau's *Governmental Finances* series and in the national income and product accounts in the *Survey of Current Business*. The other series exclude some components of the budget series, such as aid to Puerto Rico and U.S. territories, payments to private, nonprofit entities operating under state auspices, and certain payments in kind such as food for school lunch programs. Conversely, some items excluded from the budget series—federal payments for research conducted by public universities, for example—are included in the others. Payments for low-rent public housing are treated as federal aid in the budget and census series but as subsidies in the national income accounts. The result of these differences in scope in fiscal 1976 was a budget series that showed federal grants-in-aid to be $59.0 billion, a census measure that placed them at $58.4 billion, and a national income accounts figure of $57.5 billion. See *Special Analyses, Budget of the United States Government, Fiscal Year 1979*, p. 185.

Table 4-2. Relation of Federal Grant-in-Aid Outlays to Federal and State and Local
Expenditures, Selected Fiscal Years, 1950–78

		Federal grants as a percent of		
Fiscal year	*Total grants (billions of dollars)*	*Total federal outlays*	*Domestic federal outlays*[a]	*State and local expenditures*[b]
1950	2.3	5.3	8.8	10.4
1955	3.2	4.7	12.1	10.1
1960	7.0	7.7	15.9	14.7
1965	10.9	9.2	16.5	15.3
1970	24.0	12.2	21.1	19.4
1973	41.8	16.9	24.8	24.3
1975	49.8	15.3	21.3	22.9
1978	77.9	17.3	22.9	26.7

Source: *Special Analyses, Budget of the United States Government, Fiscal Year 1980*, p. 225.
a. Excludes outlays for national defense and international affairs.
b. As defined in the national income and product accounts.

of federal outlays in 1950 and 1955, grants exceeded 10 percent by
1970 and stood at 17 percent of total federal outlays in fiscal 1978
(table 4-2). In relation to federal domestic outlays, however, grants
reached a peak in their relative importance of nearly 25 percent in
fiscal 1973 and then receded slightly. For state and local governments, federal grants represented only 10 percent of total expenditures in 1950 and 1955; they were close to 20 percent by 1970 and
over 26 percent in 1978.[4] This period of rapid growth also witnessed
some major changes in functional allocations of federal grants (table
4-3). Apart from the rise in significance of general-purpose aid, there
was a marked expansion of grants for education, training, and health,
while grant aid for agriculture, transportation, and income security
declined in relative importance.

Grant-in-aid programs can be evaluated quite specifically on the
basis of their performance and prospects in each functional area or
very broadly by their contributions to economic stability and growth
and their effects on wage rates in the public sector and prices in the
private sector. The intermediate approach adopted here emphasizes
the use of alternative grant instruments to achieve different public

4. Measured in relation to state and local general revenue from own sources,
federal aid rose from 11 percent of those funds in fiscal 1954 to an estimated 30
percent in 1976. U.S. Advisory Commission on Intergovernmental Relations (ACIR),
Significant Features of Fiscal Federalism, 1976–77 Edition, vol. 1: *Trends,* Report
M-106 (U.S. Government Printing Office, 1976), p. 53.

Table 4-3. Percentage Distribution of Federal Grant Outlays by Function, Fiscal 1957, 1967, and 1978

Function	1957	1967	1978
Agriculture	9	3	1
Community and regional development	1	6	9
Education, training, employment, and social services	8	25	26
General-purpose fiscal assistance	3	2	12
Health	4	10	16
Income security	49	25	18
Natural resources and environment	1	2	5
Transportation	24	27	11
Other	1	*	1

Source: *Special Analyses, Budget of the United States Government, Fiscal Year 1979*, p. 182, and *Fiscal Year 1980*, p. 223. Figures are rounded.
* 0.5 percent or less.

purposes across functional lines. Applied to the long-established and complex area of federal categorical grants, this approach directs attention to the strengths and weaknesses of existing programs and to ways and means of improving them. With general revenue sharing it focuses on the philosophy and gradual development of a program established in 1972 to provide exactly the opposite kind of aid from the familiar categorical programs. It raises similar questions about a concurrent development in the federal grant system, the late-blooming block grant programs that were called special revenue sharing in President Nixon's 1971 budget message to Congress.[5]

Another major segment of the U.S. grant system is state aid to local governments. Financed in part by the federal government, state grants-in-aid have grown from 42 percent of local general revenue from own sources in fiscal 1954 to nearly 60 percent in 1977 (table 4-4).[6] If direct federal-to-local government aid, which has grown rapidly in recent years, is added to state grants, the total intergovernmental aid received by local governments rose from 43 percent of local own-source general revenue in 1954 to an estimated 75 percent

5. ACIR, *Special Revenue Sharing: An Analysis of the Administration's Grant Consolidation Proposals*, Information Report M-70 (GPO, 1971).

6. Ratios of intergovernmental aid to own-source general revenue may be converted to ratios of total general revenue by dividing them by their value plus 1.00. For example, state aid equal to 0.6 of local own-source general revenue in 1977 means that state aid provided $0.6/1.6 = 0.375$ of total local general revenue in that year.

Table 4-4. Federal and State Aid to Local Governments, Selected Fiscal Years, 1954–77

	State aid		State and federal aid	
Fiscal year	*Amount (billions of dollars)*	*Percent of local general own-source revenue*	*Amount (billions of dollars)*	*Percent of local general own-source revenue*
1954	5.7	41.7	5.9	43.5
1964	13.0	42.9	13.8	45.7
1969	24.8	54.0	26.1	56.9
1974	45.6	59.4	54.8	71.3
1977	61.1	59.9	76.9	75.4

Source: U.S. Advisory Commission on Intergovernmental Relations, *Significant Features of Fiscal Federalism, 1978–79 Edition*, Report M-115 (U.S. Government Printing Office, 1979), pp. 81–83, and earlier editions.

in 1977.[7] Clearly, there has been a dramatic change throughout the nation in the dependency of local governments on outside funds.

Categorical Grants-in-Aid

Categorical grants, the oldest and still the predominant form of federal aid to state and local governments, have long been a favorite target of fiscal reformers. Their problems, difficult under the best of circumstances, are compounded by the multidimensional nature of the issues at stake. All three branches of government—legislative, administrative, and judicial—at all levels of public activity—federal, state, and local—are involved in varying degrees in the operation of such a maze of programs that simply counting them has developed into a numbers game with highly variable answers. While some have placed the number of federal categorical grants at well over 1,000, David Walker, in the ACIR's comprehensive study of the U.S. grant system, identified 442 funded programs for which state and local governments were eligible in fiscal 1975.[8] For many critics, that creates a prima facie case for both extensive consolidation and greater coordination of federal grant programs. Such improvements, however, cannot be arrived at directly. Rather they must emerge from an

7. The ACIR estimates that of $68.8 billion in intergovernmental aid to local entities in fiscal 1976, $14.3 billion was direct federal aid, about $12 billion indirect federal aid passed through state governments as intermediaries, and $42.5 billion direct state aid. *Trends*, p. 55.

8. David B. Walker, "Categorical Grants: Some Clarifications and Continuing Concerns," *Intergovernmental Perspective*, vol. 3 (Spring 1977), p. 14.

analysis of grant instruments and goals, the relations between them, and the impact of different program designs on equity, economic efficiency, and the processes of public choice. The nature of the controls and constraints built into different federal grant programs is an important aspect of any such study.

Grant Instruments and Goals

Like many government programs, federal grants have developed in response to perceived needs with only cursory attention being paid to alternative means of achieving the desired goals, such as different program designs. Moreover, even the goals themselves are exceedingly difficult to specify precisely, and as instruments to achieve them, grants are seldom the only or the most suitable choice. Fiscal reformers are thus probably well advised to eschew the idealistic task of identifying society's major economic goals and determining the best instruments to attain them. Their efforts are likely to be more fruitful, at least in the short run, if they accept a significant federal involvement in grant programs as given and then proceed first to specify the different grant instruments that could be used and finally to relate these to particular public purposes.

In general terms there are three features of grant programs that may be designated by grantors and that will have an important influence on the results. These are the definition of the aided program area, the means by which funds are to be allocated to grantees, and the controls or constraints to be imposed on the grantees' operation of the activities in question. Specifying the functions to be aided by federal grants raises difficult questions about the nature of the national interest, the service of which has long been regarded as the raison d'être of the categorical grant programs. Is it the benefit spillouts that provide the real reason for federal grants, or is it something else? In particular, may not grant programs exist simply because state and local beneficiaries found the programs too expensive, or even impossible, to establish and operate locally?[9] If so, it is presumably the nation's political institutions and processes that need reforming,

---

9. A related question concerns the conditions under which a majority of voters would opt for federal provision of a collective service that could be provided more efficiently at the state or local level. See Kenneth V. Greene, "Some Institutional Considerations in Federal-State Fiscal Relations," *Public Choice*, vol. 9 (Fall 1970), pp. 1–18; reprinted in James M. Buchanan and Robert D. Tollison, eds., *Theory of Public Choice: Political Applications of Economics* (University of Michigan Press, 1972), pp. 236–54.

rather than the grant programs themselves. Be this as it may, it seems clear that the meaning of national purpose, as reflected in federal categorical grant programs, has become broader and broader in recent years, and that these developments must be taken into account by grant reformers.[10]

The critical question is whether or not the relative degrees of national interest in different functional areas can be identified objectively, at least on a rank order basis. If they can be, the case for either categorical or block federal grants is strong, and both federal financial support and controls should vary directly with a program's standing on the national interest scale. Reformers should then concern themselves with determining the levels of federal matching and management merited by programs on the basis of this scale, and also with weeding out unmerited differentials. In those areas where the national interest is highly uncertain, or even nonexistent, the case for categorical federal grants is seriously weakened but not necessarily destroyed. Instead of benefit spillouts, fiscal partnership may be the appropriate rationale for grants. The criterion then becomes simply whether or not a given program can be most effectively operated on a cooperative multilevel basis, without regard to how much (or little) it serves the national interest. The reform question for those enterprises should focus on the particular nature and extent of the federal contribution. Presumably something more than federal money is needed, since otherwise an unrestricted grant would be the appropriate instrument. Federal help for some governmental functions with highly localized benefits may be needed to provide expert knowledge and skills or to coordinate related activities throughout the country. In such cases, federal grant programs should embody negotiated agreements that set forth each party's contributions and responsibilities. These should be very specifically tailored to the individual situation, varying according to the purpose served and the nature of the grantee government so as to attain the greatest efficiency of operation. It is entirely relevant in such instances to raise serious questions about the equity of using federal money, collected broadly from the nation's taxpayers, for operations that benefit groups in narrowly defined geographical areas. The justification is not that the benefits of these programs are widely available to federal taxpayers but rather that such support is a cost of making opportunities available everywhere in the country to operate local or regional programs more efficiently. The test is not

10. See Walker, "Categorical Grants," p. 18.

what is being done but *how* it is being done—that is, not the services themselves but the means of providing them. There may be a national interest in federal grant programs of this kind, but it is operational rather than functional. Both the case for establishing new categorical grants and for continuing established programs should be evaluated on these basic efficiency grounds.

Once the functional areas to be aided by federal grants have been identified, the next question concerns the manner in which the funds are to be allocated to recipients. This may be done either by explicit formulas incorporating standards for measuring the relevant characteristics of potential grantees or on a project-by-project, application basis. Recipient matching may or may not be required and, if required, may be allowed to operate freely on an open-ended basis or be restricted to a fixed amount of grantor funds (closed-end basis). To minimize the leakage of grant funds into unintended uses, maintenance-of-effort requirements of varying kinds may be imposed on recipients, or grant funds may be targeted at particular population groups that otherwise would receive less governmental aid.

Allotted Formula Grants

Allotted formula grants are much less numerous than project grants in the federal system but disburse almost as much money. In fiscal 1975, for example, 97 of the 442 federal categorical grant programs identified by the ACIR were allotted formula grants; they disbursed an estimated 23 percent of the total outlays of $37.4 billion compared with 31 percent disbursed by 296 project grants.[11]

Formula grants are an appropriate instrument for programs aimed at a clearly defined population of eligible recipients, all of whom have some need for the aid in question, if an objective measure of need is available for use as a factor in the allocation formula. Where need is conceived not in absolute but in relative terms, objective measures of both fiscal need and fiscal capacity are required.[12]

11. ACIR, *Categorical Grants: Their Role and Design: The Intergovernmental Grant System: An Assessment and Proposed Policies,* Report A-52 (GPO, 1978), p. 92. In addition, there were 35 mixed formula-project grant programs with 7 percent of total outlays and 14 open-ended reimbursement programs with 39 percent of total outlays.

12. Guidelines for setting up such allocation formulas are suggested in chapter 3. These, of course, apply to all formula grant programs, whether they be categorical, block, or completely unrestricted. For a discussion of the factors used in the allocation of federal categorical grant monies see ACIR, *Categorical Grants,* pp. 100–03, 202–29.

If matching requirements are used with allotted formula grants, they are not likely to serve as a price incentive at the margin of grantee choice of program level. Rather, they should be seen as a substitute for grantor management controls designed to increase operating efficiency. If some minimum contribution by grantees could be established as an important determinant of efficiency in grantee-operated categorical grant programs, its use in place of grantor regulations and controls would reduce paperwork and simplify the administration of these joint enterprises. Seen in this light, matching requirements that appear low in relation to the degree of national interest may instead look efficient, or even excessive. In fiscal 1975 nearly 39 percent of federal categorical grant programs had no statutory matching requirements, 12 percent required nonfederal matching of only 5–10 percent, and only 13 percent required donee matching of 50 percent or more.[13] Another simplification that might be made possible by an efficiency matching requirement is the elimination of any need to vary grantee matching ratios inversely with hard-to-derive measures of fiscal capacity.[14]

Matching requirements may be added to closed-end categorical grants simply as a matter of equity on the assumption that each partner should contribute something to a joint venture. Even when statutory matching is absent, the authorizing legislation often specifies that recipients should share in the costs of the aided activity, the amounts being left to the discretion of grant administrators.[15] Equity considerations may also be dominant in programs that allow grantees to fulfill their matching obligations by contributions in kind rather than in cash. The degree of grantee participation that these soft matches, as they are called, elicit as compared to cash matches is a matter of considerable controversy.[16]

A final function of matching, shared by both closed-end and open-ended categorical grants, is to stimulate grantee expenditures on the aided programs. Unfortunately, it is very difficult to determine the stimulative powers of matching when the grants are closed-end and when all recipients completely use up their allotments. In such cases,

13. Ibid., p. 111.
14. For a discussion of federal experience with variable matching grants see ibid., pp. 170–71.
15. Even fixed statutory matching ratios may be variable in practice if administrators have considerable discretion over which grantee expenditures qualify for matching.
16. Ibid., pp. 172–73.

price incentives are likely to have few, if any, effects at the margin, and the fungibility of grant funds may be both high and rising over time. Such, at least, are the early findings of the pioneering studies of Martin McGuire designed to develop empirically testable models that distinguish the income and price effects of closed-end categorical grants.[17] When these models were applied to state intergovernmental expenditures for education, the proportion of grants converted by recipients into fungible resources rose from an estimated 45–55 percent in 1964–67 to 51–79 percent in 1968–71.[18]

Uncertainty about the stimulative powers of the standard kind of matching grant has induced a continuing search for more effective instruments. One possibility that is appropriate whenever the federal grant is applied to new experimental programs, and can therefore be viewed as seed money, is to use a formula that increases the non-federal matching share gradually as the programs mature, until most, if not all, of the funding depends on state and local sources.[19] Another, more generally applicable, instrument is a maintenance-of-effort or nonsupplant requirement.[20] Grantees typically must maintain their own-source spending at specified levels in order to qualify for aid, a requirement that is equivalent to a quantitative match that varies from one recipient to another but not over time. Maintenance-of-effort requirements, like price and wage controls, may have perverse initial effects unless they are quickly enacted without extended preliminary discussion. In addition, they are patently unfair to grantees

17. Martin McGuire, "An Econometric Model of Federal Grants and Local Fiscal Response," in *Financing the New Federalism: Revenue Sharing, Conditional Grants, and Taxation*, Papers by Robert P. Inman and others, The Governance of Metropolitan Regions no. 5, ed. Wallace E. Oates (Johns Hopkins University Press for Resources for the Future, 1975), pp. 115–38.

18. Martin C. McGuire, "A Method for Estimating the Effect of a Subsidy on the Receiver's Resource Constraint: With An Application to U.S. Local Governments 1964–1971" *Journal of Public Economics*, vol. 10 (August 1978), p. 43, and "The Analysis of Federal Grants Into Price and Income Components," in Peter Mieszkowski and William H. Oakland, eds., *Fiscal Federalism and Grants-in-Aid*, COUPE Papers on Public Economics no. 1 (Washington: Urban Institute, 1979), pp. 31–50.

19. The 1975 ACIR tabulation showed 19 grant programs with rising matching requirements. *Categorical Grants*, pp. 112, 192–93.

20. The ACIR tabulations show that 20 percent of all federal categorical grants and at least 40 percent of formula grants funded in fiscal 1976 had statutory maintenance-of-effort or nonsupplant requirements. Ibid., p. 174.

who have been innovators in the aided program area and whose base levels are therefore higher than other recipients'. If a recession follows shortly after a program's adoption, maintenance-of-effort requirements are likely to reinforce the adverse fiscal pressures on state and local governments unless exceptions are made or other federal grant programs, such as antirecession fiscal assistance, take up the slack. These difficulties can be dealt with, more or less effectively, by flexible program design and by sensitive administration. A much more intractable problem is the steadily decreasing effectiveness of a match based on any given year's spending level in a growing or inflationary economy. Under such conditions expenditures by grantees are bound to rise to or beyond the point at which the outlay of their own funds equals the required match plus the federal funds. At that point the grant funds will have become fully fungible.

One way around this difficulty is a requirement, used in a number of federal grant programs, that grantees show they are spending no less of their own funds on the aided program than they would have spent in the absence of the grant. Such a nonsupplant requirement is fine in principle but virtually impossible to administer unless good objective evidence exists concerning grantees' spending behavior. If own-source spending on the aided program could be estimated accurately for all grantees, say, on the basis of real income, relative price, and other elasticities of response, a rising matching requirement based on observed determinants of state and local government spending could be written into the law. This kind of control may now be no more than a dream of fiscal economists—and possibly a nightmare for state and local officials—but it is one long-term goal whose desirability and feasibility might well be considered in any review and assessment of maintenance-of-effort and nonsupplant requirements.[21]

Another instrument that may serve as an effective stimulant of program activities is targeting. Title I of the Elementary and Secondary Education Act, for example, requires grantees to spend different amounts on two different groups of the client population and then monitors the observable difference between the two programs. In a

21. The ACIR's comprehensive study recommends that Congress request the General Accounting Office or other appropriate agency to research and report on the effects of maintenance-of-effort requirements in federal grants. Ibid., p. 313.

study of this "differential add-on grant," Feldstein estimated that about 72 cents of every title I dollar is used to increase school spending and concluded that this is much greater stimulus than could be expected from a grant lacking this feature.[22]

Project Grants

When neither a well-defined client population nor reasonably objective measures of fiscal need and capacity are available, the grantor may simply invite applications for the funding of particular projects in some specified area of public service. This effectively screens out any governments that neither need nor desire the services in question. If applicants' requests exceed the funds available, grant administrators will be in a position to pick projects with the greatest promise of success and favor applicants with the greatest need.[23] They may also be able to stimulate grantees' spending by varying effective matching ratios inversely with their elasticities of demand for the aided output. Project grants are particularly well suited for undertakings of limited duration that involve research, development of new techniques for producing and delivering services, or capital construction.

Project grants, of course, are not without drawbacks. They may discourage deserving governments who regard the costs of application as too high or the chances of success in the competition as too low. Those with high fiscal capacities or relatively low needs for program benefits may be best at discovering grant programs and creating proposals for them. When project grants are ubiquitous, the much touted art of grantsmanship[24] is a quality well worth the cultivating. Even if no special expertise were demanded for grant application, however, project grant programs would typically require more

22. Martin Feldstein, "The Effect of a Differential Add-On Grant: Title I and Local Education Spending," *Journal of Human Resources,* vol. 13 (Fall 1978), pp. 443–58.

23. These two criteria often conflict. Since aided projects may have virtually no chance of success in the neediest jurisdictions and may make their greatest contributions in communities that are sufficiently well off to be able to take full advantage of their benefits, grant administrators may be sorely tempted to misallocate project funds. The solution, presumably, is to find credible means of broadening administrators' perspectives so that they realize that the neediest applicants will qualify for more effective aid under other federal programs. See ACIR, *Categorical Grants,* p. 315.

24. See, for example, Deil S. Wright, *Understanding Intergovernmental Relations* (Duxbury Press, 1978), pp. 188–92.

paperwork and entail higher administrative costs for all parties than allotted formula grants.

A basic issue in federal grant reform, then, concerns the relative use of allotted formula and project grants. Each type is well suited for certain kinds of objectives and unsuited to others. A systematic and continuing analysis of these interrelationships is an indispensable part of any long-run program of structural grant-in-aid reform. One vehicle for its implementation would be enactment of a sunset system for federal grants, as the ACIR has recommended.[25]

Open-Ended Matching Grants

Though few in number (fourteen programs in the 1975 ACIR tabulation), open-ended matching grants disburse a significant share of all federal categorical grant outlays (39 percent in fiscal 1975).[26] Dominated by aid to families with dependent children and medicaid, these reimbursement grants are deeply enmeshed in two of the most difficult policy issues faced by the federal government in recent years —welfare reform and the adoption of national health insurance. This particular kind of grant instrument may be best used for well-defined governmental functions where there is a true joint national-regional-local interest and the donees' price elasticities of demand for the service are both relatively high and predictable. While questions could be raised about how well income support meets these tests, the critical issue is the public interest in those programs at other than the national level.

Those who view the distributive function as the responsibility solely of the federal government[27] would seek welfare reforms that established uniform nationwide levels of income support, adjusted for regional differences in the cost of living, and that provided for full

25. *Categorical Grants*, pp. 305–08. Sunset laws provide for automatic termination of specified government programs at regular intervals or on particular dates unless the programs are reviewed, evaluated, and explicitly reauthorized by legislative enactment.

26. Ibid., p. 92.

27. Richard A. Musgrave, *The Theory of Public Finance: A Study in Public Economy* (McGraw-Hill, 1959), pp. 181–82; Wallace E. Oates, "The Theory of Public Finance in a Federal System," *Canadian Journal of Economics*, vol. 1 (February 1968), pp. 45–48.

federal financing.[28] There would then be no need for any grant-in-aid instruments. Those who oppose the view that income redistribution should be left entirely to the federal government see it as a public function with subnational dimensions, either because people care more about the welfare of low-income families close to home than of those farther away,[29] or because income redistribution is a complex issue involving significant geographical diversities of taste. Either rationale would create a case for the use of federal grants. If decentralized management aimed at satisfying diverse local tastes is a major goal, a fiscal partnership with minimum matching requirements to assure efficient operation might be the preferred instrument. If local autonomy over the level of income support is a major concern, however, an open-ended matching program would offer the only means of equating local costs with perceived local benefits at the margin. To minimize the migration of low-income families from low- to high-support level areas, federal funds could be targeted at areas with above-average numbers of low-income families, and matching requirements could be set at higher levels for jurisdictions with below-average concentrations of poor.

The future importance of federal open-ended matching grants is likely to be decided as part of any major reform of federal welfare programs or of the establishment of national health insurance. Rejection of the instrument in these policy areas would not eliminate this type of federal grant, but it would reduce its importance greatly. Wherever price incentives are an effective means of stimulating state and local spending programs of national interest, however, open-ended matching grants will remain an attractive possibility.

28. Welfare reform options available to the Carter administration are discussed by George J. Carcagno and Walter S. Corson, "Welfare Reform," in Joseph A. Pechman, ed., *Setting National Priorities: The 1978 Budget* (Brookings Institution, 1977), pp. 249–81; John L. Palmer, "Employment and Income Security," in Joseph A. Pechman, ed., *Setting National Priorities: The 1979 Budget* (Brookings Institution, 1978), pp. 66–74. For more general treatments see Henry J. Aaron, *Why Is Welfare So Hard to Reform?* (Brookings Institution, 1973); John L. Palmer and Joseph J. Minarik, "Income Security Policy," in Henry Owen and Charles L. Schultze, eds., *Setting National Priorities: The Next Ten Years* (Brookings Institution, 1976), pp. 505–82.

29. See, for example, Mark V. Pauly, "Income Redistribution as a Local Public Good," *Journal of Public Economics,* vol. 2 (February 1973), pp. 35–58.

The Problem of Controls

"What makes me tear my hair in frustration is when people like you come and say there are not controls," Mr. Goodell said. "You call it control. I refer to it as objectives of the legislation," Mr. Celebrezze replied.[30] This exchange of views between Representative Charles E. Goodell of New York and Anthony J. Celebrezze, secretary of health, education, and welfare, illustrates nicely the disagreement that is possible when two people look at the same federal grant program with different theories in mind about the role of intergovernmental grants. If the main purpose is to support state and local government programs, particularly in areas of high need and low fiscal capacity, federal controls are not called for, and to adopt them is to imply, as Mr. Goodell suggested, that the states are not to be trusted to know their own interests.

The situation is quite the contrary with joint enterprises. Since the public benefits to be supported by grants accrue jointly to the citizens of two different levels of government, responsibility for operating the programs should also be shared. Partnership arrangements, to be sure, are not always easy for the participants to live with, but increasingly that kind of approach is called for in the operation of important governmental activities. With persistence and goodwill, the difficulties should be surmountable; states can, in any case, simply withdraw from any program that they feel interferes unduly with their freedom to act. If the needs for fiscal equalization are taken care of by other means, as they should be, no state could plead poverty as a reason for having to accept a grant on terms it did not like.

Controls that have to do with the efficient management of federal programs[31] are by no means the only source of concern for state and local government officials. During the 1960s and 1970s a new, and potentially more frustrating, kind of controls developed. These general requirements, not related closely to the specific purposes of any grant program, are intended to further other national policy goals.

---

30. *Aid to Elementary and Secondary Education,* Hearings before the General Subcommittee on Education of the House Committee on Education and Labor, 89 Cong. 1 sess. (GPO, 1965), p. 148. The point under discussion was President Johnson's 1965 education proposals.

31. ACIR, *Improving Federal Grants Management: The Intergovernmental Grant System: An Assessment and Proposed Policies,* Report A-53 (GPO, 1977).

The ACIR sees these attempts to use the leverage of federal grant monies to implement unrelated national policies as "new sources of delays, confusion, costs, and controversy."[32] The steadily growing list includes policies dealing with civil rights and nondiscrimination, environmental protection, planning and project coordination, wage rate and procurement standards, public employee standards, access to government information and decision processes, and obligations to provide relocation assistance and make acquisitions of real property (the latter two injunctions designed to deal with unwanted side effects of urban renewal and other grant programs).[33] The result has been what the ACIR calls a three-way tug-of-war with program-specific controls competing with general policy requirements, and both conflicting with efforts to create greater administrative simplicity and efficiency.[34] State and local officials have reacted to these developments with mixed feelings of uncertainty, frustration, support, and irritation.[35] Particularly troublesome for them have been requirements that are mandated but not funded by the federal government. As a result the effectiveness of federal matching ratios is reduced and the possibility of distortions in state and local participation in grant programs is increased. These are compliance costs that may be undervalued, or even ignored, in congressional evaluations of grant programs and their allocation among the different levels of participating governments may be inappropriate.[36]

Federal grant controls pose the dilemma of choosing between highly specific requirements that may overlook the diversity in need and incentives among governments and very general guidelines that allow unintended and counterproductive actions on the part of federal administrators or grant recipients. Some ambiguity and uncertainty in federal grant programs appears to be an inevitable result of the politics of dealing with complex social and economic problems. The bargaining process is likely to be protracted and, in the absence of effective grantor control mechanisms, to confer considerable dis-

32. ACIR, *Categorical Grants*, p. 40.

33. Ibid., p. 235.

34. Ibid., p. 234.

35. For a detailed discussion of the attitudes of government officials at all levels to grant programs see ACIR, *The Intergovernmental Grant System as Seen by Local, State, and Federal Officials*, Report A-54 (GPO, 1977).

36. ACIR, *Categorical Grants*, pp. 238–39.

cretionary power on grantees.[37] Unintended uses of grant funds may
then occur, and the courts are likely to play an important role, for
better or worse, in the settlement of disputes between grantors and
grantees and between both and program beneficiaries.[38]

Coordination and Consolidation

Reform of the control mechanisms built into federal grant programs[39] is part of the more general problem of bringing the proliferat-
ing maze of programs under better control. The mere existence of a
large number of categorical grant programs with their highly diverse
features suggests strongly that consolidating those with closely related features and coordinating the operation of others might yield
valuable gains in efficiency. Though those have been important federal objectives in recent years, accomplishments appear to many
observers to have been decidedly few. Whether this is because we
haven't tried hard enough, or because our anticipation has greatly
exceeded the potentialities of these two reform measures, or because
grant coordination and consolidation, while desirable on occasion,
conflict with too many more important policy goals is a matter of
continuing, unresolved controversy.

In the mid-1960s three multifunctional, target grant programs—
community action, regional development in Appalachia, and model
cities[40]—were adopted with coordination as one of their explicit
objectives. Each of these important undertakings attempted to bring
together a wide variety of grant-assisted public services in order to
focus them on the solution of complex social and economic problems
of a specific target population or geographical area. Their very limited
successes, as the ACIR puts it, "highlight the perennial force of the

37. For the development of theoretical models capable of dealing with these
complexities and an application to several federal grant programs see Frederick C.
Doolittle, "Intergovernmental Relations in Federal Grant Programs: The Case of
Aid For Families With Dependent Children" (Ph.D. dissertation, University of California—Berkeley, 1977).

38. Ibid., chap. 12.

39. See ACIR, *Improving Federal Grants Management*, pp. 255–87, and *Categorical Grants*, pp. 316–19. See also Congressional Budget Office, *Federal Constraints
on State and Local Government Actions*, Background Paper (GPO, 1979).

40. Authorized by the Economic Opportunity Act of 1964, the Appalachian
Regional Development Act of 1965, and the Demonstration Cities and Metropolitan
Development Act of 1966, respectively.

'functional fiefdoms' in the Federal government. They suggest the difficulty—perhaps the impossibility—of achieving concerted action by a wide range of agencies, each of which is limited by its own organizational needs, bureaucratic traditions and procedures, internal administrative weaknesses, and separate legislative authorizations."[41] Apart from the expected opposition from potential losers, coordination was criticized for conflicting with more important program goals, for unduly preserving the status quo and diverting attention from the development of entirely new solutions to the problems under attack, and even for producing exactly the opposite of its intended results.[42]

Grant coordination has also been a general federal policy objective, particularly in the last fifteen or so years, pursued by the Office of Management and Budget (OMB), the ten federal regional councils created in 1969, the Domestic Council established in 1970, various interagency committees, and the General Services Administration.[43] The procedures outlined in OMB circular A-95 were created to implement the provisions of title IV of the Intergovernmental Cooperation Act of 1968, which requires applications for certain federal grant funds (150–200 programs, depending on who is doing the counting) to be reviewed by state, regional, and local governments whose activities might be affected by those grant-aided projects,[44] and the Joint Funding Simplification Act of 1974, which is designed to help grantees obtain federal grants and integrate them with related programs.[45] None of these administrative initiatives, it appears, has made more than "marginal improvements . . . in the operation of a system of Federal assistance programs characterized by fragmentation, inconsistency, duplication, and complexity."[46]

That there are strict limits to the effective use of grant coordination policies is a message that has been increasingly heard in recent years. The skeptics, who stand in direct opposition to the standard admin-

41. ACIR, *Improving Federal Grants Management*, p. 78.
42. Ibid., pp. 79–83.
43. Ibid., pp. 162–205.
44. Ibid., pp. 216–34; Wright, *Understanding Intergovernmental Relations*, pp. 377–87.
45. The act had the same purposes as the integrated grant administration program, an experiment initiated by OMB in 1972. See ACIR, *Improving Federal Grants Management*, pp. 240–47.
46. Ibid., p. 207.

istrative theories stressing the virtues of coordination and rational centralization,[47] have raised fundamental questions about the ways in which governmental budgetary choices should be made and also about the efficiency with which they are carried out. Those concerned about decisionmaking emphasize the difficulties of applying any rational procedures in a pluralistic society with multiple, conflicting, and frequently ambiguous goals operating in a highly uncertain environment.[48] In their view coordination is just as unworkable and dangerous as the much-discussed planning, programming, and budgeting systems.[49] Critics addressing the operational problems stress the virtues of competition among separate government agencies supplying similar, or even identical, services and the inefficiencies that can be expected to characterize bureaus with unchecked monopoly powers.[50] Coordination, it seems, is to the federal grant system what garlic is to a stew. Applied with finesse it can sharpen the focus of categorical grants and enhance their productivity. Applied injudiciously, however, it can blunt the functional fine-tuning that is the hallmark of the categorical grant instrument and increase the inefficiency and unresponsiveness of government operations.

If coordination is an unreliable means of rationalizing the perceived chaos of the federal grant system, consolidation offers an alternative way. It too is a prime objective of grant reformers, recommended by the ACIR in 1967 and again in 1978.[51] The commission in its detailed 1974–78 study of all of the categorical programs concluded that the problem was less one of duplication and overlap than of fragmentation. Fitting the small pieces of highly specific programs

47. Ibid., pp. 146–56. The standard work is Luther Gulick, "Notes on the Theory of Organization," in Luther Gulick and L. Urwick, eds., *Papers on the Science of Administration* (Institute of Public Administration, Columbia University, 1937), pp. 1–45.

48. See, for example, Dennis A. Rondinelli, *Urban and Regional Development Planning: Policy and Administration* (Cornell University Press, 1975), p. 15.

49. See, for example, Charles L. Schultze, *The Politics and Economics of Public Spending* (Brookings Institution, 1968).

50. See, for example, William A. Niskanen, Jr., *Bureaucracy and Representative Government* (Aldine-Atherton, 1971); Martin Landau, "Redundancy, Rationality, and the Problem of Duplication and Overlap," *Public Administration Review,* vol. 19 (July-August 1969), pp. 346–58; Richard E. Wagner, *The Public Economy* (Markham, 1973), pp. 112–23.

51. ACIR, *Fiscal Balance in the American Federal System,* Report A-31 (GPO, 1968), vol. 1, p. 14, and *Categorical Grants,* pp. 298–304.

together, it reasoned, did promise to create a stronger mosaic. For merging programs, it suggested correlation according to functional area covered, to objectives sought, or to types of recipient served. Applying these criteria to the 442 categorical grant programs operating in fiscal 1975, the commission concluded that "the merger of at least 170 programs into no more than 24 grant consolidations appears to be both feasible and desirable."[52] It considered consolidation in those twenty-four functional areas so important that it recommended legislation authorizing the president to submit appropriate plans which Congress would be required to approve or disapprove by resolution within ninety days of submission.[53] Many functional fiefdoms and client interest groups must give way if these proposals are followed. Developments, however, may point in the opposite direction. Revenue sharing has yet to become a permanent part of the federal grant system, and block grants still exist in a somewhat unstable state of challenge, reaffirmation, and redesign, always facing the frontal threat of greater internal controls or the prospect of being outflanked, and perhaps stifled, by new, related categorical grant programs.

General Revenue Sharing

Conceived in an environment of fiscal drag and fiscal mismatch, both of which provided strong reasons for its creation, federal revenue sharing was a long time coming to birth. By the time it saw the light of day the fiscal drag had disappeared, and before it began to mature the fiscal mismatch, if not gone, had ceased to be so worrisome. Not that unrestricted revenue sharing was really a new idea when it became the watchword of the national political arena in the fall of 1964. Such distributions had in fact been made by the federal government in 1803 and 1837, have been a part of state aid systems throughout the twentieth century, and are extensively used in other countries such as Canada and Australia. In 1938, as part of his cogent advocacy of the use by the federal government of a progressive, comprehensively based personal income tax, and its elimination from state and local tax systems, Henry C. Simons proposed a completely

52. ACIR, *Categorical Grants,* p. 301.
53. Ibid., pp. 301–04.

unrestricted sharing of personal income tax revenues, on the basis of source, with the states.[54] Foreshadowing today's policy issues, he commented: "The revenues from the personal taxes should be shared unconditionally; and the rules determining the relative shares should be designed to prevent both discretionary, administrative manipulation and frequent or substantial alteration by future Congresses. In other words, the initial legislation should serve to settle definitely the basic question of policy."[55]

In 1964 a number of factors combined to make federal revenue sharing especially attractive, and its time seemed clearly to have come. It was sponsored in different forms by both conservatives and liberals—by presidential candidate Barry Goldwater, by economic adviser Walter Heller, and by a task force appointed by President Johnson under the chairmanship of Joseph Pechman.[56] These proposals enjoyed a period of celebrity under the klieg lights and then suddenly retired, somewhat battered, into the quieter academic regions from which they had come. But not for long. Gradually revenue sharing picked up endorsements from important organizations, including the ACIR, during the late 1960s.[57] It was recommended by a Republican preelection task force in 1968 and included in that party's platform for that year. Yet it took four more years of debate and discussion, designing and redesigning, before federal revenue sharing was finally adopted by Congress and signed by President

54. *Personal Income Taxation: The Definition of Income as a Problem of Fiscal Policy* (University of Chicago Press, 1938), pp. 214–18. Most of the income tax revenue was to be raised by a single basic, or normal, tax rate; the revenue from this rate, rather than from the higher surtax rates, was to be distributed to the states of residence or domicile of the individual taxpayers.

55. Ibid., p. 216.

56. The original impetus came from Walter W. Heller, who recommended unrestricted federal grants to the states as a method of reducing the "fiscal drag" generated by rising federal receipts under conditions of rapid and sustained economic growth ("No More Depressions?" *U.S. News and World Report,* June 29, 1964, p. 59). The task force's report, submitted in November 1964, was never released. The views of Joseph A. Pechman are given in "Financing State and Local Government," *Proceedings of a Symposium on Federal Taxation* (American Bankers Association, 1965), pp. 717–84 (Brookings Reprint 103). For Walter W. Heller's views, see *New Dimensions of Political Economy* (Harvard University Press, 1966), chap. 3.

57. ACIR, *Fiscal Balance in the American Federal System,* vol. 1, pp. 5–12. See also ACIR, *Revenue Sharing—An Idea Whose Time Has Come,* Information Report M-54 (GPO, 1970).

Nixon in October 1972.[58] Authorized then for a five-year period ending in December 1976, the so-called "main jewel in the New Federalism crown of the Nixon administration"[59] had barely begun to achieve its full brilliance before the time came round to consider its renewal. Though that process was accomplished with relative ease, the mandate was extended only until September 30, 1980. Whether the true potentialities of a program as far-reaching as revenue sharing can be read from a record produced under the constraint of such a temporary, two-stage authorization is one of the dilemmas confronting fiscal researchers.

In the early 1960s the federal government found itself faced with "the serious inconvenience of an overflowing Treasury," to borrow a description applied by a Senate committee to a similar situation in 1826.[60] The "inconvenience" of having more money generated each year by a growth-sensitive tax system than needed to be spent on its own programs might not seem troubling to everyone. To macroeconomists, however, it was a worrisome manifestation at a time of high national unemployment because it posed the threat that the automatically generated federal surpluses could, unless deftly handled, depress aggregate demand to the point of preventing an early return to full employment conditions. This potential fiscal drag was not the only concern of Walter Heller in his capacity as chairman of the Council of Economic Advisors. State and local governments were facing exactly the opposite kind of problem because their revenues were rising less rapidly each year than their perceived spending requirements. Where the high-priority public service needs were, the money was lacking; and where the money was ample, the high-priority needs were lacking. What more attractive federal initiative could there be than to deal with this fiscal mismatch, and to eliminate fiscal drag at the same time, by a distribution of federal monies, without strings, to state and local governments?

In the event, of course, the Johnson administration did not embrace the idea of revenue sharing but instead turned to various Great So-

58. As the State and Local Fiscal Assistance Act of 1972. For a detailed discussion of the development of this legislation see Richard P. Nathan, Allen D. Manvel, and Susannah E. Calkins, *Monitoring Revenue Sharing* (Brookings Institution, 1975), pp. 344–72.

59. Wright, *Understanding Intergovernmental Relations*, p. 147.

60. James A. Maxwell, *The Fiscal Impact of Federalism in the United States* (Harvard University Press, 1946), p. 12.

ciety programs, with strong categorical features, that did much both to eliminate fiscal drag and fiscal mismatch and to set the stage for a new kind of federal aid program.[61] Certainly there were many who looked to revenue sharing as a simple and attractive solution to problems created or exacerbated by a burgeoning categorical grant program. Some saw the federal government's power and influence on the economy as excessive and the proliferation of categorical grant programs as an alarming stimulus to this trend. Some feared the consequences of the accelerating shift of political power from elected or appointed policy generalists to professional program specialists operating in each functional area. For these and other reasons,[62] revenue sharing was enacted in 1972 and, rather singularly, without any explicit statement of purposes in the law. Presumably the goals of the program's supporters were too many and diverse to allow any simple enumeration by legislative leaders.[63]

This implied diversity of purpose became an inherent problem for the new program since it could hardly be expected to satisfy all expectations at once. A more immediate problem, however, was the considerable change in the fiscal environment between 1964 and 1972. In the earlier year the obvious alternative to the adoption of revenue sharing had been larger federal tax reductions. This increased the program's attractiveness to those who saw the public sector as underfinanced, as compared to the private economy. In addition, it meant that even in the absence of any substantial shift of resources to government, in the event that state and local governments chose to use the revenue sharing funds to reduce their own tax rates, the result would simply be a substitution of federal for state and local tax burdens—a development that would increase the progressivity of the nation's total tax system. By 1972, however, the situation was quite different. The most probable alternative to the enactment of revenue sharing was higher spending on other federal programs, including

61. In his wide-ranging discussion of five phases of intergovernmental relations in the United States Deil Wright characterizes the Johnson administration years as a period of "project-categorical grant explosion." *Understanding Intergovernmental Relations*, p. 55. For a general economic assessment of the period see Henry J. Aaron, *Politics and the Professors: The Great Society in Perspective* (Brookings Institution, 1978).

62. See Nathan, Manvel, and Calkins, *Monitoring Revenue Sharing*, pp. 352–72; Wright, *Understanding Intergovernmental Relations*, pp. 148–52.

63. Wright, *Understanding Intergovernmental Relations*, pp. 153–56.

categorical grants-in-aid. What had been looked on in 1964 as an additional infusion of federal aid, and with good reason, suddenly began to appear more and more as a substitute for existing aid funds. No wonder mayors and governors, who had strongly supported revenue sharing, began to question what they had attained thereby, particularly when in 1973 President Nixon began to make vigorous use of his impoundment powers in an effort to stem the flow of categorical grant funds.[64]

Whatever the fiscal effects that its enactment may have generated, the program was under way. Soon to become known as general revenue sharing to distinguish it from the Nixon administration's concurrently proposed special revenue sharing plan for the consolidation of a hundred and twenty-nine categorical grants into six block grant programs,[65] the new kind of federal aid raised a number of important policy questions. The most fundamental of these, which would apply to any firmly established unrestricted grant program, have to do with the level of support provided, the rules for allocating funds among the different recipients, and the attendant changes, if any, in the political processes, allocation of power, and structure of intergovernmental relations generally. In principle the uses to which the funds are put by recipients should have no policy significance, since the basic purpose of revenue sharing is to give free rein to the priorities of state and local governments, whatever they may be. This independence on the part of recipients, however, was greatly diminished by the short-term basis on which general revenue sharing was enacted. The necessity of reevaluation clearly gave importance to fund uses, as the cases for and against renewal were patently affected by people's perceptions of which state and local programs gained support and which lost and of the program's potential impact on the level and structure of state and local tax burdens.

Allocation Rules

The critical feature of any unrestricted grant program is the definition of the qualified recipient group and the selection of formulas by

64. For an interesting discussion of the changed perceptions and plans of local government officials during this period see Bruce A. Wallin, "Economic and Political Rationality: General Revenue Sharing and Local Finance" (Ph.D. dissertation, University of California—Berkeley, forthcoming).

65. Both were proposed in the State of the Union and budget messages in early 1971.

which the funds are to be allocated within that group. The choices are difficult and controversial, and general revenue sharing nearly foundered on those rocks. Inevitably, the final solution in 1972 was a complicated one, its principal attraction being its acceptability to a wide diversity of interest groups. Experience in 1976, and again in 1980, indicates that the allocation rules cannot fail to be a controversial feature of any debate over renewal. So far preserving the status quo has proven to be the line of least resistance, but that fact has not discouraged the proliferation of suggested improvements.

The drafters of the general revenue sharing law had to walk a delicate political tightrope in choosing the set of local governments to be made eligible for the grants. Efficiency suggested a small number of populous cities and counties—as few as five hundred had two-thirds of the total population at the time[66]—but political salability required a much larger group of beneficiaries. In the event, funds were made available to all general-purpose local governments—nearly thirty-nine thousand.[67] In a simpler age such a massive distribution would have been unthinkable, but modern computers, the inconspicuous midwives of the allocational procedure, can handle the task without difficulty.[68]

Distribution of general revenue sharing funds to state and local governments is done in a series of steps. First, amounts due each of the fifty state areas and the District of Columbia are calculated on the basis of two alternative formulas (for each recipient the more favorable of the resulting allocations is adopted). One formula, devised by the Senate, assigns equal weight to population, general tax effort as measured by the ratio of total state and local tax revenue to state personal income, and inverse income status as measured by the ratio of nationwide per capita personal income to state per capita income. The alternative House formula assigns different weights to those three factors plus two others—urban population and state in-

66. Nathan, Manvel, and Calkins, *Monitoring Revenue Sharing*, p. 40.

67. The situation has not changed much. Census data for 1977 show 3,042 counties, 18,856 municipalities, and 16,822 townships, for a total of 38,720 general-purpose local governments. In addition there were 15,260 school districts and 26,140 special districts. U.S. Census Bureau, *1977 Census of Governments, Governmental Units in 1977, Preliminary Report no. 1* (October 1977), p. 1.

68. In 1978 the Treasury Department's Office of Revenue Sharing employed about 200 people and spent $7 million to distribute $6.9 billion to all state and local governments. *The Budget of the United States Government, Fiscal Year 1980—Appendix*, pp. 750–52.

come tax collections.[69] One-third of each state allocation goes to the
state government and two-thirds to all eligible local governments. The
local government portion for each state is first assigned to county
areas on the basis of an appropriately adjusted Senate formula.
These allocations are then, where appropriate, adjusted to conform
to both maximum and minimum per capita limits, with any deficiencies or remainders being spread proportionately among the other
areas.[70] Within each county area, allocations are first made to Indian
tribes and Alaskan native villages on the basis of relative population.
The remaining funds are then allocated to the county government
and to all municipalities and townships on the basis of nonschool tax
revenue; the distribution to municipalities and townships employs a
three-factor, Senate-type formula. Again there are per capita limits
on allocations and a ceiling that restricts revenue sharing funds to
50 percent of the local government's nonschool tax revenue and intergovernmental grant receipts.[71]

Need, Capacity, and Revenue

The most difficult and critical problem in setting up any unrestricted grant program is that of identifying and measuring recipients'
fiscal need and their capacity to meet that need on their own. In the
allocation formulas for revenue sharing, both population and per
capita personal income can be viewed as measures of fiscal need.
Critics, who stress the imprecision of these factors, have sought to
supplement or to supplant them with better measures. But such factors as the percentage of families within the jurisdiction below official
poverty lines[72] may prove too much. If a community's fiscal needs are

69. For the details see Nathan, Manvel, and Calkins, *Monitoring Revenue Sharing*, pp. 45–50.
70. Ibid., pp. 51, 52. No county area may receive less than 20 percent or more
than 145 percent of the statewide average per capita amount for local distribution.
71. Ibid., p. 53. Any local allocation above the ceiling reverts to the state government, which may therefore receive slightly more than a third of the state's allocation. In distributions to county areas or allocations among municipalities and townships, or both, the state may modify the three-factor Senate allocation formula by
dropping either the relative income measure or the relative effort measure or both.
As late as 1979, no state had done so.
72. See John P. Ross, "Alternative Formula For General Revenue Sharing:
Population-Based Measures of Need," in National Science Foundation (NSF), *General Revenue Sharing: Research Utilization Project*, Research Applied to National
Needs (RANN), vol. 1: *Summaries of Formula Research* (GPO, 1975), pp. 117–
25; see also ibid., vol. 3: *Synthesis of Formula Research* (GPO, 1975), pp. 37, 75.

mainly related to large concentrations of low-income people, unrestricted grants would surely be less useful instruments than either direct government transfers to low-income families or categorical grants supporting public programs whose benefits are largely confined to poverty groups. Since the purpose of revenue sharing is to support state and local programs in general, the needs it responds to should be correspondingly broad. Several researchers advocate the use of an index based on each state or local government's cost of providing some standard or average menu of public services[73] in the belief that it would improve the vertical equity of the revenue sharing program.

Measures of fiscal capacity based on per capita personal income[74] are widely criticized for their failure to take account of the differing abilities of state and local governments to export some of their tax burdens to outsiders. In a closed economic system, personal income would be a good measure of an area's ability both to impose and to bear tax burdens. However, in open systems that give taxing priority to jurisdiction of origin, as is the common practice, income origination becomes an important component of the ability to impose tax burdens. Between 1974 and 1979, for example, the six major oil-exporting states enjoyed rapidly rising revenues from that source. Total collections from severance taxes and oil and gas rents and royalties during the six-year period ranged from $410 per capita in Oklahoma to $2,040 per capita in Alaska, compared to only $17 per capita from the same sources in all other states.[75] Personal income, which is normally a residence-based concept, is a comprehensive measure of ability to bear tax burdens but only a partial measure of ability to impose them.

A good measure of an area's taxing potential, then, would take into account both income originating in the area and income received there, as the ACIR's representative tax system index does. When that

73. Gregory Schmid, "An Alternative Approach to General Revenue Sharing: A Needs-Based Allocation Formula," and Stephen M. Barro, "Equalization and Equity in Revenue Sharing: An Analysis of Alternative Interstate Distribution Formulas," in NSF, *Summaries of Formula Research*, pp. 41–53, 55–74.

74. Used alone as an allocation factor, per capita personal income may be viewed as a measure of need when it is relatively low and as a measure of capacity when it is relatively high. Used in relation to tax collections to measure tax effort it is unambiguously a capacity factor.

75. Allen D. Manvel, "Some U.S. Beneficiaries of OPEC," *Tax Notes*, February 4, 1980, pp. 166–67.

measure was substituted for personal income in the revenue sharing formula for state allocations in 1972, ten states showed gains in their allocations of 5 percent or more and twenty-two showed losses of corresponding size. The gaining states tended to rank high in per capita personal income and degree of urbanization, while the losing states were typically mining, farming, or tourist oriented.[76]

The ACIR's representative tax system as a measure of tax capacity, however, is not without its critics, many of whom would prefer to use a standard derived from the kind of behavioral study discussed earlier. Barro, however, in a comparison of two such alternatives found large enough differences in the gross allocations among states to recommend against any change in the factors measuring fiscal capacity until a single best measure of taxing potential can be determined.[77] The immediate question is whether the ACIR measure is sufficiently better than the personal income measure of tax potential to warrant a concerted effort to change the allocation formulas.[78]

Measures of local taxing capacities are not only more difficult to derive and to keep current than are state measures but more difficult to compute. Different capacity indexes typically show wide variations for local governments.[79] Though property taxes provide about 80 percent of all tax revenue collected by local governments, some jurisdictions, especially large cities, make extensive use of income, sales, and other levies. The property tax base alone, then, will often not be a good indicator of taxing potential. The growing evidence that different kinds of property affect local spending choices differently strongly suggests that capacity measures should take account of the composition, as well as the size, of the property tax base.

Another factor in allocation formulas that is closely related to fiscal capacity is tax effort, normally defined as the ratio of tax collections to some measure of a jurisdiction's tax capacity. Tax effort,

76. Nathan, Manvel, and Calkins, *Monitoring Revenue Sharing*, pp. 137–40.

77. Barro, "Equalization and Equity," p. 66.

78. If the answer is affirmative, a simplified version of the representative tax system, developed by Halstead and Reischauer, is available; it provides measurements that can be updated annually from regularly published data. D. Kent Halstead, *Tax Wealth in Fifty States*, U.S. Department of Health, Education, and Welfare, National Institute of Education (GPO, 1978); Robert D. Reischauer, "Rich Governments—Poor Governments: Determining the Fiscal Capacity and Revenue Requirements of State and Local Government" (Brookings Institution, December 1974).

79. Reischauer, "Rich Governments—Poor Governments," provides striking evidence on the size of these differences.

however, is not a good means of distinguishing relatively deserving from undeserving recipients. High tax effort may indeed be a sign of above-average fiscal need or below-average fiscal capacity, but it may also be the result of wasteful management, of exploitation of passive local taxpayers by powerful special interest groups, or simply of strong voter tastes for public services.[80] Moreover, measures of tax effort based on personal income may assign high values to jurisdictions with above-average abilities to export tax burdens, thereby rewarding not those who most help themselves, which is one of the attractive features of tax effort as an allocation factor, but rather those most able to push the cost of their public benefits onto other jurisdictions. This bias could be handled by shifting to a representative tax system as a measure of fiscal capacity. Or tax effort could simply be dropped from the formulas for allocating revenue sharing funds. Barro's simulations indicate that dropping the tax effort factor from state distributions would strengthen the inverse relation between fund allocations and per capita personal income, reduce entitlements to rural states, and increase them for states with the largest concentrations of black and poor people.[81] Dropping tax effort as a factor in distributions to both county areas and to municipalities and townships—which states may elect to do under section 108(C)(1) of the 1976 revenue sharing law—would reduce the shared revenues of central cities by more than 20 percent and increase those of neighboring suburban communities by more than 10 percent.[82]

The narrowness of the revenue measures used is another criticism of revenue sharing formulas. User charges and fees are excluded generally, thereby providing some incentive for local governments to move away from direct benefits-received financing.[83] Any significant move in that direction would, in the view of many experts, cause an important loss in the equity and efficiency of state and local financing systems. It is not easy, however, to decide exactly how much the revenue factors should be broadened. Presumably they should

80. James A. Maxwell, "Tax Effort as a Determinant of Revenue Sharing Allotments," *Harvard Journal on Legislation*, vol. 11 (December 1973), pp. 63–67.

81. NSF, *Synthesis of Formula Research*, p. 71.

82. Richard P. Nathan and Jacob M. Jaffee, "Effects of the Statutory Formula Alternatives," in NSF, *Summaries of Formula Research*, p. 10.

83. For a discussion of the reactions that allocation formulas may induce on the part of state and local governments, see Robert D. Reischauer, "General Revenue Sharing—The Program's Incentives," *Financing the New Federalism*, pp. 40–87.

include all kinds of revenue received to finance the standard and ordinary government activities, but those activities are difficult to delineate precisely. The Nixon administration's inclusion of total "own-source general revenue" in its revenue sharing plan has been criticized as too broad.[84] Revenue measures of narrower scope, which include the most standard kinds of user charges and fees rather than taxes only, have been estimated to shift revenue sharing funds from counties to municipalities, sometimes in significant amounts.[85]

Questions have also been raised about what the use of nonschool rather than total local taxes in the county area distributions of revenue sharing funds does to the competition for funds among local jurisdictions that draw upon the same tax base. What a school district gets may come at the expense of other local general-purpose governments; total local taxes may thus be a better measure of county area fiscal effort than nonschool taxes alone. Simulations show that changing to a total tax basis would make revenue sharing formulas somewhat more redistributive but would tend to reduce allocations to central cities and to increase them for suburban and rural areas.[86] Omission of school taxes from allocation formulas also creates opportunities for some jurisdictions to manipulate their nonschool tax totals in order to qualify for more funds.[87] The incentives to do so are unlikely to be strong, however, and in any case could probably be combatted by less stringent measures than changes in revenue sharing formulas.[88]

When all is said and done, the most important feature of the distribution formula for revenue sharing may be its complexity. That widens its political appeal, frustrates attempts by individual recipient jurisdictions to improve their own entitlement qualifications, and impedes the development of systematic reactions designed to take advantage of its loopholes.

Intergovernmental Fiscal Relations

In recent years the federal government has shown a notable propensity to bypass states in order to concentrate its aid on local govern-

84. Nathan, Manvel, and Calkins, *Monitoring Revenue Sharing*, pp. 145–48.
85. NSF, *Synthesis of Formula Research*, pp. 74–75.
86. Reese C. Wilson and others, "General Revenue Sharing Formula Alternatives," in NSF, *Summaries of Formula Research*, p. 80.
87. Nathan, Manvel, and Calkins, *Monitoring Revenue Sharing*, pp. 148–50.
88. Reischauer, "General Revenue Sharing," pp. 72–74.

ments. The general revenue sharing law is no exception to this trend. Whereas in 1970–71 state and local governments' percentage shares of direct general expenditures were 39–61 and of own-source revenues 53–47, the revenue sharing law of 1972 imposed a uniform 33–67 sharing of its funds on those two levels of government. How much bias toward local governments this represents can be determined by comparing the two levels' ratios of revenue sharing funds to their direct general expenditures. The resulting index of local budget preference in the 1972 distribution of shared revenue was 3.2 for the country as a whole, varying from a high of 7.8 in Hawaii to a low of 1.4 in New York.[89] Since an index value of unity would indicate neutrality between the two levels of government, it is apparent that some local preference exists in every state.

A more serious aspect of the revenue sharing formula is its use of a uniform rule for splitting funds between state and local levels, regardless of how fiscal responsibilities are actually shared. In fact, this division varies greatly from state to state. The effect of this rule is to create, for no apparent reason, wide differentials among the states in the relative importance of shared funds to the two levels of government. The most direct solution to this problem would be to relate the division of funds within each state to the relative fiscal responsibility carried by each jurisdiction. This could be measured by direct general expenditures, or own-source revenues, or both. A combined responsibility index constructed by G. Ross Stephens, for example, showed an average state-local division of funds in 1972 of 53–47 for the country as a whole, with a range from 80–20 for Hawaii to 38–62 for New York.[90]

The tiered distribution system of the revenue sharing law is so complex that the original Heller-Pechman proposal seems all the more appealing. Funds would simply be divided up among the fifty states and the District of Columbia, and they would shoulder the responsibility of allocating the money between themselves and their own subordinate local government units. Distrust of the fairness and efficiency with which such a distribution system might operate has greatly complicated the legislated apparatus. More fundamentally, it has af-

89. Nathan, Manvel, and Calkins, *Monitoring Revenue Sharing*, pp. 152–53, 336–41.
90. "State Responsibility for Public Services and General Revenue Sharing," in NSF, *Summaries of Formula Research*, p. 99.

fected, for better or worse, the recent development of intergovernmental relations in the United States.

Statutory Floors and Ceilings

Distributional constraints on revenue sharing are designed to assure that no beneficiary gets relatively too little or too much, as compared either to others or to its own revenue from other sources. Whether these intangible gains in equity come at the expense of too much operational effectiveness is an important policy question. Unfortunately, like the main program effects, these are hard to quantify because no one can be sure of what would have happened had there been no statutory floors and ceilings from the start, or if their dimensions had been different.

Nevertheless, some potential efficiency gains and losses should receive further study as the revenue sharing program develops. The 20 percent per capita floor, which in 1972 benefited one-third of all townships and one-sixth of all municipalities,[91] provides small jurisdictions with support that may slow their absorption into larger, more efficient units.[92] The 145 percent per capita ceiling diverts funds from some hard-pressed central cities, leaves others unaffected, and keeps down benefits to industrial, commercial, and tourist enclaves.[93] It may also inhibit potentially beneficial mergers of municipal and county governments in metropolitan areas.[94] The 50 percent revenue ceiling, which affected about 10 percent of all general-purpose local governments in 1972, provides the strongest incentive for jurisdictions to increase their tax effort; their entitlements go up by one-half of every additional dollar of nonschool taxes raised. Both the high uncertainty about the future operation of the complex allocation process and the slowness with which entitlements actually respond to higher tax effort, however, may blunt the impact of this incentive.[95] Lowering the revenue limit, from 50 percent to, say, 20 percent,

91. Nathan, Manvel, and Calkins, *Monitoring Revenue Sharing,* p. 160.
92. For a general discussion of the program's effects on government structure, see Reischauer, "General Revenue Sharing," pp. 74–79; Nathan, Manvel, and Calkins, *Monitoring Revenue Sharing,* chap. 11; Richard P. Nathan, Charles F. Adams, Jr., and associates, *Revenue Sharing: The Second Round* (Brookings Institution, 1977), chap. 5.
93. NSF, *Synthesis of Formula Research,* pp. 76–77.
94. Nathan, Manvel, and Calkins, *Monitoring Revenue Sharing,* p. 160.
95. Ibid., p. 165.

would reduce these incentives and also lower allocations to small units and to jurisdictions that are relatively inactive.[96]

The statutory floors and ceilings on revenue sharing, then, generate a variety of effects whose mixed nature, uncertain importance, and highly interrelated operation make reform a very delicate matter indeed. Even the sequence with which the constraints are implemented, concerning which the law allows more than one interpretation, is important, as Strauss has shown.[97] He suggests a set of implementation rules that would in general reduce allocations to many relatively inactive Midwestern townships and might thereby strengthen moves toward a more efficient structure for local government in that region.

The fact that revenue sharing has not had a strong impact on the structure of state and local government should be interpreted with caution. Its effectiveness as an inducer of structural change, either good or bad, would be strengthened if the program were given greater financial support and more permanent status.

Regional Gains and Losses

The gross flow of funds to different state and local governments provides only a frontal view of the fiscal effects of revenue sharing. These monies are not manna from heaven but distributions that come at the expense of other federal fiscal activities. These offsetting effects —which are hard to identify, let alone measure—make up the other side of the picture. Only when both sides are considered together can patterns of regional net gains and losses be discerned. Trying to figure out who gains and who loses is a game that many attempt, but few play well.

One problem, which is more readily resolved under some economic and political conditions than others, is that of identifying the federal fiscal activities that the presence of revenue sharing precludes. In general, revenue sharing grants may be financed by higher federal taxes than otherwise would be levied, by lower federal expenditures than otherwise would be made, or by higher federal deficits and borrowing. At times it is impossible to tell which of the many permuta-

96. Wilson and others, "General Revenue Sharing Formula Alternatives," p. 76.
97. Robert P. Strauss, "The Impact of Alternative Interpretations of the Floor and Ceiling Provisions of the State and Local Fiscal Assistance Act of 1972," in NSF, *Summaries of Formula Research*, pp. 107–15.

tions is the most likely. When probable trade-offs can be discerned, measurement of potential state or regional net gains and losses may provide important insights into the operational effects of revenue sharing. But the best measurements may only be rough approximations to the true answer, and poor measurements may be more misleading than none at all.

Among the easiest of the program's effects to simulate is the distributional pattern that would be created if shared revenue came entirely, and proportionately, at the expense of money paid to state and local governments under other federal aid programs. In 1971–72 a 17 percent reduction in federal grants would have financed the $5.3 billion shared revenue allocation of that year. Twenty-nine states and the District of Columbia (together comprising two-thirds of the nation's population) would have been worse off, and twenty-one states better off. The largest losses would have been $82 and $76 per capita in the District of Columbia and Alaska, respectively, while the largest gains—$9 and $10 per capita—would have accrued to Mississippi and Wisconsin.[98] In general, revenue sharing was more generous than other federal grant programs to low-income, rural states, but not consistently so.

Probably the most frequently encountered assumption is that shared revenue grants are financed by higher federal taxes. This may well be the case, at least to some extent and under most circumstances. If so, it bears out the hopes of those who looked to it to promote redistribution of resources from high-income to low-income states and regions. Per capita shared revenue received in 1972 by Mississippi, the lowest per capita income state, for example, amounted to 153 percent of the U.S. average, while Connecticut, the highest per capita income state, got only 85 percent of the U.S. per capita average. In that same year, however, shared revenue was 284 percent of Mississippi's prorated share of total federal receipts and only 57 percent of Connecticut's.[99]

Venturing much beyond these qualitative impressions of the net redistributive effects of a tax-financed revenue sharing program is a hazardous undertaking. To say precisely which states would gain, and which lose, one must first identify the federal taxes that would be reduced if the program were terminated. Customs duties, federal excises, and the payroll tax for social security seem most unlikely to be affected. That leaves mainly the corporation and individual income taxes. There is no consensus on how the burdens of the corporation income tax are distributed, and it would be impossible to get any general agreement on the allocation of them among residents of particular states.[100] The geographical distribution of burdens is relatively easy to plot for the individual income tax, but the specific structure of any tax reductions likely to be made will always be highly uncertain. Generally, the federal tax reductions made since 1964 have increased the progressiveness of the tax, though the Revenue Act of 1978 may be a major turning point in that trend.[101] Simply to assume a proportionate reduction in each person's federal income tax liability would be only a first approximation. Given the revenue-sharing program's small size relative to total federal individual income tax revenue, however, even a rough approximation might suffice for most purposes.

A third major assumption about the fiscal impact of revenue sharing is that the grants reduce other federal expenditures more or less proportionately. While allocating transfer expenditures geographically is not difficult, distributing the government component of gross national product by region is another matter. One approach to this task is to trace out the regional incidence of the government's expenditures on goods and services.[102] Another is to allocate the benefits generated by the programs to people in different parts of the country.[103] Only the former promises any very clear answers, and even it encounters such intractable complications as the need to follow all

100. Joseph A. Pechman and Benjamin A. Okner, *Who Bears the Tax Burden?* (Brookings Institution, 1974), used five alternative incidence assumptions (p. 38) with significantly different results (p. 61).

101. Benjamin Bridges, Jr., *Intertemporal Changes in Tax Rates, Studies in Income Distribution*, no. 11 (U.S. Department of Health, Education, and Welfare, Social Security Administration, Office of Research and Statistics, 1978); Benjamin A. Okner, "Distributional Aspects of Tax Reform During the Past Fifteen Years," *National Tax Journal*, vol. 32 (March 1979), pp. 11–27; and Rudolph G. Penner, "Carter Income Tax Proposals: How Much Progression Is Desirable?" *Tax Notes,* June 26, 1978, pp. 707–09.

102. For a theoretical analysis of this option see Charles E. McLure, Jr., "The Theory of Expenditure Incidence," *Finanzarchiv* (Tübingen, West Germany), vol. 30, no. 3 (1972), pp. 432–53.

103. See, for example, Richard A. Musgrave and Peggy B. Musgrave, *Public Finance in Theory and Practice*, 2d ed. (McGraw-Hill, 1976), pp. 395–98.

government payments to prime contractors through to various layers of subcontractors around the country.[104]

The net distributional effects of revenue sharing, then, are somewhat of an enigma—too important to be ignored, yet often too imprecise to serve as a guide to action. Handled skillfully, they can make an important contribution to policymaking. Considered alone, for example, a simple allocation of grant funds on the basis of population appears to be only mildly redistributive in nature. Combined with, and financed by, a progressive tax system, however, such a grant program would be significantly redistributive. Carelessly measured net distributional effects, however, may give rise to completely unjustifiable, and even counterproductive, interregional disputes in the event that states that are really gainers regard themselves as losers and act accordingly.

Economic and Political Effects

Visible or not, the net distributional effects of revenue sharing are ever active in influencing recipients' reactions to the program. Especially important is the program's impact on the size of the public sector. To measure this the portion of shared funds used to reduce taxes must first be determined. These reductions in state and local taxes induced by revenue sharing can then be compared with the proportion of a reduction in federal taxes that would remain in the private sector rather than being transferred back to the public sector by whatever state and local tax increases are induced by the federal tax reduction. If there is indeed a flypaper tendency for money to remain in the sector in which it is first received, a federal tax reduction would mainly stimulate private spending and revenue sharing would mainly stimulate public spending. If so, one important effect of a tax-financed program of revenue sharing is to enlarge the state and local government sector of the economy.

Pinning down the effects of revenue sharing on the spending patterns of recipient governments is a difficult and intriguing problem. Some governments simply merge shared revenue with other monies; their spending patterns can be predicted from estimates of the marginal propensities of state and local government to spend on different

104. Shared revenue allocations in 1972 are compared with the interstate distribution of federal expenditures in Nathan, Manvel, and Calkins, *Monitoring Revenue Sharing*, pp. 77–81.

programs. Other governments treat shared revenue as a special kind of increment, to be spent differently; shared funds change the scope and nature of their activities. Which governmental units react in which ways and under what circumstances is one of the pivotal issues in revenue sharing.

Among the many standard research methods applied to these questions,[105] surveys of government officials, by mailed questionnaire or personal interview, have been widely used and had unusually high rates of response. Econometric behavioral models have been applied both to standard fiscal data collections and to various special survey research tabulations. A particularly interesting approach is the Brookings monitoring program under which a small group of experts has carried out closely coordinated studies of the behavior of a selected sample of state and local governments since the revenue sharing program began. From budget data, special government reports, newspaper stories, and personal interviews with a wide variety of people, these monitors try to determine what recipients have done differently because of the existence of the program. Though there presumably are no precise answers to that difficult question, the estimates thus obtained are of considerable value.

TAX REDUCTION EFFECTS. Receipt of shared revenue may enable a state or local government to avoid a tax increase, or even to lower tax rates. How sensitive a government is to the tastes of the median voter-taxpayer in its jurisdiction may be estimated by comparing that household's marginal propensity to spend its income on state or local public goods with the proportion of shared revenue the government uses to increase its expenditures. If these two proportions are the same, a tax-financed program would make no change in the size of the public sector in the jurisdiction. The maximization of consumer utility would then be the dominant factor in state and local finance. But if the shared funds are more likely to be used for increased government spending than would an equal increase in the incomes of people in the private sector, the presence of other countervailing forces would be indicated. These might arise from fears of the median voter that higher local taxes would adversely affect their communities or from misperceptions on their part of the full cost of grant-assisted

105. NSF, *General Revenue Sharing*, vol. 5: *Ancilla to Revenue Sharing Research*, contains a listing of all sponsored research reports, a detailed index, and an annotated bibliography.

local spending.[106] Alternatively, taxpayer groups may lose out in the competition over use of revenue sharing funds to bureaucratic and special interest groups.

Any range of estimates of the revenue sharing program's propensity to reduce state and local tax burdens that lies significantly below the range of household propensities to keep additional income within the private sector can be assumed to confirm the tendency for the funds brought in by the program to remain in the public sector. Such appears to be the case with federal revenue sharing. Brookings' monitors estimate that through mid-1974 both state and local governments in their sample used 20 percent of revenue sharing funds either to reduce taxes or to avoid tax increases.[107] Juster and Anton's analyses of survey data obtained by personal interview of some two thousand state and local officials with basic responsibilities for administering the revenue sharing program show that local governments used 17–24 percent of shared funds to reduce taxes in fiscal 1974 and 16–25 percent in fiscal 1975, and state governments used slightly over 20 percent for that purpose in both years. The estimates when weighted by population were even higher, with averages at 29 percent for fiscal 1974 and 36.5 percent for fiscal 1975.[108] The marginal propensity to spend private income on state and local government services, on the other hand, is consistently 5–10 percent.[109] Clearly a tax-financed revenue sharing program does achieve the goal of growth in the public sector that many of its supporters advocated.

The impact of revenue sharing on tax levels does appear to vary by type of recipient. The Brookings estimates, for example, show that

106. Paul N. Courant, Edward M. Gramlich, and Daniel L. Rubinfeld, "The Stimulative Effects of Intergovernmental Grants: or Why Money Sticks Where it Hits," and Wallace E. Oates, "Lump-sum Intergovernmental Grants Have Price Effects," in Mieszkowski and Oakland, *Fiscal Federalism and Grants-in-Aid*, pp. 5–21, 23–30.

107. Nathan, Adams, and associates, *Revenue Sharing*, p. 31.

108. F. Thomas Juster and Thomas J. Anton, "Introduction and Summary," Irene Hess, Amaury de Souza, and F. Thomas Juster, "Sample and Survey Design," and F. Thomas Juster, "Fiscal Impact on Local Governments," in F. Thomas Juster, ed., *The Economic and Political Impact of General Revenue Sharing*, National Science Foundation, Research Applied to National Needs (GPO, 1976), pp. 2–3, 191–300, 27–30, 20–21. Juster's best-judgment estimates are 20–25 percent for 1974 and 30–35 percent for 1975. Ibid., p. 13.

109. Edward M. Gramlich, "Intergovernmental Grants: A Review of the Empirical Literature," in Wallace E. Oates, ed., *The Political Economy of Fiscal Federalism* (Lexington Books, 1977), p. 230.

tax reductions were larger in local governments with over 100,000 population than in smaller units through the second round, though the differential narrowed greatly in the third round (mid-1974 to the end of 1975). They were most likely to occur in jurisdictions where fiscal pressures were either extreme, implying that tax rates were already too high, or completely absent, implying that demands for public services were already well satisfied.[110] In general, econometric studies have identified per capita income, city size, regional location, fiscal pressure, per capita grant revenue, and uncertainty about the continuation of revenue sharing as the most important factors determining the uses to which the funds are put.[111]

SPENDING EFFECTS. Revenue sharing sometimes plays a supportive role, enabling recipient governments to do more of what they are already doing. At other times they are enabled, or induced, to do something different, either because the revenue sharing allotment is much larger than any normal revenue increment to which they are accustomed or because shared revenue, for a variety of reasons, is regarded in a special light. Recipients may also spend shared revenue funds differently because they are seen as less burdensome in terms of cost to local taxpayers than revenue generated in other ways, because they are regarded as temporary, or because they are subject to the special political processes specified in the law.

Though empirical research cannot draw a very precise distinction between the supportive and innovative effects of revenue sharing, it has produced some interesting evidence. The Brookings study indicated that, through mid-1974, new spending on capital projects, expanded current operations, and increased pay and benefits absorbed 47 percent and 65 percent, respectively, of shared revenue for the state and local governments sampled. The balance of the funds was devoted to supportive uses—program maintenance, restoration of federal aid, avoidance of borrowing, and increased fund balances.[112]

110. Nathan, Adams, and associates, *Revenue Sharing*, pp. 35–41; Charles F. Adams, Jr., and Dan L. Crippen, *The Fiscal Impact of General Revenue Sharing on Local Governments* (U.S. Treasury Department, Office of Revenue Sharing, 1979), pp. 16–27.

111. Gail R. Wilensky, "Modeling the Fiscal Impact of Revenue Sharing," and Harvey E. Brazer, "The States and General Revenue Sharing," in Juster, *Economic and Political Impact*, pp. 69–79, 127–29.

112. These percentages exclude the "tax reduction," "tax stabilization," and "not categorized" items in the Brookings tabulations. See Nathan, Adams, and associates, *Revenue Sharing*, p. 31.

During the third round, 52 percent of shared funds spent by local governments was in the new spending category.[113] Local governments have used the funds in ways that differ only moderately from their typical spending patterns, with an observed tendency to favor programs not already supported by federal and state grants.[114] In general, public safety, transportation, and recreation programs have enjoyed greater than usual support from shared revenue, and education less. State governments have allocated funds in more unusual ways, supporting education much more strongly, and welfare, health, and transportation less strongly, than typical spending patterns would have suggested.[115]

PROCESS AND STRUCTURAL EFFECTS. In the minds of many supporters, the major objective of revenue sharing in 1972 was to shift political power to underrepresented governments and groups of people and thereby to make some basic structural improvements in the U.S. federal system. This ambitious political plan envisioned a shift of program responsibilities from the federal to state and local governments, a transfer of operational power from bureaucratic specialists to elected generalists, a broadening of public participation in state and local government decisionmaking processes, elimination of discrimination against minorities and women in the operation of state and local government programs, and a general strengthening of the local government sector. Such strengthening might involve consolidations of inefficient and unresponsive governmental units, decentralization of local government operation where needed to satisfy diverse tastes for public services, or increased intergovernmental cooperation

113. Adams and Crippen, *The Fiscal Impact*, p. 11.
114. Wright, *Understanding Intergovernmental Relations*, p. 91.
115. Ibid., p. 118. Reports submitted regularly to the Treasury Department's Office of Revenue Sharing on planned and actual use of funds provide information that may be misleading. Those on planned use sometimes sacrifice accuracy in the pursuit of timeliness, and those on actual use show only the particular accounts to which recipients have assigned funds. The reports do not, of course, identify the true programmatic effects of revenue sharing. Juster, "Fiscal Impact on Local Governments," pp. 34–35; Patrick D. Larkey, "Process Models and Program Evaluation: The Impact of General Revenue Sharing on Municipal Fiscal Behavior—A Summary," in National Tax Association—Tax Institute of America, *Proceedings of the Sixty-Ninth Annual Conference on Taxation, 1976* (Columbus, Ohio: NTA-TIA, 1977), pp. 167–78; Nathan, Adams, and associates, *Revenue Sharing*, pp. 75–78; NSF, *General Revenue Sharing*, vol. 4: *Synthesis of Impact and Process Research*, pp. 57–58.

in urban areas to improve the provision of services with areawide benefits. Some of these goals, at least, retained their attraction, for when the revenue sharing program was extended in 1976, there was no change in its allocation formulas but its civil rights and public participation provisions were tightened. At the same time programmatic strings were loosened; the categories enumerating expenditure priorities were eliminated as was the prohibition against using shared funds to match other federal grants.[116]

Of course, revenue sharing was not expected to accomplish all of the hoped-for goals on its own. It was one of several important instruments available for use, and it has to be judged accordingly. Even these scaled-down expectations, however, appear to have been over-ambitious. In general it has had little or no impact on either political processes or governmental structure. Few significant changes have been effected for the gratification of reformers, but at the same time few of the fears of those concerned about undesirable structural incentives have been realized either.

This is not to say that the program has had no important effects on government process. In one-fifth of the Brookings sample of local governments, for example, significant shifts in political power benefiting either particular government officials or certain interest groups were observed and attributed to the program. Generalist officials were also found to have strengthened and broadened their political influence.[117] Other studies have credited revenue sharing with some degree of increased public participation in budgetary choices, especially in the largest cities, although over time these effects appear to have diminished as shared revenue has become a less distinguishable element in the budgetary process.[118] As for the adverse structural effects that many anticipated, Brookings monitors reported little impact on the use of special districts, no appreciable increase in annexation activity, no significant decline in intergovernmental cooperation in urban areas, and no major increases in the scope of the activities carried out by small governments.[119] Nor has the structure of state-

116. Nathan, Adams, and associates, *Revenue Sharing,* chap. 1.
117. Ibid., p. 131.
118. Edie Goldenberg, "Citizen Participation in General Revenue Sharing," in Juster, *Economic and Political Impact,* pp. 165–82; NSF, *Synthesis of Impact,* chap. 3.
119. Nathan, Adams, and associates, *Revenue Sharing,* chap. 5.

local relations been much shaken up, though revenue sharing has apparently stimulated state aid to local governments.[120] Of course, these findings might change if revenue sharing were made a permanent part of the U.S. fiscal system.

ANTIRECESSION FISCAL ASSISTANCE. In 1976, Congress enacted antirecession fiscal assistance (ARFA) in an effort to reverse the responses to recession by state and local governments that were undermining federal attempts to stimulate the economy.[121] To revenue sharing jurisdictions whose unemployment rates exceeded 4.5 percent, it allocated funds in proportion to the product of the excess rate and their latest revenue sharing allocation—but only as long as the national unemployment rate stayed at 6 percent or higher. As with revenue sharing one-third of the antirecession funds was allocated to states and two-thirds to local governments, but the funds were to be spent to maintain basic public services and not for the creation of new ones or for new construction.[122]

The principle of federal antirecession assistance for state and local governments has long had a strong, broadly based appeal. Working out the specific details that such a program should possess, however, is no easy task. The 1976 act, in the eyes of its critics, represented a serious mismatch of public policy goals and instruments. For the two national goals conceivably served by the program, they argue, its instruments were suboptimal, and the one goal that the program did appear to further was clearly not the one it was set up to serve.[123]

The two national goals that the 1976 act presumably sought to

120. Ibid., p. 156; Thomas J. Anton, "General Revenue Sharing and State-Local Governmental Structure," in Juster, *Economic and Political Impact,* pp. 131–42.

121. Public Law 94–369, title II of the Public Works Employment Act of 1976; amended by title VI of P.L. 95-30, the Intergovernmental Antirecession Assistance Act of 1977 (91 Stat. 164). Specifically mentioned in P.L. 94-369 were state and local tax increases that offset federal tax reductions, and construction cutbacks and employee layoffs that offset federal public works and public service employment stimulants. Ironically, in spite of this, studies of state and local government behavior during postwar recessions consistently show it to be countercyclical rather than procyclical. ACIR, *Countercyclical Aid and Economic Stabilization,* Report A-69 (GPO, 1978), and *State-Local Finances in Recession and Inflation: An Economic Analysis,* Report A-70 (GPO, 1979).

122. U.S. Treasury Department, Office of Revenue Sharing, *What Is ARFA?* (Treasury Department, 1978).

123. Margaret Jess and Dennis Zimmerman, "Targeting Anti-Recessionary Assistance to States: An Evaluation of Public Law 94–369, Title II," in NTA-TIA, *Proceedings, 1977,* pp. 69–78.

serve were stabilization of the economy and minimization of any budgetary disruptions forced on state and local governments by national recessions. As a stabilization device, this antirecession program has had mixed reviews. Some critics regard the expansionary effects of its grants on aggregate demand as significantly more uncertain than those of higher federal direct expenditures or lower federal taxes;[124] others give relatively high ratings to their employment-generating powers.[125] The importance of these ambiguous findings depends on what is expected of the program. They need not be discouraging if aggregate demand management is only a secondary purpose of the grants, and if any net contribution to that goal is to be welcomed.

If stabilization is of secondary importance, the program's main contribution is to economic efficiency by preventing undue cutbacks in basic public services during a recession. Since state and local governments operate under balanced budget constraints, such cutbacks can occur either because other expenditure obligations, such as aid to families with dependent children, automatically increase during recessions or because tax revenues automatically decline. Using these two nondiscretionary changes in expenditures and receipts as a measure of budgetary disruption during recessions, Jess and Zimmerman have shown that the targeting mechanism of the antirecessionary fiscal assistance program did not perform well.[126]

The indicated solution would be to replace the excess unemployment rate allocation factor used in the 1976 program with some measure of state and local budgetary disruption. Several difficult design problems would then have to be faced. Since the goal is not the prevention of all program cutbacks but only those severe enough to create disruptive economic inefficiencies, federal funds would presumably reimburse state and local governments for only some part of their total built-in, recession-induced fiscal pressures. That proportion would have to be specified and an index of budgetary disruption devised for all eligible jurisdictions. The index would have to take account of the possibility that inflation and recession might occur simultaneously and incorporate the effects of both. In 1973–76, for

124. Ibid., p. 69.

125. U.S. Congressional Budget Office, *Temporary Measures to Stimulate Employment: An Evaluation of Some Alternatives* (CBO, 1975), and *Short-Run Measures to Stimulate the Economy* (GPO, 1977).

126. "Targeting Anti-Recessionary Assistance," pp. 71–76.

example, state and local governments had an estimated annual average net revenue gain from inflation of $5.8 billion which partially offset their loss from recession of $8.7 billion.[127] It is quite possible during recessionary periods that some state and local budgets might experience no disruption at all while others were being placed under considerable financial stress.[128]

There would be a risk in any redesigned antirecession assistance program of creating certain undesirable fiscal incentives. State and local governments have behaved countercyclically in recent years in part by drawing down accumulated surpluses during recessions. The promise of federal stabilization aid might induce beneficiaries to accumulate smaller surpluses during good times, shifting their responsibility for dealing with potential budgetary disruptions to the federal government.[129] Similarly, expectations of reimbursement for the effects of inflation on budgets might induce beneficiaries to be less resistant to the wage demands of employees, thereby making it harder for the federal government to control inflation.

State and local governments might also react to allocations based on budgetary disruption by increasing their use of tax sources with high built-in flexibilities. This would presumably mean some shift from retail sales to individual income taxes at the state level and possibly a shift from property taxes at the local level.[130] How desirable such changes would be is a matter of considerable controversy.

The goal that the antirecessionary assistance program apparently

127. ACIR, *Countercyclical Aid and Economic Stabilization*, pp. 12–13.

128. See, for example, Bernard Jump, Jr., and David Greytak, *The Effects of Inflation on State and Local Government Finances, 1967–1974*, Metropolitan Studies Program (Maxwell School, Syracuse University, 1975); David Greytak and Bernard Jump, *The Impact of Inflation on the Expenditures and Revenues of Six Local Governments, 1971–79*, Metropolitan Studies Program (Maxwell School, Syracuse University, 1975); Roy Bahl and others, *The Impact of Economic Base Erosion, Inflation, and Employee Compensation Costs on Local Governments*, Metropolitan Studies Program (Maxwell School, Syracuse University, 1975).

129. Jess and Zimmerman have suggested handling this problem by adding a budgetary surplus factor to the assistance allocation formula and increasing antirecession aid by some fraction of past measured surpluses. "Targeting Anti-Recessionary Assistance," p. 76.

130. Estimates of the income or growth elasticity of state and local taxes consistently place the individual income levy above the general sales tax. Property tax elasticity measures are more variable because they depend on the accuracy and frequency of assessment and reassessment. For a summary of elasticity estimates see ACIR, *Significant Features of Fiscal Federalism, 1976–77 Edition*, vol. 2: *Revenue and Debt*, Report M-110 (GPO, 1977), p. 254.

did further—though that is clearly not what it was set up for—was direction of federal aid to jurisdictions suffering the ill effects of secular decline. Such areas while going through the long, slow adjustment process, typically experience relatively high unemployment rates.[131] If federal assistance is an appropriate means of dealing with service disruptions that are either cyclical or secular, programs specifically aimed at one goal or the other would be better instruments. Antirecession fiscal assistance should be redesigned to deal more effectively with short-run inefficiencies and a new program established to cope with secular decline. Antirecession assistance could at the very least be greatly improved by the use of better allocation factors than local area unemployment rates.[132]

A special problem common to all programs of federal antirecession aid is the maze of difficulties likely to be encountered when a recession is over and the time for withdrawing or phasing out assistance has arrived. The more abundant the aid supplied during periods of high national unemployment, the more will recipients come to count on its continuation. Antirecession assistance was enacted as part of a package that included local public works grants, authorized by title I of the Public Works Employment Act of 1976, and public service employment grants, authorized by titles II and VI of the Comprehensive Employment and Training Act (CETA) of 1973.[133]

131. U.S. General Accounting Office, Comptroller General of the United States, *Antirecession Assistance—An Evaluation, Report to the Congress* (GAO, 1977), pp. 103–23.

132. Many experts believe that these unemployment rates are little better than pure guesses, and that their use to allocate federal grant monies creates gross inequities in the programs involved. The U.S. National Commission on Employment and Unemployment Statistics recommended in 1979 that the monthly unemployment sample survey be expanded, at an annual cost of $34 million, so as to improve the accuracy of measured state and local area unemployment rates. *Counting the Labor Force* (GPO, 1979). See also ACIR, *Countercyclical Aid and Economic Stabilization*, pp. 47–48.

133. Analyses of the stimulus package include ACIR, *Countercyclical Aid and Economic Stabilization*, pp. 15–28; Edward M. Gramlich, "Stimulating the Macro Economy Through State and Local Governments," *American Economic Review*, vol. 69 (May 1979, *Papers and Proceedings, 1978*), pp. 180–85; Robert D. Reischauer, "Federal Countercyclical Policy—the State and Local Role," in NTA-TIA, *Proceedings, 1978*, pp. 53–64; U.S. Treasury Department, Office of State and Local Finance, "Report on the Fiscal Impact of the Economic Stimulus Package on 48 Large Urban Governments" (January 23, 1978). A more general analysis of grants as countercyclical instruments is Congressional Budget Office, *Countercyclical Uses of Federal Grant Programs*, Background Paper (GPO, 1978).

Budget outlays on the three programs rose from $4.6 billion in fiscal 1977 to $9.2 billion in 1978, but then declined as economic conditions improved. Sensitivity to short-term fluctuations in both directions will continue to be a highly desirable, but perhaps elusive, feature of countercyclical revenue sharing programs.

Block Grants

Block grants constitute a third major component of the federal grant system, intermediate in scope between categorical grants and general revenue sharing and more ambiguous in design and unstable in structure than either. Though the unique advantage of block grants has been stressed by experts for a long time, their political appeal in the United States has been small until quite recently.[134] In part this change resulted from growing disenchantment with the rapid proliferation of categorical grants and in part from a strengthening trend toward decentralization within the federal system as a whole.

The first steps toward the creation of a tripartite federal grant system were taken with the consolidation of nine categorical grants into the partnership for health program in 1966 and the establishment of a grant program in the area of crime prevention and administration of justice on a broad functional, rather than a categorical, basis in 1968.[135] Consolidation of existing categorical programs is clearly more difficult than formation of new block grants because of the need to satisfy a variety of firmly established special interest groups. Not much room is left for the easier approach, however, as few functional areas are without existing programs.

134. For a discussion of earlier attempts to create federal block grants, partly in response to the recommendations of the first Hoover Commission (1949), see Selma J. Mushkin, "Barriers to a System of Federal Grants-in-Aid," *National Tax Journal*, vol. 13 (September 1960), pp. 193–218; Selma J. Mushkin and John F. Cotton, *Functional Federalism: Grants-in-Aid and PPB Systems* (George Washington University, State-Local Finances Project, 1968), pp. 112–33.

135. The health grants were established by P.L. 89-749, the Comprehensive Health Planning and Public Health Services Amendments of 1966, and the crime control grants were created by title I of P.L. 90-351, the Omnibus Crime Control and Safe Streets Act of 1968. See ACIR, *The Partnership for Health Act: Lessons From a Pioneering Block Grant: The Intergovernmental Grant System: An Assessment and Proposed Policies,* Report A-56 (GPO, 1977), and *Safe Streets Reconsidered: The Block Grant Experience 1968–1975: The Intergovernmental Grant System: An Assessment and Proposed Policies,* Report A-55 (GPO, 1977).

A major stimulus to consolidation came in early 1971 when President Nixon proposed, under the title of special revenue sharing, the grouping of one hundred and twenty-nine categorical grant programs into six block grants in the broad functional areas of education, law enforcement, manpower training, rural community development, transportation, and urban community development.[136] His objectives were to reduce grant administration and compliance costs, to increase state and local governmental freedom of choice in the use of federal aid funds, to strengthen state and local fiscal positions by removing matching and maintenance-of-effort requirements, and to shift political power from functional specialists to political generalists in elected positions. Accomplishing these goals required a complex mixture of improvements in technical efficiency and fundamental structural changes. To consolidate a number of closely related categorical grants into a closely controlled aid program is one thing; it requires a set of well-articulated national goals best pursued by fiscal partnerships in which the federal government is the dominant member. To merge an equal number of categoricals into a formula-allocated, broad-scope grant allowing recipients great freedom in spending the proceeds is quite another matter; this presumes not only a set of broad, nonspecific national objectives that are best implemented, in a diverse society, by decentralized fiscal operations but also a state and local public sector that is at least capable of operating in an efficient and responsive fashion. Such exigent requirements have long been the very essence of fiscal federalism, and there was nothing particularly new about them in the early 1970s.[137] The Nixon proposals for special revenue sharing, however, probably did set the development of federal grants on a new course. The first result was the creation of four important block grant programs. They made the federal grant system, for the time being at least, a truly tripartite one.

In 1973 seventeen categorical grants were consolidated into the comprehensive employment and training program (CETA), and in 1974 six urban aid programs were combined under the community

136. ACIR, *Special Revenue Sharing*.
137. Two interesting discussions of these trade-offs, one in a general context and the other with reference to a specific program, are Robert D. Reischauer, "Special Revenue Sharing," in Charles L. Schultze and others, *Setting National Priorities: The 1972 Budget* (Brookings Institution, 1971), pp. 158–71; and Nonna A. Noto, "Simplifying Intergovernmental Transfers: The Lessons of Community Development Block Grants," *National Tax Journal*, vol. 30 (September 1977), pp. 259–67.

development block grant program (CDBG).[138] Later that same year
social services grants, after a checkered and difficult period of early
development, were made into a block grant program by title XX of
the Social Security Act.[139] Another group of grants to fund a wide
variety of state and local capital projects was authorized by the Public
Works Employment Act of 1976; they have no matching requirements, but state and local governments must apply and compete for
these grants, which are administered by the Economic Development
Administration. Because of the different administrative requirements
the ACIR (unlike the Office of Management and Budget) does not
include public works grants in its block grant grouping,[140] although
they have the block grant characteristic of allocating funds by formula—in this case one using unemployment rates.

These components of the federal block grant system are a mixed
lot. As Carl Stenberg has reported, the results of the ACIR staff
studies of them indicated that they "are not as well defined structurally or as stable politically as other instruments. They are neither
widely understood nor widely accepted. They have emerged through
historical accident and the politics of compromise, as well as by
deliberate design. And they often rest upon unstated premises, un-
clear intentions, and untested assumptions."[141] Nevertheless, the Advisory Commission concluded in 1978 "that the block grant is a
necessary component of federal intergovernmental assistance."[142] It
also identified seven program qualities that would make block grants

138. ACIR, *The Comprehensive Employment and Training Act: Early Readings
From a Hybrid Block Grant: The Intergovernmental Grant System: An Assessment
and Proposed Policies,* Report A-58 (GPO, 1977), and *Community Development:
The Workings of a Federal-Local Block Grant: The Intergovernmental Grant System: An Assessment and Proposed Policies,* Report A-57 (GPO, 1977).

139. Social Services Amendments of 1974 (P.L. 93-647). On the early development vicissitudes of social services grants see Martha Derthick, *Uncontrollable
Spending for Social Services Grants* (Brookings Institution, 1975).

140. The ACIR definition of a block grant is "a program in which funds are
provided chiefly to general purpose governmental units in accordance with a statutory formula for use in a broad functional area largely at the recipient's discretion."
See Carl W. Stenberg, "Block Grants: The Middlemen of the Federal Aid System,"
Intergovernmental Perspective, vol. 3 (Spring 1977), p. 9. As shown in table 4-1,
the OMB includes school aid in federally affected areas in its category of broad-
based aid.

141. Ibid., p. 8.

142. ACIR, *Summary and Concluding Observations: The Intergovernmental
Grant System: An Assessment and Proposed Policies,* Report A-62 (ACIR, 1978),
p. 24.

a preferred fiscal instrument and suggested guidelines for developing new legislation concerning their design and use.[143] How much appeal these recommendations will have is an open question. The issues are complex and the conflicting pressures great. The effects of block grants are as mixed as their components, sometimes similar to those of general revenue sharing, sometimes more like those of the categorical grant group, and sometimes, as one would expect, intermediate between the two.[144]

Process and Structural Effects

A basic goal of both general revenue sharing and block grants is the devolution of fiscal and political power to state and local governments, a process that many people in the federal government, not surprisingly, have supported reluctantly and haltingly. Block grant programs have not been as free of strings, earmarking, and discretionary federal powers as purists would have liked, and they have often been surrounded by categorical grants that logically might have been consolidated with them. Nevertheless, the five programs established between 1966 and 1974 have structural features that have contributed significantly to the devolution process, and the antirecession programs of 1976 and 1977 added a good deal more.[145]

The extent of the shift of spending authority from the federal to state and local governments cannot be judged solely from the legislative and administrative characteristics of different grant programs. One additional factor is the fungibility of grant funds that permits recipients to spend earmarked funds in any way they please. If block grants are really fully fungible, they should be looked at simply as adjuncts to general revenue sharing distributed by different formulas. Though messy in structure, such a combination of programs may well have more political appeal than a single unrestricted grant program using a fixed distribution formula.

Working in the opposite direction to fungibility is another factor that the ACIR calls "intrusiveness," embodied in "some 31 separate requirements, enacted by the Congress to carry out national policy objectives, which apply more or less across the board to all grant

143. Ibid., pp. 24–25.
144. Attention here is centered on the characteristics of the block grant instrument rather than the specific benefits and costs of each program.
145. Ibid., pp. 36–39.

programs."[146] These impose significant cost burdens on federal grant-ees. Although of relatively recent origin, they have proliferated rapidly and raised serious doubts in the minds of many state and local officials not only about the size of the real contribution of federal aid to their budgets but even about the desirability of accepting it at all.

It is not easy to judge the net impact of these conflicting pressures, to say nothing of foreseeing their future development. The crosscurrents are many, making progress toward devolution difficult and even doubtful.

A second major goal of revenue sharing is to improve the structure of local government and the fiscal relations between state and local governments. In part the aim is to favor general rather than special-purpose governments as recipients and elected officials and administrative generalists, rather than functional specialists, as participants. The eligibility provisions of the block grant programs are structured to encourage generalists, but the tendency to center control there has characterized some programs more than others.[147] Other effects of the programs are similarly mixed. Several programs do tend to strengthen general-purpose local governments and urban counties, but regional planning agencies are strengthened in some ways and weakened in others. Both the CETA and CDBG programs focus directly on local governments and expand their financial capabilities, but the Safe Streets Act assigns a dominant role in the crime prevention program to state governments.[148]

Economic Effects

Since block grants come in a wide variety of sizes—being anything broader than categorical grants but narrower than general revenue sharing—their economic effects are bound to be highly diverse. Detailed estimates of the effects of the community development block grant program are being made at the Brookings Institution in conjunction with the monitoring service set up to study general revenue sharing. The research sample selected in early 1975 includes thirty central cities, twelve "satellite" metropolitan cities with populations over fifty thousand, ten urban counties, and ten nonmetropolitan

146. Ibid., p. 39.
147. Ibid., pp. 44–48.
148. Ibid., pp. 51–61.

Table 4-5. Use of First-Year Allocations of Funds under Community Development
and General Revenue Sharing Programs

	Percent of first-year allocation	
Use of grant funds	Community development block grants	General revenue sharing grants to local governments
New spending	53.0	56.0
Program maintenance	32.0	13.0
Substitutions	7.0	30.0
Tax stabilization or reduction	0.5	18.0
Other or unallocated	8.0	1.0

Sources: Richard P. Nathan and others, "Monitoring the Block Grant Program for Community Development," *Political Science Quarterly*, vol. 92 (October 1977), pp. 225–26; Richard P. Nathan, Charles F. Adams, Jr., and associates, *Revenue Sharing: The Second Round* (Brookings Institution, 1977), p. 31. Figures are unweighted means for all sample jurisdictions.

jurisdictions.[149] During the first year of the program these governments put 85 percent of their CDBG funds into new spending and program maintenance. The contrast with the first year's use of general revenue sharing funds is particularly notable in their relative effects on the level of local taxes (table 4-5).

A special feature of the CDBG program is its stated intention to use federal funds as a lever to attract large amounts of private and other public capital to urban development projects. During the first year that feature of the program was apparently rather ineffective.[150] However, an action grant program of $400 million a year authorized in 1977 to promote private construction projects in distressed areas began to draw private investment.[151]

A special CDBG feature is the explicit, though vague, directive in the 1974 act that the program should give "maximum feasible priority to activities which will benefit low- or moderate-income families

149. Richard P. Nathan and others, "Monitoring the Block Grant Program for Community Development," *Political Science Quarterly*, vol. 92 (Summer 1977), p. 220 (Brookings Reprint 326).

150. Richard P. Nathan and others, *Block Grants For Community Development*, Report Prepared for the U.S. Department of Housing and Urban Development (GPO, 1977), chap. 9.

151. The first $150 million, allocated in April 1978 to forty-five cities, attracted nearly $1 billion of private capital. *Business Week*, May 1, 1978, p. 36.

or aid in the prevention or elimination of slums or blight."[152] It was
estimated that during the program's first year, 52 percent of CDBG
funds in fifty of the Brookings sample jurisdictions was spent for the
benefit of low- and moderate-income families.[153] Official estimates
put this share at 64 percent of total allocations in fiscal 1975 but
showed it falling to 57 percent in 1976. The response of the Department of Housing and Urban Development was to draft regulations in
late 1977 requiring that 75 percent of the CDBG money received by
any locality be used to provide direct benefits of this kind. The in-
flexibility of this rule, in the light of the diversity of potential CDBG
beneficiaries, stirred up so much criticism that when the regulations
were issued in the spring of 1978, provisions were added allowing for
the acceptance, and evaluation on their specific merits, of applications falling short of the 75 percent target.

Here again is the familiar dilemma of second-best policymaking.
The best way to benefit low-income groups is not by intergovernmental grants but by direct transfer payments or subsidies. Intergovernmental grants are well suited to the financing of urban public
goods and collective services, but these, by their very nature, confer
their benefits on all people in a given geographical area. There is no
precise way of measuring the rate at which the benefits of public
goods accrue to poor people, and even when it can be estimated
reasonably well, a policy aimed at a target as high as 75 percent risks
eliminating many projects that offer valuable collective services. As
a result the poor may receive direct public benefits that are inferior
both to the private goods and services they would have bought with
government transfers and to the collective services that could have
been financed by unrestricted grants.

Another dilemma that federal grant programs often face is the
resolution of multiple, conflicting objectives. The Brookings monitoring study of the public service employment component of the
CETA program, for example, dealt separately with three major goals
—the creation of jobs in an underemployed economy, the provision
of useful local public services, and the targeting of assistance to economically disadvantaged and structurally unemployed individuals.
In spite of the obvious conflicts among these objectives, the "striking
conclusion" for the analysts was "the degree to which the balancing

152. 88 Stat. 639.
153. Nathan and others, "Monitoring the Block Grant Program," p. 227.

of the goals of governmental jurisdictions at all levels has produced a workable bargain that has allowed the program to function."[154] The balance achieved may not be the best possible, but some progress toward each goal clearly indicates the presence of valuable benefits to be compared with the program's costs.

Distributional Effects

The allocation of funds to state and local governments, always a controversial aspect of intergovernmental grant design, has two distinctive features in the case of block grants. One tries to enforce compliance with the federal government's intention in awarding the grant, either by adopting the categorical feature of earmarking some of the funds for particular purposes or by designating some of the funds for the discretionary use of federal administrators. Either arrangement restricts the spending powers of grant recipients unless the funds in question can somehow be converted into fungible resources.[155]

The design of the allocation formulas is another special feature of block grants. Here two different, potentially conflicting, approaches are used. The first simply ties the formula to the particular purposes of the program, relating manpower service grants to unemployment rates, for example, or community development grants to clear evidence of overcrowded or substandard housing. The seemingly simple logic of this approach breaks down if the funds are highly fungible. In that case the programs are simply another form of general revenue sharing, and the allocation formula ought to be tailored to complement the formulas used for unrestricted grants. By its very nature this second approach to block grant formula design is not one that is likely to be used openly and explicitly. It does, however, provide a valid and important perspective on the usefulness of alternative proposals for allocation formulas. Some logical connection with specific

154. Richard P. Nathan and others, *Monitoring the Public Service Employment Program: The Second Round*, Special Report of the National Commission for Manpower Policy, no. 32 (GPO, 1979), p. 105.

155. Significant discretionary funds are available to federal administrators under the crime control and safe streets, CDBG, and CETA programs, and some of the funds provided under the partnership for health and CETA programs are earmarked. Congress has also sometimes tried to increase its control by putting funds into related categorical grant programs instead of increasing block grants. See the ACIR studies of the individual block grant programs cited in notes 135, 138.

program goals may well be essential, though not all related factors would be equally effective in complementing revenue sharing allocation rules.

Looked at in this light, the allocation formulas for block grants might profit from study and redesign. The most frequently used allocation factor is population. The partnership for health, crime control and safe streets, and social services grant programs use it exclusively, and community development grants include it along with other measures of urban need. A population factor has the virtues of simplicity and availability, and it also serves as a redistributive allocator, especially if the grants can realistically be said to be financed by federal income taxes. When revenue sharing and block grants are viewed together as a single unrestricted program, it is clear that population is a very important allocation factor. Whether its role should be increased or decreased is a question for future researchers to tackle, particularly since it has heretofore not been asked in so broad a context.

Block grants under title I of the Comprehensive Employment and Training Act are allocated partly on the basis of unemployment rates and partly on the basis of the incidence of low-income families.[156] Both of these factors are clearly related to the program's broad goals, and they add two new dimensions to the fiscal need criterion for allocating general revenue sharing funds. How well the two factors would serve a more precisely targeted CETA program, however, is open to question. Much of the debate over federal policies regarding the labor market has concerned the different means required to deal with structural unemployment on the one hand and cyclical unemployment on the other. A loosely designed, compromise program, it seems clear, is likely to deal badly with both problems.[157] When funds for

156. Eighty-five percent of the funds in the basic CETA training programs (title II) are allocated by a three-factor formula, 50 percent of the weight being given to previous funding levels of each recipient, 37.5 percent to the relative number of unemployed persons, and 12.5 percent to the relative number of low-income adults. ACIR has recommended elimination of past funding level as a factor. *Comprehensive Employment and Training Act*, pp. 17, 67.

157. John L. Palmer, "Employment and Income Security," in Joseph A. Pechman, ed., *Setting National Priorities: The 1979 Budget* (Brookings Institution, 1978), pp. 74–87; John L. Palmer, ed., *Creating Jobs: Public Employment Programs and Wage Subsidies* (Brookings Institution, 1978); Michael Wiseman, "Public Employment as Fiscal Policy," *Brookings Papers on Economic Activity, 1:1976,* pp. 67–104, and "Comments and Discussion," ibid., pp. 105–14.

the various CETA programs were either cut back or stabilized in 1978 and 1979, greater emphasis was given to targeting the aid on persons with low incomes and long-term unemployment records and to ways of increasing the private sector's contribution to the total effort.[158]

The allocation process for block grants that has received the greatest attention is that used in the community development program. Apart from the complications created by a "hold harmless" provision and a certain amount of administrative discretion, fund allocations for the program were initially based in a straightforward fashion on a three-factor formula. Population and the number of overcrowded housing units each had a weight of 25 percent, and the number of persons with incomes below a designated poverty level a weight of 50 percent. Two of these factors have considerable appeal—population because of its obvious political advantages, and the poverty index because it is probably a reasonable proxy for both physical and fiscal need. Overcrowded housing is a questionable factor, however, because it is closely correlated with the poverty index but not with the general state of a community's physical environment.[159] Among suggested alternatives to this factor are census measures of the housing stock built before 1939,[160] an index of the number of households that are inadequately housed,[161] a measure of housing abandonments, and the rate of population decline.[162] The Brookings monitoring study, after simulating the distributional effects of eight different formulas, recommended an approach similar to the state allocation process for general revenue sharing: each eligible community could use whichever of two formulas was more favorable to it, one being the original CDBG formula, and the other a formula containing population,

158. In 1977, employers were offered a two-year employment tax credit for hiring additional unskilled and part-time workers; in 1978 a $400 million "private-sector jobs initiative" program was begun. See Jeffrey M. Perloff and Michael L. Wachter, "The New Jobs Tax Credit: An Evaluation of the 1977–78 Wage Subsidy Program," *American Economic Review*, vol. 69 (May 1979, *Papers and Proceedings, 1978*), pp. 173–79.

159. Nathan and others, "Monitoring the Block Grant Program," pp. 239–40.

160. Ibid., p. 240.

161. Richard DeLeon and Richard LeGates, *Redistribution Effects of Special Revenue Sharing for Community Development*, Institute of Governmental Studies, Working Paper 17 (University of California—Berkeley, 1976).

162. ACIR, *Community Development*, p. 89; Comptroller General, *Report to the Congress*, pp. 103–23.

poverty, and a double-weighted pre-1939 housing factor.[163] The Housing and Community Development Act of 1977, which extended the CDBG program for three years, did add an alternative formula and adopted the dual approach.[164]

All of this pulling and hauling over the allocation formula is mainly a reflection of the difficulties inherent in providing federal grants directly to a highly diversified group of local governments. Satisfactory and stable solutions are necessarily hard to come by. Worse still, it may all be much ado about nothing. If the community development funds are really highly fungible, formula reform is not a matter of finding better measures of physical degradation but rather of giving greater weight to general measures of community need.[165] For those who favor decentralization this strategy would have the advantage of eliminating any need for the federal government to determine the optimal means of dealing with declining cities. One approach, exemplified by a tightly targeted community development block grant, is to "put the money where the distress is." Another, a "put the people where the distress isn't" strategy, would require a completely redesigned urban development grant, probably of a categorical nature. Alternatively, cities could be given the financial freedom to seek their own solutions by an expanded set of loosely targeted community development block grants.

Conclusion

Whatever its programmatic merits and future promise, block grants have added a new dimension to the federal grant system. More funding for the established programs and creation of new block grants of the same type may further increase the financial flexibility of state and local governments even if general revenue sharing remains a relatively static component of the system. If this should happen, as Reischauer has noted, congressional appropriation decisions would become "less important in determining *what* the funds were ultimately

163. Nathan and others, *Block Grants,* pp. 191–222. The study also recommended that regional differences in program costs be taken into account; pp. 226–37.

164. The alternative formula uses measures of population growth lag with a weight of 20 percent, poverty with a weight of 30 percent, and age of housing with a weight of 50 percent.

165. Unless in the best second-best tradition the specific need factors in the CDBG program are seen as offsetting the effects of unduly specific allocation factors in other fungible block grant programs.

spent for, but critical in determining *who* got them."[166] On the other hand, block grant programs may be badly outflanked by new categoricals in related areas and eroded internally by earmarking, discretionary fund set-asides, priority guidelines, and administrative pressure. If so, congressional attention would again focus on what is done with federal money, and program supporters and lobbyists would tend to return to the nation's capital from their current "discover America" forays into the various states and large cities.

State Grants-in-Aid

State governments are deeply involved in the intergovernmental grant business, partly as recipients of federal funds, partly as intermediaries for the transfer of federal funds to local governments, and partly as dispensers of grants to local governments. In this last capacity, states distributed $62 billion is fiscal 1977, a sum that was only slightly smaller than the nonrecession-related federal grants made in that year.[167] Like federal grants, state aid has been a strong growth component of the U.S. fiscal system, rising from only 6 percent of local government revenue at the beginning of the century to 25 percent in the early 1940s and to 30 percent in 1950 (table 4-6). Between 1950 and the mid-1960s there was little relative growth, then a spurt to just over 35 percent of local revenue in 1970, and then stability again.

The structure of state grants has also been remarkably stable since the mid-1950s. This is true in the functional areas served, the types of local government financed, and the particular grant instruments used. In both 1957 and 1977, for example, about the same percentages of state grants to local governments went for general support, schools, and public welfare. The only important functional change between those two years occurred in highway support, which fell from 15 percent of total state grants in 1957 to 6 percent in 1977 (table 4-6). Total state intergovernmental expenditures rose from 29 percent of local revenues in 1957 to 34 percent in 1977, with counties, municipalities, and school districts all participating in that relative growth.

166. Reischauer, "Special Revenue Sharing," p. 171.
167. In fiscal 1977 total federal grants were $68.4 billion; $4.6 billion of the total was for economic stimulus. *Special Analyses, Budget of the United States Government, Fiscal Year 1980,* p. 214.

Table 4-6. Role of State Grants-in-Aid in Local Finance, Selected Fiscal
Years, 1902–77

Fiscal year	Total grants (billions of dollars)	Percent of total local revenue	Percent of aid used to finance			
			Education	Public welfare	Highways	General government
1902	0.1	6.1	86	...	4	10
1922	0.3	8.1	65	1	22	11
1927	0.6	10.1	49	1	33	16
1932	0.8	14.1	50	4	29	18
1942	1.8	25.0	44	22	19	13
1950	4.2	30.1	49	19	14	11
1952	5.0	29.8	50	19	14	11
1957	7.4	29.1	57	15	15	9
1962	10.9	28.4	59	16	12	8
1967	19.1	32.7	62	15	10	8
1970	28.9	35.7	59	17	8	10
1972	36.8	33.4	58	19	7	10
1977	61.1	34.1	60	14	6	10

Sources: U.S. Advisory Commission on Intergovernmental Relations, *The States and Intergovernmental Aids: The Intergovernmental Grant System: An Assessment and Proposed Policies*, Report A-59 (GPO, 1977), pp. 9–10, and *Significant Features of Fiscal Federalism, 1978–79 Edition*, Report M-115 (GPO, 1979), p. 81; U.S. Census Bureau, *Governmental Finances in 1976–77*, series GF, no. 5 (GPO, 1978), p. 19.

Grant Instruments

There are sharp contrasts between the different instruments used to dispense state aid and those used for federal grants. One important reason for these differences, quite apart from the diversity of state grant systems,[168] is the strong state commitment to the support of education. Making up more than half of the total, state school grants have their own special features and for many purposes should be analyzed separately.[169] Another important reason for the dissimilarities between state and federal grants, but one that has received little attention from economists, is the basic difference in the political rela-

168. In 1975, for example, state intergovernmental expenditures were 38 percent of state general expenditures in the nation as a whole, but the range was from lows of 2 percent and 15 percent in Hawaii and South Dakota, respectively, to a high of 55 percent in New York. ACIR, *The States and Intergovernmental Aids: The Intergovernmental Grant System: An Assessment and Proposed Policies*, Report A-59 (GPO, 1977), pp. 2–3.

169. See, for example, Robert P. Inman, "Optimal Fiscal Reform of Metropolitan Schools: Some Simulation Results," *American Economic Review*, vol. 68 (March 1978), pp. 107–22.

tionship between the contracting parties. While federal grants to states are agreements made between equal partners, state grants to local governments flow down the political hierarchy to subordinate administrative units. This would not necessarily have to make a difference in grant design, but it would be surprising if it did not.

Whatever the reasons, the major variations between the two grant systems are clear enough. Federal aid is more functionally diverse, and in recent decades has been more changeable in pattern, than state aid. Project grants are numerous at the federal level, but scarce at the state level where formula-allocated categorical grants are the dominant mode (87 percent of total state aid in 1972). Both systems make substantial use of general revenue sharing, which accounted for 12 percent of the federal aid total in 1978 (table 4-1) and 10 percent of total state aid in 1977 (table 4-6). In 1972, 45 states operated 209 programs providing general support to local governments. Much of this support came from shared taxes allocated by their origin; some was paid to local governments in lieu of taxes on state property; and nearly half was allocated on a straight population basis as redistributive aid.[170] Another distinctive characteristic of state aid, and one that has had a critical impact on the design of federal grants, is a relative disregard for municipal and urban problems. In 1969 the ACIR noted that states had a minimal role in urban development programs but one that did appear to be growing.[171] By 1979 it could report that "the states have become increasingly attentive to local growth and development concerns—particularly over the past two years," but also noted that it was too early to tell how productive this awakened interest might turn out to be.[172] Finally, though very few state grants have formal matching requirements of the kind often used in federal categorical grants, nearly 33 percent of state aid is provided on a cost-reimbursement basis whereby the state undertakes to finance a

170. For further details see ACIR, *The States and Intergovernmental Aids,* pp. 27–30. Colorado, Delaware, Montana, Vermont, and West Virginia had no general assistance program in 1972. Of total state general support grants of $3.8 billion in 1972, $1.2 billion (32 percent) was allocated by population, $0.5 billion (13 percent) by other equalization factors, and $1.0 billion (26 percent) by origin, while $0.8 billion (21 percent) took the form of in lieu payments.

171. ACIR, *State Aid to Local Government,* Report A-34 (GPO, 1969), pp. 97–104.

172. ACIR, *State Community Assistance Initiatives: Innovations of the Late 70s,* Report M-116 (GPO, 1979), p. 1.

stated percentage of local expenditures on specified programs.[173]
These arrangements, like their federal counterparts, may be viewed
either as administrative partnerships set up to carry out public functions both governments desire or as incentive devices adopted in a
decentralized government system to stimulate grantee spending on
programs to which grantors give high priorities.

The States as Grant Intermediaries

In 1972 state governments received $26.8 billion in federal aid and
paid out $35.1 billion in grants to local governments. In addition
local governments received grants of $4.6 billion directly from the
federal government. The total grants by the federal government
amounted to $31.3 billion and the receipts by local governments to
$39.7 billion. These figures fail to clarify the role played by the state
governments. They leave unanswered the question of how much of
the federal aid to states was passed through directly to local governments, and the even more difficult question of what effect the remaining portion had on the amount of aid provided by the states. How
much federal categorical and block grant money, in other words,
though spent nominally on state programs, in fact substituted for and
thus released state funds that were then used to raise the amount of
state aid to local governments?

No one expects any very precise answer to the latter question since
it involves both the fungibility of federal grant funds and the spending
priorities of state governments. The question concerning the amount
passed through to local governments is more manageable. In 1972, as
estimated by the Maxwell School of Citizenship and Public Affairs of
Syracuse University, it was $7.1 billion, most of which was designated
for public welfare ($3.6 billion) and education ($3.0 billion).[174]
With this important flow-through taken into account, the intergovernmental aid picture for 1972 is considerably clarified. Of the $39.7
billion received by local governments, $11.6 billion rather than $4.6
billion came from the federal government. And of the $31.3 billion
paid out by the federal government only $19.7 billion went to the
states. States transferred $28.1 billion of their own funds to local gov-
ernments, but how much of that came from own-source revenues and
how much indirectly from federal grant funds is unknown.

173. ACIR, *States and Intergovernmental Aids,* p. 32.
174. Ibid., pp. 14–21.

State Grant Reform

Because the state grant system is composed of fifty distinctive and independent parts, the problem of a nationwide reform is rarely tackled. The ACIR, however, after an intensive four-year study of the whole U.S. grant system that began in the spring of 1974, made fifty-nine specific recommendations for grant reform, six of them applying to state aid programs.[175] They supplement two earlier commission recommendations, even more important for the future structure and scope of the state grant system, that deal with the financing of schools and welfare. The ACIR position, announced in 1969, is that the federal government should assume full financial responsibility for public welfare broadly defined (including general assistance and medicaid) and that each state should assume "substantially all" responsibility for the financing of local schools.[176] Such functional reassignments would have a major impact on the state grant system. In 1975, 60 percent of state grant funds ($31.1 billion) went to support local education and 16 percent ($8.1 billion) went for public welfare.[177] Early action on either fiscal reassignment is unlikely. However, with the adoption of Proposition 13 in 1978, California has moved much closer to the ACIR's goals. In 1976–77 the state government financed two-thirds of total state and local expenditures on public welfare; by 1979–80 it was financing everything except minor amounts of general welfare relief. Whereas in 1976–77 the state share of state and local revenue for schools was 42 percent, in 1979–80 it was expected to be 75 percent.[178] Sudden changes of these dimensions are not a surprising response to the passage of tax or expenditure limitations of Proposition 13 dimensions. Program complexities and conflicting group interests can be overcome when they have to be. Under less pressing circum-

175. ACIR, *Summary*, pp. 15–32. For an overview of the summary report and thirteen detailed studies of the subject, see *In Brief: The Intergovernmental Grant System: An Assessment and Proposed Policies* (ACIR [1978]).

176. ACIR, *State Aid to Local Government*, pp. 14–16.

177. ACIR, *States and Intergovernmental Aids*, p. 10. States could assume substantially all responsibility for the financing of local schools either by expanding their grant programs or by eliminating them entirely and converting the school system into a regular state department.

178. See ACIR, *Significant Features of Fiscal Federalism, 1978–79 Edition*, Report M-115 (GPO, 1979), pp. 19, 25; David J. Levin, "Proposition 13: One Year Later," *Survey of Current Business*, vol. 59 (November 1979), p. 17.

stances, however, the reform of welfare and school finance is likely to proceed at a more leisurely pace.

Four of the ACIR state aid recommendations bear a close resemblance to the commission's more detailed recommendations for federal grant reform.[179] This is not surprising since the same evaluation criteria—fiscal equity, economic efficiency, administrative effectiveness, and political accountability—were applied. In general, the ACIR opts for a more precise separation of grant goals and instruments, a greater degree of fiscal equalization, more consolidation and simplification, greater certainty, and systematic periodic review and evaluation of programs. The most controversial of these objectives is the reduction of fiscal disparities between jurisdictions. To accomplish this the commission would rely exclusively on general support grants by states to local jurisdictions according to an allocation formula that would give equal weight to population, tax effort, and municipal overburdens.[180]

This redirected and reinvigorated role for state unrestricted grants raises a number of important issues. Clearly, this reform[181] would be less important for highly centralized than for highly decentralized states, and its importance everywhere would diminish with more federal or state assumption of the financing of education and welfare. Though the ACIR report mentions the need for shared taxes and in lieu payments by states, its model system apparently does not call for either of these instruments. Yet shared taxes may be the most efficient way of diversifying local revenue systems. Moreover, if local finance is given a stronger benefits-received basis, as many people have long advocated and an increasing number may favor in an environment of tax and expenditure limitations, state payments in lieu of explicit user charges for city services provided to state government enterprises would be an indispensable part of any equitable and efficient state-local fiscal system.

179. The other two deal with ways of strengthening the role played by state governments in the management of federal grants. ACIR, *The States and Intergovernmental Aids*, pp. 72–83.

180. Tax effort would be measured by the ratio of a jurisdiction's tax revenue to the sum of the personal income of its residents and its property tax base. Municipal burden would be measured by the excess of a jurisdiction's per capita tax revenue over 1.5 times the statewide average per capita local tax burden. See ACIR, *State Legislative Program*, pt. 3: *State and Local Revenues*, Report M-94 (GPO, 1975).

181. See ACIR, *States and Intergovernmental Aids*, pp. 72–75.

The ACIR report does not discuss the issue of whether there is a need for state equalizing grants—a debatable one because of uncertainties over the extent to which land markets can be relied on to adjust for environmental advantages and disadvantages, including low and high tax prices for local public services. Assuming there is such a need, as appears to be widely believed, the commission's allocation formula is still open to question. A basic philosophic objection is that it is founded (implicitly) on an ability-to-pay model of local finance, notwithstanding the fact that a benefits-received model might not only be preferable but would call for a completely different allocation formula for state redistributive grants. More pragmatic objections might accept the commission's basic ability-to-pay orientation but argue for different components or different weights for allocation formulas to be used in state revenue sharing.

The ACIR's state revenue sharing recommendations, then, are likely to receive a mixed reception. For any state wishing to reduce local fiscal disparities there would be one advantage in implementing the commission's recommendations. Its functional grants could then be directed entirely at program support and grant funds allocated according to the relative program needs of different jurisdictions. Fiscal equalization would then be the objective of its general support grants, and program support the objective of its categorical grants.

The remaining ACIR state aid recommendations may appear relatively unobjectionable, but experience indicates that they too will be difficult to implement. A prima facie case for grant consolidation is made by the ACIR's count of 2,121 separate state aid programs in 1972, but conflicting interests will be aroused by any attempt to reduce that number. Sunset laws, benefit-cost program analyses, and zero-based budgeting, which are the essence of the ACIR's third recommendation, all have reform track records, and they are unimpressive indeed. Perhaps the most likely to succeed is the proposal that advocates providing grantees with more funding certainty in the interest of achieving better local government planning and budgeting. Uncertainty about how much money is to be received and when could be reduced by providing multiyear advance budgeting for some of the largest grant programs, especially those dealing with capital projects, and by integrating the state legislature's appropriations cycle more closely with the fiscal years of all local governments receiving significant amounts of state grant money.

Conclusion

Whether such a potentially kaleidoscopic universe as the state grant system can remain relatively quiescent seems a rather high-risk bet. Factors that are bound to disturb the equilibrium are coming into play, and whether the effect will be to rectify or confuse the shape of things depends on one's point of view. As they make themselves fully felt, however, such explosive forces as *Serrano* v. *Priest* and similar court decisions concerning the financing of schools, and Proposition 13 together with its predecessors and progeny cannot fail to produce significant changes in urban fiscal systems. The pattern of intergovernmental grants may never look the same again.

CHAPTER FIVE

Urban Fiscal Systems

WHATEVER it may have lost in urbanity, twentieth century America has certainly gained in urbanization. The decline and fall of the urbane in American society is beyond the scope of this study; the steady increase in urban concentration may have peaked out. In the United States 75 percent of the people live on 2 percent of the land, mainly in 276 standard metropolitan statistical areas (SMSAs).[1] Urbanization, however, is a quality of life that is very unevenly distributed. Whereas in California and New York 93 percent and 86 percent of the population, respectively, live in SMSAs, in Vermont and Wyoming there are no SMSAs at all, though there are, of course, urban areas.[2] Similarly large differences are found in growth rates in

1. U.S. Advisory Commission on Intergovernmental Relations, *Improving Urban America: A Challenge to Federalism,* Information Report M-107 (U.S. Government Printing Office, 1976), p. 1.

2. About 70 percent of the people in the United States live in "urban places," defined by the Census Bureau as communities with at least 2,500 people; about 60 percent live in "urbanized areas," defined to include at least one central city of over 25,000 people and the surrounding closely settled area; and some two-thirds live in SMSAs, defined basically to include any county, however rural some of its areas may be, that includes or is functionally related to a central city of at least 50,000 population. See Richard P. Nathan and Paul R. Dommel, "The Cities," in Joseph A. Pechman, ed., *Setting National Priorities: The 1978 Budget* (Brookings Institution, 1977), p. 284. The number of SMSAs increased from 264 in 1971 to 276 in 1975, partly because of population growth and partly because of changes in definition that to some extent reflect pressure from localities anxious to be designated as "metropolitan." ACIR, *Improving Urban America,* p. 25, n. 1.

metropolitan population—a rise of 86 percent in Nevada between 1960 and 1970, while the nation's metropolitan population was increasing by only 17 percent and West Virginia's was declining by 0.5 percent.[3] Diversity in the degree and rate of urbanization, then, is a quality that both federal and state policymakers need to keep continuously in mind. What may be particularly important for the future are some trends away from metropolitan living. Between 1970 and 1975, for example, nonmetropolitan counties gained 6.9 percent in population while metropolitan counties gained only 4.0 percent.[4] Such shifts of population to sparsely settled areas are something new in the nation's recent experience, and their continuation would pose some interesting policy issues.

Population trends of still other kinds, as Downs has emphasized, are affecting U.S. cities in important ways. The nation's overall population growth rate is slowing down; Americans are migrating from the Northeast and Midwest to the South and West, and moving out of large cities and close-in suburbs to farther out suburbs, though high energy costs may soon reverse this; the number of households has increased rapidly since 1970 while the average size of households has declined; and racial segregation continues in nearly all metropolitan areas.[5] The demographic environment in which city governments operate is clearly changing, sometimes in ways that reduce their problems and sometimes in ways that make them worse. These population trends, combined with the mixture of economic and social factors that attend them, offer a considerable challenge to American federalism.

Urban Social and Economic Problems

The urban areas of the United States are highly diverse entities. Some are densely settled and some are not;[6] some are growing rapidly

3. ACIR, *Improving Urban America*, p. 207.
4. Anthony Downs, "Urban Policy," in Joseph A. Pechman, ed., *Setting National Priorities: The 1979 Budget* (Brookings Institution, 1978), p. 163.
5. Ibid., pp. 161–65.
6. Between 1950 and 1970 the average density in urbanized areas fell from 5,408 per square mile to 3,376, in central cities from 7,786 to 4,463, and in suburban areas from 3,167 to 2,627. In Manhattan, where the density was 102,711 per square mile in 1910, the average for 1970 was 67,160. ACIR, *Improving Urban America*, p. 211.

in population and economic activity while others are declining; and some are highly specialized economies that export the bulk of their output while others are largely self-contained and inner-directed economies.[7] Those urban qualities that are of special interest to inter-governmental policymakers are, not surprisingly, those by which urban need and distress can be identified and measured. Which cities stand in the greatest need of federal and state assistance? What are the causes of their fiscal problems? What are the prospects of their being able to deal with the problems on their own? What kinds of intergovernmental assistance should be offered, to whom, and under what circumstances? These are the questions that bedevil policy-makers and occupy the time of countless bureaucrats and legislative staff members.

The identification of cities most deserving of federal and state assistance is one of the more difficult exercises in the measurement of jurisdictional needs and resources. Some qualities of urban life, both good and bad, are too intangible to be quantified;[8] some can be measured but only at such great cost that they can be observed clearly only at infrequent intervals; some cannot be measured directly but can be gauged by more or less satisfactory proxies; and some can be mea-

7. Ibid., pp. 214–15.
8. Quantifying the unquantifiable is, of course, one of the favorite activities of researchers; and many policymakers, anxious to avoid the biases inherent in decisions based only on measurable variables, have encouraged these endeavors. In 1966 President Johnson directed the secretary of health, education and welfare to develop a set of social indicators to supplement the country's well-established set of economic indicators. A panel of experts was appointed under the chairmanship of Daniel Bell and Alice M. Rivlin, and their findings, *Toward a Social Report,* were released by the U.S. Department of Health, Education and Welfare in January 1969 (GPO, 1969). More recent research has been stimulated by national concern over the environment and government requirements concerning environmental impact statements and analyses. See, for example, U.S. Environmental Protection Agency, Office of Research and Monitoring, *The Quality of Life Concept: A Potential New Tool for Decision-Makers* (1973); Don Dedera, "Computing the Quality of Life," *Exxon USA* (Third Quarter, 1977), pp. 2–6; Werner Z. Hirsch, Sidney Sonenblum, and Jerry St. Dennis, "Estimating the Quality of Urban Life with Input-Output," in A. Brody and A. P. Carter, eds., *Input–Output Techniques,* Proceedings of the Fifth International Conference on Input–Output Techniques, Geneva, January 1971 (Amsterdam: North-Holland, 1972), pp. 44–60; and Lowdon Wingo and Alan Evans, eds., *Public Economics and the Quality of Life* (Johns Hopkins University Press for Resources for the Future and the Centre for Environmental Studies, 1977). For an effort to quantify interstate differences in the quality of life, see Ben-chieh Liu, "Differential Net Migration Rates and the Quality of Life," *Review of Economics and Statistics,* vol. 57 (August 1975), pp. 329–37.

sured directly and objectively at reasonable cost. The most promising single proxy may well be geographical differences in the real wages paid for given qualities of labor services. In well-functioning labor markets these differentials should reflect the differences in the quality of life that people care about when deciding where to live and work. In less attractive locations, employers should have to pay more to attract a given quality of worker, and in more attractive places, less. By relating observed differences in wage rates to various urban characteristics, researchers should be able to estimate the importance of individual qualities of life and then combine them into intercity and intertemporal indexes.[9] Great practical difficulties are involved, however, in obtaining sufficiently accurate readings of these variables to permit construction of indexes reliable enough to be used as a basis for policymaking. Until that can be accomplished, emphasis will remain on those factors that can be measured directly. They must first be combined into a weighted composite index in some reasonable fashion. Then both levels and trends of these indexes must be taken into account.[10] And some recognition must be given to those nonmeasurable factors that are of comparable importance to the measurable variables.

To those who suffer the effects of urban distress, all of this is likely to sound maddeningly academic. Like the poverty that is one of its chief causes, urban degradation is both unpleasant and self-reinforcing. An urban area that is declining secularly, for whatever reasons, will gradually (or even rapidly) lose its most able and prosperous citizens as the downward trend becomes more and more apparent. With increasing concentration of high-need households, the area's tax and crime rates rise and the quality of its public services falls. New businesses avoid the area, established ones expand elsewhere or leave, and the flight of affluent families continues. Crime rates and the tax cost of local government services rise further, and the debilitating cycle continues on and on for some time. The story is all too familiar.

Fortunately, the situation is not as dire as such sad stories of the

9. Sherwin Rosen, "Wage-Based Indexes of Urban Quality of Life," in Peter Mieszkowski and Mahlon Straszheim, *Current Issues in Urban Economics* (Johns Hopkins University Press, 1979), pp. 74–104.

10. The importance of looking at both levels and trends is stressed in ACIR, *Measuring the Fiscal "Blood Pressure" of the States—1964–1975*, Information Paper M-111 (GPO, 1977).

death of cities would suggest. Urban hardship, as Nathan and Dommel have stressed, "is a localized infection, confined to certain cities and within these cities to certain areas that have been characterized in recent years by a rapid process of deconcentration."[11] It is a disease that requires not just effective treatment of existing cases but careful analysis of the causes of urban stress so that its future incidence may be reduced. The very rarity of the infection, however, may seriously weaken the political will to stamp it out. Cities may have to solve their own problems, a strategy that some would prefer in any case.[12] The federal government could help simply by adopting tax reforms that remove some of the distortions imposed on urban economies.[13] If intergovernmental grants are to be used, the many different strains and intensities of the urban disease make it difficult for the specialist to produce timely and effective treatments. Early prescriptions may waste aid or worsen matters. Delayed assistance, on the other hand, may come too late to do much good. Somewhere in between lies an intergovernmental urban plan, or set of plans, that will be beneficial and cost-effective.[14]

The first step in the process of diagnosis is to identify the measurable dimensions of urban welfare or distress and to combine them into quantitative indexes that rank jurisdictions on a scale of relative needs. No fully comprehensive set of indicators yet exists. What such a set might look like, what compromises and omissions its derivation might require, and what values it might have for intergovernmental policymakers are all well illustrated by studies of urban hardship at Brookings and at the Congressional Budget Office.[15]

In the Brookings study Nathan and Adams focus on central city problems in fifty-five of the nation's largest metropolitan areas.[16]

11. "The Cities," p. 283.
12. Gurney Breckenfeld, "It's Up to the Cities to Save Themselves," *Fortune,* March 1977, pp. 194–206.
13. George E. Peterson, "Federal Tax Policy and Urban Development," *Tax Notes,* vol. 8 (January 1, 1979), pp. 3–9.
14. For a discussion of some of the dimensions of such an urban plan see Downs, "Urban Policy," pp. 170–94; James L. Sundquist, "Needed: A National Growth Policy," *Brookings Bulletin,* vol. 14 (Winter-Spring 1978), pp. 1–5; William H. Oakland, "Central Cities: Fiscal Plight and Prospects for Reform," in Mieszkowski and Straszheim, *Current Issues in Urban Economics,* pp. 322–58.
15. See also Touche Ross and Co. and First National Bank of Boston, *Urban Fiscal Stress: A Comparative Analysis of 66 U.S. Cities* (New York, 1979).
16. Richard P. Nathan and Charles Adams, "Understanding Central City Hardship," *Political Science Quarterly,* vol. 91 (Spring 1976), pp. 47–62.

Their measurement of the social and economic status of these areas is based on 1970 census data on the percentages of the civilian labor force that is unemployed, of the population that is over sixty-four or under eighteen years old, of persons over twenty-four years old with less than a twelfth-grade education, of occupied housing units with more than one person per room, and of families whose incomes are below 125 percent of poverty-level income, as well as per capita income adjusted for regional differences in the cost of living. Per capita income, which varies inversely with a city's economic or social need, is inverted and combined with the other factors, which vary directly, to form a composite index.

The intrametropolitan hardship index, a comparison of central cities and their suburban areas, is the dynamic element in the picture, since the greater the disparity in favor of better-off suburbs, the higher is the likelihood that migration trends will intensify whatever central city distress already exists. The intercity, intersuburban, and intrametropolitan indexes give a three-dimensional measure of urban hardship. The indexes show clearly the cities that stand at opposite ends of the affluence-hardship scale. Worst off are Newark, Cleveland, Baltimore, Hartford, Atlanta, Philadelphia, and Detroit, where the index of internal disparity is high, the central city ranks high on the intercity hardship index, and its suburbs rank low on the intersuburban hardship index. In these central cities, distress already exists and future prospects are unfavorable. In sharp contrast are Portland (Oregon), Dallas, Fort Lauderdale, Seattle, and Allentown, where internal disparities are either small or favor the central city and where both city and suburbs rank low on their respective hardship indexes. Between the extremes lie numerous shades and gradations of need blending together in a complex pattern that different observers may well interpret differently. In addition to the problems involved in interpreting the quantitative evidence, there are the inevitable questions concerning the use of only six socioeconomic factors, the appropriateness of the simple, standardized weighting system used,[17] and the relative importance that should be assigned to the three composite indexes when they show conflicting pictures of urban distress. Nonetheless, quantitative measurement of urban needs is indispensable, if only to pinpoint areas that otherwise would not be the object of special attention. Among the twenty-nine central cities that face

17. Ibid., pp. 61–62.

significant amounts of relative hardship the presence of such cities as Atlanta, Miami, and Sacramento may be surprising. The absence of New York City from the group of highest need may also be unexpected, though New Yorkers are likely to derive scant comfort from the knowledge that others face even greater problems than themselves.

A more comprehensive study of urban needs by the Congressional Budget Office, building on the work of Nathan and Adams, is based on composite indexes of social needs, arising from the problems of a city's resident population; economic needs, created by the problems of local business; and fiscal needs, reflecting the problems of city government.[18] The social index is constructed from a 1973 measure of per capita income, the 1976 unemployment rate, and Nathan and Adams's indexes of intrametropolitan and intercity hardship; each factor is given equal weight with need ranging from zero (least need) to 100 (most need).[19] The economic index is built on a similar combination of factors—1963–72 change in manufacturing jobs, 1960–73 population change, 1960–73 change in residents' per capita incomes, 1970–75 change in total employment, 1970 population density, and proportion of the housing stock built before 1940. The index of fiscal need is constructed from a measure of local tax effort, the amount of the property tax base per capita, and a composite measure relating local public service requirements and tax effort to local fiscal capacity.[20]

The scores and rankings of forty-five cities on each of the needs indexes are shown in table 5-1. Only Newark and St. Louis are among the ten neediest cities on all three scores. Nine cities rank in that category on two needs dimensions, as figure 5-1 shows, and six more

18. Peggy L. Cuciti, *City Need and the Responsiveness of Federal Grants Programs,* a report prepared for the Subcommittee on the City of the House Committee on Banking, Finance and Urban Affairs, 95 Cong. 2 sess. (GPO, 1978).

19. Ibid., p. 81. This is the same averaging procedure as that used in Nathan and Adams, "Understanding Central City Hardship."

20. Two alternative composite measures were developed by the U.S. Department of Housing and Urban Development to evaluate the community development block grant program; they are based on indexes developed to study the allocation of general revenue sharing funds in Gregory Schmid, Hubert Lipinsky, and Michael Palmer, *An Alternative Approach to General Revenue Sharing: A Needs Based Allocation Formula* (Menlo, California: Institute for the Future, 1975). One index is equal to the product of need and tax effort divided by fiscal capacity and the other is the sum of the three factors with need receiving twice the weight of the other two factors. See Cuciti, *City Need,* pp. 34–38.

Table 5-1. Composite Measures of Social, Economic, and Fiscal Need for Forty-five Large U.S. Cities

City	Social need Score	Social need Rank	Economic need Score	Economic need Rank	Fiscal need Score	Fiscal need Rank
Northeast						
Albany	n.a.	...	59	21	28	28
Boston	45	15	74	8	72	2
Buffalo	61	6	77	5	44	13
Jersey City	48	13	78	3	47	8
Newark	100	1	84	1	65	4
New York	41	21	80	2	67	3
Patterson	n.a.	...	72	9	45	12
Philadelphia	49	12	70	12	53	6
Pittsburgh	43	20	71	10	37	18
Rochester	44	19	70	11	36	19
Midwest						
Akron	37	25	64	17	27	29
Chicago	46	16	76	6	n.a.	...
Cincinnati	45	17	65	16	44	14
Cleveland	67	2	78	4	42	16
Columbus	34	26	51	28	28	26
Detroit	62	4	66	15	46	9
Gary	58	8	58	22	31	24
Indianapolis	21	35	37	37	22	32
Kansas City	29	30	56	24	n.a.	...
Milwaukee	37	23	64	18	n.a.	...
Minneapolis	20	37	62	20	23	31
Oklahoma City	30	29	34	39	n.a.	...
St. Louis	64	3	74	7	61	5
South						
Atlanta	47	14	45	30	n.a.	...
Baltimore	55	9	63	19	52	7
Birmingham	51	11	45	31	46	10
Dallas	11	39	35	38	n.a.	...
El Paso	n.a.	...	30	41	34	21
Houston	21	34	26	43	n.a.	...
Louisville	45	18	51	27	35	20
Miami	60	7	42	34	31	23
New Orleans	61	5	53	26	45	11
Norfolk	30	28	40	36	44	15
Tampa	51	10	29	42	29	25
Washington	n.a.	...	54	25	84	1
West						
Anaheim	n.a.	...	31	40	10	38
Denver	20	36	41	35	33	22
Los Angeles	27	31	57	23	18	34

Table 5-1 (*continued*)

City	Social need		Economic need		Fiscal need	
	Score	Rank	Score	Rank	Score	Rank
Phoenix	24	32	16	45	18	33
Sacramento	40	22	43	33	24	30
San Bernadino	n.a.	. . .	49	29	28	27
San Diego	30	27	43	32	17	35
San Jose	37	24	24	44	12	37
San Francisco	22	33	68	13	39	17
Seattle	16	38	66	14	13	36

Source: Peggy L. Cuciti, *City Need and the Responsiveness of Federal Grants Programs,* a report prepared for the Subcommittee on the City of the House Committee on Banking, Finance and Urban Affairs, 95 Cong. 2 sess. (U.S. Government Printing Office, 1978), p. 53.
   n.a.   Not available.

Figure 5-1. Overlapping Needs of Cities among the Ten Highest in Social, Economic, and Fiscal Need

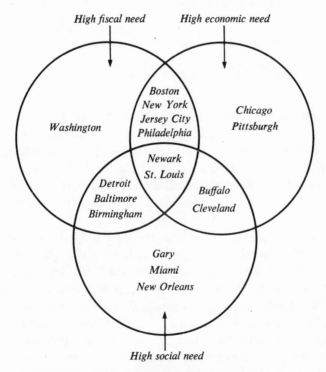

Source: Peggy L. Cuciti, *City Need and the Responsiveness of Federal Grants Programs,* a report prepared for the Subcommittee on the City of the House Committee on Banking, Finance and Urban Affairs, 95 Cong. 2 sess. (U.S. Government Printing Office, 1978), p. 52.

Table 5-2. Correlation between Per Capita Distribution of Federal Grant Programs and Measures of Social, Economic, and Fiscal Urban Need

	Correlation coefficient		
Program	*Social need index*	*Economic need index*	*Fiscal need index*
General revenue sharing			
City governments only	0.378	0.401	0.769
City and overlying governments	0.528	0.354	0.516
Community development block grants			
1977 distribution	0.328	0.361	0.609
Dual formula	0.548	0.786	0.517
Antirecession fiscal assistance			
City governments only	0.714	0.620	0.656
City and overlying governments	0.731	0.524	0.481
Local public works	0.546	0.608	0.546
Comprehensive employment and training			
Title I	0.616	0.428	0.417
Title II	0.509	0.399	0.028[a]
Title VI	0.446	0.372	0.168[a]

Source: Cuciti, *City Need*, p. 76. Measure used is a Pearson correlation coefficient.
a. Correlation coefficient not statistically significant at the 0.05 level.

on one dimension only. To determine how well these cities were served by federal urban grant programs, the CBO study correlated the per capita grant allocations of five major programs with each of the three composite indexes of urban need (table 5-2). It is particularly notable that none of the correlation coefficients is negative—that none of the programs, in other words, distributed funds in an inverse relation to urban needs. And in only two instances—the correlation of CETA title II and title VI grants and the CBO index of fiscal need —is no significant relation to need found. All of the other correlation coefficients are positive and statistically significant. By this quantitative test the best targeted grants are those for antirecession fiscal assistance, local public works, and community development block grants distributed under the dual formula. The first two of these programs, ironically, were established to alleviate cyclical rather than secular urban distress. Of course, better measures of urban need for a wider range of areas may show different results. What matters here, however, is not the findings of the specific studies but the methodology they have developed. Both the Brookings and CBO studies are helpful guides over that difficult terrain.[21]

Urban Fiscal Systems

A simple two-sector model of unbalanced growth developed by William Baumol has generated important insights into the problems of cities.[22] The model assumes that output per unit of labor input grows at a steady rate in one sector but not at all in the other and derives the broad macroeffects of these differential growth rates. It is not stretching the point too much to use the private and public sectors of the economy as examples of the two Baumol sectors.

One of the main propositions derived from this application of the model is that the cost of output per unit in the public sector will rise steadily without limit. This means that consumers of local government output will find themselves paying more and more for exactly the same, or even deteriorating, services. Government workers with limited alternative opportunities will find themselves under steadily increasing pressure to accept wage increases that are lower than those in the private sector. Zero growth in productivity in the public sector, in other words, traps both consumers and producers in a no-win situation that is not of their own making and about which they can do nothing. An escape from the dilemma is possible if productivity can be increased to some degree or in some part of the public sector so that a cap or governor can be placed on explosive cost trends. Reorganizing bureaucratic incentive systems so as to stimulate such gains in efficiency is one of the continuing challenges for government managers.

A second proposition suggested by the Baumol model is that any outputs of the public sector for which the price elasticity of demand is not very low or the income elasticity of demand very high will decline steadily in quantity and may eventually vanish. Proponents of California's Proposition 13 take heart! How common these threatened segments of the public sector may be is, of course, an empirical question. It may be that they are relatively unimportant, in which case

21. For an application of the Nathan-Adams indexes, see Richard P. Nathan and others, *Block Grants for Community Development* (GPO, 1977).

22. William J. Baumol, "Macroeconomics of Unbalanced Growth: The Anatomy of Urban Crisis," *American Economic Review*, vol. 57 (June 1967), pp. 415–26.

Table 5-3. Relation of Federal Baseline Expenditures to Nonrecession GNP, Selected Fiscal Years, 1955-77

Fiscal year	Federal baseline expenditures as a percent of GNP[a]	
	Current dollars	Constant dollars
1955	18.2	18.2
1960	18.1	17.0
1965	18.1	16.4
1970	19.0	16.1
1975	19.9	15.9
1977	20.1	15.8

Source: Charles L. Schultze, "Federal Spending: Past, Present, and Future," in Henry Owen and Charles L. Schultze, eds., *Setting National Priorities: The Next Ten Years* (Brookings Institution, 1976), p. 331.
a. Both series have been standardized to remove the effects of recession and the Vietnam War.

a third proposition takes on significance: if the ratio of the outputs of the two sectors is held constant, a greater and greater proportion of the labor force will have to be allocated to the public sector, and the rate of growth of the total economy will decline steadily toward zero. Strong desires for public services when their productivity growth rate is zero, in other words, are costly. On the other hand, the very process that creates this cost disease in the public sector—namely, a high rate of increase in productivity in the private sector—also creates greater aggregate wealth and hence a more affluent society. As Baumol and Oates have emphasized, that kind of society can, if it wishes to do so, afford to maintain or even increase its consumption of personal services of all kinds, even those with low rates of productivity growth.[23]

If the Baumol hypothesis of unbalanced growth does describe accurately the performance of the private and public sectors, one basic implication is that the relative price of public output will steadily increase. Under these circumstances, policy goals that set some target share for the public sector in the total economy must be interpreted with care. If government expenditures are kept in a constant relation to gross national product when both are measured in current dollars, for example, the relative size of the government sector in real terms will steadily fall. Conversely, to keep the public sector's share of real GNP constant it will be necessary to increase its share of nominal GNP steadily, as table 5-3 illustrates. Between 1955 and 1965 the

23. William J. Baumol and Wallace E. Oates, *Economics, Environmental Policy, and the Quality of Life* (Prentice-Hall, 1979), chap. 10.

ratio of expenditures to gross national product was stable in current dollar terms but steadily falling in constant dollar terms, while the reverse was true between 1965 and 1977. Over the entire period the price of what the federal government buys or finances rose annually about 1.0–1.3 percent faster than the general price index for the whole economy.[24] Greater or smaller differentials in the future will of course produce different results.

Tests of the Baumol hypothesis, like all research dealing with government expenditures, face the formidable task of measuring public output in physical terms. No entirely satisfactory solution is possible, and analyses must utilize proxies for the quality of output that have varying degrees of suitability. One good example of what can (and cannot) be done in this area is the Bradford, Malt, and Oates study which estimates that unit costs of the major local services between World War II and the mid-1960s rose at annual compound rates of 5–7 percent and total spending of local governments at nearly 9 percent.[25] Though the estimates do contain some unknown amounts of quality improvement, it is clear that rising unit costs, as predicted by the Baumol hypothesis, were indeed a major source of fiscal pressure on local governments.

Since the mid-1960s these trends, which have presumably continued, have been joined by another, general price inflation. The troublesome question that inflation poses is whether city expenditures for a given market basket of public services increase more or less than do the receipts generated by a given revenue system. Clearly, much is likely to depend on the specific structures of both sides of a city's budget. On the expenditure side the cost of labor-intensive services will increase at a rate faster than the inflation rate if the Baumol hypothesis holds. Contributions to employee pension funds will be affected directly by their statutory relations to wages and salaries and

24. Official price indexes are computed for the public sector on the same assumption as the Baumol hypothesis—that there is no productivity growth in the government sector. Measurement difficulties mandate this but it produces an upwardly biased measure of the price change in public output if there is any productivity increase there. In 1978, for example, the implicit price deflator for personal consumption expenditures (1972 = 100) was 150.0, while those for federal and state-local purchases of goods and services were 154.8 and 162.1, respectively. *Survey of Current Business,* vol. 59 (July 1979), p. 61.

25. D. F. Bradford, R. A. Malt, and W. E. Oates, "The Rising Cost of Local Public Services: Some Evidence and Reflections," *National Tax Journal,* vol. 22 (June 1969), pp. 185–202.

indirectly, with varying lags, by actuarial calculations of future fund earnings and benefit entitlements. Both of the latter will be increased by inflation but not necessarily at the same rates. On the revenue side, intake from most local personal income and retail sales taxes can be expected to increase more than proportionately and from specific excises less than proportionately. What is highly uncertain, however, is the sensitivity of the property tax to inflation since its fluctuations depend on the frequency and accuracy with which re-assessments are made and the extent to which process controls inhibit local governments from spending the revenues generated by reassessments.

The net budgetary impact of inflation on local governments, then, may turn out to be positive or negative, depending on individual circumstances.[26] Moreover, as some analysts have emphasized, the net impact may be different in the short and long runs.[27] If revenues react more quickly to inflationary trends than do expenditures, as is likely when wage contracts covering public employees are negotiated infrequently and include no automatic cost-of-living increases, local governments may enter an inflationary period by accumulating surpluses, react by reducing tax rates, and end up facing troublesome budgetary deficits.[28]

Urban fiscal systems are plagued not only by relentlessly rising unit costs and inflationary trends but also by internal disparities. Differentials between central city and suburbs are both the cause and the result of the decentralizing migration trend that is frequently at the heart of the process of urban decay in the United States. Theoretical

26. See, for example, David Greytak and Bernard Jump, *The Impact of Inflation on the Expenditures and Revenues of Six Local Governments, 1971–1979*, Metropolitan Studies Program (Maxwell School of Citizenship and Public Affairs, Syracuse University, 1975); Roy Bahl and others, *The Impact of Economic Base Erosion, Inflation, and Employee Compensation Costs on Local Governments*, Metropolitan Studies Program (Maxwell School, Syracuse University, 1975).

27. David J. Ott and others, *State-Local Finances in the Last Half of the 1970s* (Washington: American Enterprise Institute for Public Policy Research, 1975), chap. 5. Projecting budgetary expenditures and revenues under inflationary conditions, as is done here, is not the same thing as estimating the impact of inflation on a fixed government budget structure. A reduction in construction expenditures resulting from an inflation-induced increase in interest rates, for example, would be taken into account in the projections but not in the simulations of inflation's impact.

28. Robert A. Crider, *The Impact of Inflation on State and Local Government* (Columbus, Ohio: Academy for Contemporary Problems, 1978).

models of this flight to the suburbs have been constructed and tested,[29] and hypotheses imputing exploitation of one kind or another have been proposed and discussed. One of the most popular of these, that suburbanites typically do not pay for their fair share of the central city public services that they and central city dwellers jointly enjoy, plunges the investigator into some of the toughest empirical questions of expenditure and tax incidence, to say nothing of the problem of placing dollar values on all of the benefit and cost flows that are identified. Despite a number of valiant efforts to test this hypothesis,[30] the verdict is not yet in.

A broader approach to the exploitation question is taken by studying the differential effects that various kinds of government structure or land use controls have on equity and efficiency in urban areas.[31] This involves dealing with institutional complexities of considerable magnitude and interpreting the theoretical and empirical findings with great care. Suppose, for example, it were found that a shift from the decentralized structure of local governments to a unified system would redistribute income from rich suburbanites to poor central city dwellers. To interpret such a finding as indicating "exploitation" of the central city by those who live outside it would be to impute to

29. Richard Dusansky and Lawrence P. Nordell, "City and Suburb: The Anatomy of Fiscal Dilemma," *Land Economics,* vol. 51 (May 1975), pp. 133–38; David F. Bradford and Harry H. Kelejian, "An Econometric Model of the Flight to the Suburbs," *Journal of Political Economy,* vol. 81 (May-June 1973), pp. 566–89; William C. Wheaton, "Income and Urban Residence: An Analysis of Consumer Demand for Location," *American Economic Review,* vol. 67 (September 1977), pp. 620–31.

30. William B. Neenan, "Suburban-Central City Exploitation Thesis: One City's Tale," *National Tax Journal,* vol. 23 (June 1970), pp. 117–39, comments by D. A. L. Auld and Gail C. A. Cook and by David D. Ramsey, ibid., vol. 25 (December 1972), pp. 595–97, 599–604, and reply by Neenan, ibid., pp. 605–08; William B. Neenan, *Political Economy of Urban Areas* (Markham, 1972); and Kenneth V. Greene, William B. Neenan, and Claudia D. Scott, *Fiscal Interactions in a Metropolitan Area* (Lexington Books, 1974).

31. David F. Bradford and Wallace E. Oates, "Suburban Exploitation of Central Cities and Governmental Structure," in Harold M. Hochman and George E. Peterson, eds., *Redistribution Through Public Choice* (Columbia University Press in cooperation with the Urban Institute, 1974), pp. 43–90; Bryan Ellickson, "Jurisdictional Fragmentation and Residential Choice," *American Economic Review,* vol. 61 (May 1971, *Papers and Proceedings, 1970*), pp. 334–39; Edwin S. Mills, "Economic Analysis of Urban Land-Use Controls," in Mieszkowski and Straszheim, *Current Issues in Urban Economics,* pp. 511–41.

suburbanites motivations that may or may not exist. People may choose to live in communities where income levels are relatively homogeneous not because of urban fiscal disparities, or from a desire to escape welfare costs, but because they prefer to live among people with similar social and economic characteristics and to use housing values, which are closely related to family incomes, as an observable measure of the qualities they mutually are seeking. The motivating forces behind zoning laws and other controls on land use may also stem from a variety of fiscal and nonfiscal considerations.[32] The issue for the country as a whole, however, is not so much why such policies exist as how they affect the efficiency with which urban areas operate and the distribution of income within them. Despite the misdirection of emphasis, the exploitation hypotheses have made an important contribution to local public finance by focusing attention on these problems.

Urban Expenditure Systems

Providing local public goods in the open, interactive environment in which most urban communities operate is no easy task. Not only will the menu offered, and the means of financing it, affect the way residents vote in the next election, but it will also influence their decisions about staying there and those of outside households and businesses about moving in. Such locational choices, in turn, will affect the size of the tax base available to each community, and this will help to determine future choices of local public service menus, which in turn will affect future locational choices. Every community, in other words, reacts, sometimes knowingly and sometimes not, to what every other community does. For policymakers it is particularly difficult to foresee the full effects of their actions.[33]

Complex problems, fortunately, tend to work like magnets, attracting research attention. Economists and others with their increasing interest in urban fiscal problems have examined residential and

32. Bruce W. Hamilton, "The Impact of Zoning and Property Taxes on Urban Structure and Housing Markets" (Ph.D. dissertation, Princeton University, 1972); Edwin S. Mills and Wallace E. Oates, eds., *Fiscal Zoning and Land Use Controls* (Lexington Books, 1975).

33. See especially Robert P. Inman, "Micro-Fiscal Planning in the Regional Economy: A General Equilibrium Approach," *Journal of Public Economics,* vol. 7 (April 1977), pp. 237–60.

business property values, the locational choices of households and businesses, the level and composition of local governments' expenditures and revenues, and the size and rate of development of local communities. In addition to the standard socioeconomic determinants of these important aspects of urban life, their research has centered on such fiscal pivot points as the quality of services and the tax burdens of local governments, intergovernmental grants, and zoning and other local controls on the use of land. To study any one of these topics in isolation, which is a difficult enough task in itself, is to put aside the essential relationship with the other factors. The result of such abstraction may be to introduce biases of unknown magnitude into the empirical findings. Only a few researchers have attempted to estimate comprehensive models that simultaneously deal with urban location decisions, determination of property values, and choices about local expenditures and taxes.[34]

A very large body of professional literature now exists on most aspects of urban life. Looking at it, policymakers, like many ordinary voters looking at government activities, may be more impressed by the effort made than by the answers produced. Nevertheless, the results are by no means all esoteric and impractical. Important behavioral determinants have been quantified, and valuable insights have been gained into the operation of urban economic and fiscal systems.

The Tiebout Hypothesis

A major stimulus to economic research on urban fiscal problems was the appearance in 1956 of a modest-looking paper presenting "A Pure Theory of Local Expenditures."[35] At first glance it was simply another theoretical model with highly unrealistic assumptions and conclusions that were hard to state precisely, let alone test empirically. Yet it has had a profound influence.

In large part Tiebout's paper was a reaction to the pure theory of public expenditures then being developed by Musgrave and Samuel-

34. Howard S. Bloom, H. James Brown, and John E. Jackson, "Residential Location and Local Public Services," in John E. Jackson, ed., *Public Needs and Private Behavior in Metropolitan Areas* (Ballinger, 1975), pp. 73–98; Michael J. Lea, "Local Public Expenditure Determination: A Simultaneous Equations Approach," in National Tax Association—Tax Institute of America, *Proceedings of the Seventy-First Annual Conference on Taxation, 1978* (Columbus, Ohio: NTA-TIA, 1979), pp. 131–36.

35. Charles M. Tiebout, "A Pure Theory of Local Expenditures," *Journal of Political Economy*, vol. 64 (October 1956), pp. 416–24.

son.[36] Their theory showed that no efficient, market-type solution to the problem of choice exists in the public sector. Part of the reason for this is that public goods, by their very nature, must be consumed in equal quantities by all, and part comes from the fact that, unlike private sector pricing, there is no feasible way of charging consumers according to their individual demands for different public goods. Tiebout, however, argued that a market-type solution does exist in the special case of local public goods in urban areas. There, if consumers are rational, mobile, and well informed, they can satisfy their own tastes for particular local public services by choosing to live in the right community. Given a sufficiently large number of separate municipalities, each providing its residents with a distinctive menu of public goods tailored to their special tastes, the local public goods market might, by offering a reasonably wide choice of products, approach the efficiency levels achievable in private markets. By voting with their feet, people would reveal their true preferences for local public goods, an outcome that is conceptually impossible at the federal level and difficult at the state.[37]

While some theorists have criticized the Tiebout model of the operation of decentralized local government and stressed its limitations,[38] others have developed sophisticated theories of urban resi-

36. Richard A. Musgrave's work, which had appeared as early as 1939, was shortly to be published in *The Theory of Public Finance* (McGraw-Hill, 1959); Paul A. Samuelson's work appeared in three successive Novembers in the *Review of Economics and Statistics:* "The Pure Theory of Public Expenditure," vol. 36 (1954), pp. 387–89; "Diagrammatic Exposition of a Theory of Public Expenditure," vol. 37 (1955), pp. 350–56; and "Aspects of Public Expenditure Theories," vol. 40 (1958), pp. 332–38.

37. See, however, Robert T. Deacon, "Private Choice and Collective Outcomes: Evidence From Public Sector Demand Analysis," *National Tax Journal,* vol. 30 (December 1977), pp. 372–73, which summarizes discussions by public choice theorists of ways of inducing people to reveal their true preferences for non-local public goods.

38. See, for example, James M. Buchanan and Charles J. Goetz, "Efficiency Limits of Fiscal Mobility: An Assessment of the Tiebout Model," *Journal of Public Economics,* vol. 1 (April 1972), pp. 25–43; James M. Buchanan and Richard E. Wagner, "An Efficiency Basis for Federal Fiscal Equalization," in Julius Margolis, ed., *The Analysis of Public Output* (Columbia University Press for the National Bureau of Economic Research, 1970), pp. 139–58; Jerome Rothenberg, "Local Decentralization and the Theory of Optimal Government," in ibid., pp. 31–64; Mark V. Pauly, "A Model of Local Government Expenditure and Tax Capitalization," *Journal of Public Economics,* vol. 6 (October 1976), pp. 231–42; William C. Wheaton, "Consumer Mobility and Community Tax Bases: The Financing of Local Public Goods," *Journal of Public Economics,* vol. 4 (November 1975), pp. 377–84.

dential location and local government operation.[39] Led by Oates, numerous economists have tested empirically certain aspects of the Tiebout theory,[40] while others have discussed the great difficulties involved in testing its most fundamental efficiency properties.[41]

From this extended discussion of over twenty years, one aspect of urban fiscal policymaking that stands out is that in a decentralized urban world that provides different public services in different juris-

39. Martin McGuire, "Group Segregation and Optimal Jurisdictions," *Journal of Political Economy,* vol. 82 (January-February 1974), pp. 112–32; Richard E. Schuler, "The Interaction Between Local Government and Urban Residential Location," *American Economic Review,* vol. 64 (September 1974), pp. 682–96, Elhanan Helpman, David Pines, and Eli Borukhov, "Comment," ibid., vol. 66 (December 1976), pp. 961–67, and Richard E. Schuler, "Reply and Further Analysis," ibid., pp. 968–75; Oded Hochman and Haim Ofek, "The Value of Time in Consumption and Residential Location in an Urban Setting," ibid., vol. 67 (December 1977), pp. 996–1003; J. V. Henderson, "Theories of Group, Jurisdiction, and City Size," in Mieszkowski and Straszheim, *Current Issues in Urban Economics,* pp. 235–69.

40. Wallace E. Oates, "The Effects of Property Taxes and Local Public Spending on Property Values: An Empirical Study of Tax Capitalization and the Tiebout Hypothesis," *Journal of Political Economy,* vol. 77 (November-December 1969), pp. 957–71; Henry O. Pollakowski, "A Comment and Further Results," ibid., vol. 81 (July-August 1973), pp. 994–1003; and Wallace E. Oates, "A Reply and Yet Further Results," ibid., pp. 1004–08. J. Richard Aronson and Eli Schwartz, "Financing Public Goods and the Distribution of Population in a System of Local Governments," *National Tax Journal,* vol. 26 (June 1973), pp. 137–60; Joseph Friedman, "Housing Location and the Supply of Local Public Services" (Rand Corp., 1975); Howard Pack and Janet Rothenberg Pack, "Metropolitan Fragmentation and Local Public Expenditures," *National Tax Journal,* vol. 31 (December 1978), pp. 349–62; Jon C. Sonstelie and Paul R. Portney, "Gross Rents and Market Values: Testing the Implications of Tiebout's Hypothesis," *Journal of Urban Economics,* vol. 7 (January 1980), pp. 102–18. Aronson and Schwartz develop a fiscal map, relating community tax rates and per capita expenditures, that may aid government officials in predicting future population trends within an urban area. Friedman applies multinomial logit maximum-likelihood methods of estimation to a model that relates the probability of locating in a particular community to the characteristics of that community and the characteristics of all alternative communities. Pack and Pack find evidence in a sample of 983 medium-sized Pennsylvania towns in 1970 that households have heterogeneous rather than the homogeneous tastes for local public services predicted by the Tiebout hypothesis and that they behave so as to limit the redistributive effects of local taxation. Sonstelie and Portney criticize previous studies for using housing market values, rather than gross rents, as the dependent variable and estimate their preferred specification of the Tiebout model for 1969–70 data in San Mateo County, California.

41. Bruce W. Hamilton, "The Effects of Property Taxes and Local Public Spending on Property Values: A Theoretical Comment," *Journal of Political Economy,* vol. 84 (June 1976), pp. 647–50; and Dennis Epple, Allan Zelenitz, and Michael Visscher, "A Search for Testable Implications of the Tiebout Hypothesis," ibid., vol. 86 (June 1978), pp. 405–25.

dictions, housing is a complex, composite good with both private and public dimensions.[42] How many of the separate public goods provided by different communities significantly affect residential decisions is a matter of some dispute. The least controversial are differences in the quality of school services. There is considerable evidence that people with children do care about these differences and do take them seriously when choosing a place of residence.[43] Moreover, voters without children may support increases in local school taxes and expenditures because they expect their home values to be increased thereby.[44] In the future, however, these differences may be largely eliminated by changes in school financing systems induced by the *Serrano* and *Rodriguez* court decisions and by Proposition 13 and its followers. For most other local public services, differences in the quality of services provided are of doubtful importance. Many of these services —fire and police protection, street maintenance, traffic control, sewer and sanitation services—are basic urban housekeeping activities that tend to be carried out in more or less the same way, though not neces-

42. Empirical estimation of housing values has consequently been largely based on the theory of hedonic price indexes which relate a commodity's price to the bundle of characteristics, or attributes, that make it attractive to consumers. See Kelvin J. Lancaster, *Consumer Demand: A New Approach* (Columbia University Press, 1971); Zvi Griliches, ed., *Price Indexes and Quality Change: Studies in New Methods of Measurement* (Harvard University Press, 1971); Sherwin Rosen, "Hedonic Prices and Implicit Markets: Product Differentiation in Pure Competition," *Journal of Political Economy*, vol. 82 (January-February 1974), pp. 34–55.

43. In addition to Oates, "The Effects of Property Taxes" and the succeeding comments by Pollakowski and Oates, see Floyd J. Fowler, *Citizen Attitudes Toward Local Government, Services, and Taxes* (Ballinger, 1974); Stephen K. Mayo, "Local Public Goods and Residential Location: An Empirical Test of the Tiebout Hypothesis," in Jackson, *Public Needs and Private Behavior*, pp. 31–71; Andrew M. Reschovsky, "Intrametropolitan Residential Location and the Public Sector," in NTA-TIA, *Proceedings, 1975*, pp. 211–12. Edel and Sclar tested the hypothesis that beneficial differences in local governments' services are capitalized into higher land values in the short run but may disappear in the long run as competition from other communities eliminates the special attractions of the high-quality jurisdictions. They found the hypothesis confirmed by census data for the Boston metropolitan area for 1930–70. Matthew Edel and Elliott Sclar, "Taxes, Spending, and Property Values: Supply Adjustment in a Tiebout-Oates Model," *Journal of Political Economy*, vol. 82 (September-October 1974), pp. 941–54; criticism and extension of their model is presented by George Richard Meadows, "A Comment and Further Results," ibid., vol. 84 (August 1976), pp. 869–80.

44. Paul R. Portney and Jon C. Sonstelie, "Super-Rationality and School Tax Voting," Working Paper 84 (Graduate School of Public Policy, University of California—Berkeley, January 1978), and "Take the Money and Run: A Theory of Voting in Local Referenda," *Journal of Urban Economics* (forthcoming).

sarily at the same tax cost, everywhere. In any case, there is so far little empirical evidence that they are important factors in urban residential markets.[45]

The various transfers and services provided to low-income groups are another major program area for local governments. Though income redistribution could in principle be a local public good that would attract taxpayers with strong egalitarian tastes to particular jurisdictions,[46] the requisite conditions do not seem to exist. Indeed, there is evidence that income redistribution is one of the factors causing households to flee from the central city to the suburbs. This particular barrier to an efficient Tiebout world could, of course, be eliminated by shifting the financing of all income-support programs to state or federal governments.[47]

It appears, then, that differences in the quality of local governments' services may not play the important behavioral role that enthusiastic supporters of the Tiebout hypothesis would like. The less significant service differentials are, however, the more important will differences in local tax burdens be. In well-functioning urban residential markets, tax differences not matched by equally valuable differences in service levels—so-called onerous property tax burden differentials—will be fully capitalized into lower and higher housing values. To be sure, full capitalization will occur only where buyers expect current differentials to continue into the future. If two identical houses in two different communities bear onerous property tax burdens that currently differ by, say, $1,000 a year, the value of the two homes may differ by as little as $1,000 if the tax difference is expected to be eliminated the next year. On the other hand, they may

45. See Bloom, Brown, and Jackson, "Residential Location"; Friedman, "Housing Location"; Mayo, "Local Public Goods"; Reschovsky, "Intrametropolitan Residential Location"; Nonna A. Noto, "The Impact of the Local Public Sector on Residential Property Values," in NTA-TIA, *Proceedings, 1976*, pp. 192–200.

46. Mark V. Pauly, "Income Redistribution as a Local Public Good," *Journal of Public Economics*, vol. 2 (February 1973), pp. 35–58; James M. Buchanan, "Who Should Distribute What in a Federal System?" in Hochman and Peterson, *Redistribution Through Public Choice*, pp. 22–42; Albert Breton and Anthony Scott, *The Economic Constitution of Federal States* (University of Toronto Press, 1978), chap. 10.

47. Musgrave, *The Theory of Public Finance*, pp. 179–82; Richard A. Musgrave and Peggy Musgrave, *Public Finance in Theory and Practice*, 2d ed. (McGraw-Hill, 1976), pp. 623–24; and Wallace E. Oates, "The Theory of Public Finance in a Federal System," *Canadian Journal of Economics*, vol. 1 (February 1968), pp. 37–54.

vary by as much as $10,000 (at a 10 percent discount rate) if the tax disparity is expected to persist indefinitely. Empirical studies of the effects on housing values of onerous tax burden differentials may say more about the expectations of home buyers in the study area than they do about existence of tax capitalization.[48]

A rare opportunity to investigate tax capitalization, however, occurred in California in 1966 when the state passed a law requiring all property to be assessed at a uniform ratio of 25 percent of full market value.[49] Before 1966, single-family homes in San Francisco had been assessed at an average of only 10 percent of market value, multi-unit residential property at 14–20 percent, and commercial and industrial property at 20–25 percent. Passage of the law led to a significant increase in taxes on single-family homes within a short period of time while total city expenditures, and hence the presumed quality of local public services, remained relatively unchanged. Comparing samples of housing sales before passage of the assessment law, during the interim between passage and the announcement of San Francisco's new tax rate, and during the ensuing year, R. S. Smith found strong evidence of tax capitalization, as would be expected where the housing supply is highly inelastic. A $200 annual increase in property tax burdens which, under the circumstances, could reasonably be expected to continue indefinitely, was found to be accompanied by a $2,800 to $4,000 reduction in home values.[50]

The ubiquity and importance of the effects of tax capitalization in decentralized urban areas is the second important aspect of the Tiebout model. For policymakers these effects pose some very difficult

48. See Oates, "The Effects of Property Taxes," and the succeeding comments by Pollakowski and Oates; Robert Edelstein, "The Determinants of Value in the Philadelphia Housing Market: A Case Study of the Main Line 1967–1969," *Review of Economics and Statistics,* vol. 56 (August 1974), pp. 319–28; A. Thomas King, *Property Taxes, Amenities, and Residential Land Values* (Ballinger, 1973). The difficult problems involved in specifying an appropriate econometric model of tax capitalization are discussed in A. Thomas King, "Estimating Property Tax Capitalization: A Critical Comment," *Journal of Political Economy,* vol. 85 (April 1977), pp. 425–31; Peter Linneman, "The Capitalization of Local Taxes: A Note on Specification," ibid., vol. 86 (June 1978), pp. 535–38; Harvey S. Rosen and David J. Fullerton, "A Note on Local Tax Rates, Public Benefit Levels, and Property Values," ibid., vol. 85 (April 1977), pp. 433–40.

49. The Petris-Knox bill (AB 80) required a uniform ratio of 20–25 percent through fiscal 1970–71 and of 25 percent thereafter.

50. R. Stafford Smith, "Property Tax Capitalization in San Francisco," *National Tax Journal,* vol. 23 (June 1970), pp. 177–93.

problems. Neglecting them, which is all too easy to do, may mean enacting fiscal changes when none are needed, or adopting policies whose effectiveness is blunted by the windfall gains and losses they generate.[51]

The third important contribution of the Tiebout model has been to the debate over the desirability of decentralized metropolitan government operations. While for many economists the model provides strong support for continuing to have large numbers of independent local governments in urban areas, others are dubious about the importance of any Tiebout-type efficiency gains and concerned about various inequities that they believe are generated by a decentralized local government system.[52]

Tiebout efficiency gains, however, are not the only reason for preferring a system of multiple local governments. People who all want the same local government services may wish to choose and monitor them by different kinds of political processes. Multiple authorities provide better protection from mistaken government decisions and also from political exploitation by entrenched majorities or highly organized minorities, and from economic exploitation by public sector monopolies.[53] Active competition among independent local governments may result in more efficient provision of a standardized set of local public services and may stimulate experimentation in the

51. If a $1,000 differential property tax burden, for example, had existed for some time in two adjacent school districts whose services were of equal quality, reformers might well conclude that inequitable differences in the price of school services existed and should be eliminated. All the homes in the community with higher taxes might, however, have been purchased at reduced values that reflected the fully capitalized value of the $1,000 tax burden differential. No horizontal fiscal inequities would then exist. Moreover, any subsequent equalization of the school tax burdens between the two communities would generate windfall gains and losses to current residents rather than helping new entrants into the community where taxes had been higher to buy school services at a more equitable price. Only policy analysis that takes all capitalization effects into account can give very good guidance to urban reformers. See Gordon Tullock, "The Transitional Gains Trap," *Bell Journal of Economics,* vol. 6 (Autumn 1975), pp. 671–78. For an analysis of urban fiscal problems that does take capitalization effects into account, see Robert P. Inman and Daniel L. Rubinfeld, "The Judicial Pursuit of Local Fiscal Equity," *Harvard Law Review,* vol. 92 (June 1979), pp. 1662–1750.

52. See, for example, Buchanan and Goetz, "Efficiency Limits of Fiscal Mobility," and Inman and Rubinfeld, "Judicial Pursuit of Local Fiscal Equity."

53. On the latter see Paul N. Courant, Edward M. Gramlich, and Daniel L. Rubinfeld, "Public Employee Market Power and the Level of Government Spending," *American Economic Review,* vol. 69 (December 1979), pp. 806–17.

creation of better production and delivery systems. These and other advantages of urban decentralization must, of course, be weighed against its well-known costs. Those include the potential loss of economies of scale in production, and the creation, together with all their attendant inequities and inefficiencies, of a higher level of fiscal spillovers. While instruments exist to reduce such costs—independent community contracts with centralized, efficient producers of public services such as water supply; intergovernmental grants to control spillovers—expectations as to their successful application differ widely.[54] Finally, there is a high probability that a broad-scale move to a centralized system of metropolitan government would be likely to make for equalized spending levels considerably higher than the old areawide average of independent community expenditures.[55] In addition, a move from simple municipal revenue systems that depend largely on property taxes to a more complex and varied metropolitan one would obscure household perceptions of the local tax costs of particular programs and so probably reduce taxpayer opposition to expanding government operations.[56] The prospect of higher local spending levels, of course, will be viewed by some as an argument for centralization and by others as an argument against it.

In any case, it is clear that the choice among different governmental systems in urban areas is a complex and controversial one not likely to be settled soon or in the same way in different parts of the country.

Business Enterprises in the Urban Economy

A natural extension of the Tiebout model has recently been to apply it to the efficiency aspects of business locational decisions. This may seem a strange application because the conventional wisdom has long held that fiscal incentives used by state and local governments to attract business were either economically inefficient, diverting busi-

54. For a concise discussion of the advantages and disadvantages of urban decentralization, see Roland N. McKean, *Public Spending* (McGraw-Hill, 1968), chap. 10.

55. See Gail C. A. Cook, "Toronto Metropolitan Finance: Selected Objectives and Results," in George F. Break, ed., *Metropolitan Financing and Growth Management Policies: Principles and Practice* (University of Wisconsin Press for the Committee on Taxation, Resources, and Economic Development, 1978), pp. 138–47.

56. Richard E. Wagner, "Revenue Structure, Fiscal Illusion, and Budgetary Choice," *Public Choice*, vol. 25 (Spring 1976), pp. 45–61.

nesses from superior locations, or inequitable, resulting only in lowering business taxes without altering locational decisions. Since interregional tax differentials that are not offset by differences in the quality of public services typically rank low among the factors determining business location,[57] fiscal experts have usually viewed interstate competition for commerce and industry as a losing game, particularly since it really must be played unilaterally, as serious vying between states wipes out the stakes. It may be, however, that interstate differences in individual income tax burdens are a more important factor in location decisions than business tax differentials. Nine states do not have a broad-based personal income tax; among those that do, effective tax rates at different family income levels vary widely.[58] During the late 1970s several high-tax states—notably California, Massachusetts, and New York—enacted a variety of tax changes that improved their competitive fiscal positions. By affecting the geographical pattern of business investment, states can clearly have an important impact on household migration patterns.[59]

Where business location within a metropolitan area is being considered, however, onerous business tax differentials are likely to become relatively important simply because other key factors that vary regionally, such as wage rates, are likely to be more uniform. As Oakland has noted, intraurban tax differentials may easily constitute 10 percent of profits, both before and after federal income taxes.[60] Fiscal factors of this magnitude are clearly worth serious consideration. Whether they mainly affect relative land values or business locational choices, and in what ways, are important questions that remain largely unanswered. In his 1974 survey of the field Oakland found

57. ACIR, *State-Local Taxation and Industrial Location*, Report A-30 (GPO, 1967); Gary C. Cornia, William A. Testa, and Frederick D. Stocker, *State-Local Fiscal Incentives and Economic Development* (Columbus, Ohio: Academy for Contemporary Problems, 1978); John F. Due, "Studies of State-Local Tax Influences on Location of Industry," *National Tax Journal*, vol. 14 (June 1961), pp. 163–73; William C. Wheaton, ed., *Interregional Movements and Regional Growth*, COUPE Papers on Public Economics, no. 2 (Washington: Urban Institute, 1979).

58. ACIR, *Significant Features of Fiscal Federalism, 1978–79 Edition*, Report M-115 (GPO, 1979), p. 75.

59. Ann P. Bartel, "The Migration Decision: What Role Does Job Mobility Play?" *American Economic Review*, vol. 69 (December 1979), pp. 775–86.

60. William H. Oakland, "Local Taxes and Intraurban Industrial Location: A Survey," in Break, *Metropolitan Financing*, p. 16.

only three serious studies, and they, lacking any theoretical model of industrial location, provided little reliable evidence.[61]

A theoretical model of intraurban business location would, to be sure, be a complicated affair. In the spirit of the Tiebout model its designers would need to identify those state and local public services that would attract certain kinds of businesses to particular parts of the urban area. Where such governmental amenities were unimportant, attention would focus on differential onerous business tax burdens, their impact on land prices, and their influence on firms contemplating expansion or relocation. On the supply side would be the long-familiar economic, social, and fiscal advantages and disadvantages to community residents of having commerce and industry in their own jurisdictions. Not surprisingly, increasing attention is being paid to the total environmental impact of business on the quality of urban life. When such disamenities as increased congestion, air and water pollution, and higher crime rates have a negative impact, some balancing positive effects will be needed to induce a community to expand its nonresidential base.

These offsetting factors would include higher employment opportunities for residents, better shopping facilities, and fiscal surpluses, created whenever new businesses provide more local revenue than is needed to pay for their required public services, that can be used for such household-oriented local programs as schools, libraries, and recreational facilities. Arguing that the fiscal surpluses will typically be the most important benefits that firms can offer to suburban communities, Fischel has developed a theoretical model of business locational choices within urban areas.[62] Among his interesting hypotheses is a Tiebout-like optimality rule that in well-functioning urban markets with mobile firms and informed participants the price of a better community environment—the forgone tax benefits of having more resident business firms—will be set at competitive (that is, minimum) levels. Under such conditions there would be no net surpluses from the trade-off between fiscal gain and environmental loss

61. Ibid., pp. 13–30.

62. William A. Fischel, "Fiscal and Environmental Considerations in the Location of Firms in Suburban Communities: A Non-Technical Digest," in NTA-TIA, *Proceedings, 1974*, pp. 632–56, and "Fiscal and Environmental Considerations in the Location of Firms in Suburban Communities," in Edwin S. Mills and Wallace E. Oates, eds., *Fiscal Zoning and Land Use Controls: The Economic Issues* (Lexington Books, 1975), pp. 119–73.

in any community, and hence varying mixes of commercial and industrial property would have no impact on home values in different jurisdictions. Tax differentials might still influence the location of business, but these would reflect local perceptions of the costs they inflict on the environment rather than an inefficiently priced fiscal incentive system.[63]

How close the Fischel model comes to the real world and how close the real world comes to his optimality rule are both open questions.[64] His work, however, does suggest some new dimensions of urban behavior that policymakers will want to consider. One is that fiscal incentives for business may be an important instrument that enables local communities better to adjust the size and composition of their business sectors to the tastes of their residents for environmental amenities. Seen in this light these incentives would enhance efficiency rather than create inequities. The Fischel analysis implies also that decentralized zoning powers do have important economic functions in urban areas and that equalization of local community tax bases, which is a major goal of many school finance and property tax reformers, may make new business unattractive to many communities.

A final important effect of business property, which operates whether the Fischel model is valid or not, is to lower the perceived price of local household-oriented public services and hence to change the pattern of spending by various governments in urban areas.

Determinants of Local Government Expenditure

Nowhere is the puzzling paradox of modern economics more clearly revealed than in empirical studies of the factors that determine the composition and levels of local governments' budgets. Comparing the early, pioneering studies of Fabricant and Fisher with today's sophisticated modeling of local public choice by Bergstrom and Goodman or Borcherding and Deacon, for example, is like contrast-

---

63. Some evidence that onerous tax differentials between suburbs and central cities do not affect business locational choices is presented in Sharon G. Levin, "Suburban-Central City Property Tax Differentials and the Location of Industry: Some Evidence," *Land Economics*, vol. 50 (November 1974), pp. 380–86.

64. See the discussion of Fischel's work by Donald W. Kiefer, in NTA-TIA, *Proceedings, 1974*, pp. 657–64. Fischel's own empirical evidence, which tends to support his hypotheses, is presented in "Fiscal and Environmental Considerations," pp. 149–65.

ing a model T with a Toronado.[65] Yet the contributions of this large body of literature to the task of designing better urban policies are modest at best.[66] Some of the important factors affecting local government behavior have been illuminated, but only a few qualitative generalizations can yet be made with any high degree of confidence and large gaps remain for future research to fill.[67]

Urban expenditure systems are indeed a varied and enigmatic lot. Among the many impediments to a better understanding of local government behavior, four stand out: (1) measuring the output of local governments, (2) modeling the theoretical determinants of local public choice, (3) measuring and using price and income elasticities of demand for local government services, and (4) separating the private and public good attributes of specific local government activities and assessing the role of private sector substitutes for local government services.

65. Fabricant used population density, urbanization, and per capita income to explain per capita state and local operating expenditures in 1942, and Fisher applied the same three factors to 1956–57 data. Solomon Fabricant, *The Trend of Government Activity in the United States Since 1900* (New York: National Bureau of Economic Research, 1952), pp. 122–31; Glenn W. Fisher, "Determinants of State and Local Government Expenditures: A Preliminary Analysis," *National Tax Journal,* vol. 14 (December 1961), pp. 349–55. Later studies derive their estimating equations from explicit theoretical models of public choice, include many more explanatory factors, use highly technical statistical estimating methods, and are more explicitly aimed at testing hypotheses and producing results that are useful for public policy. See, for example, Theodore C. Bergstrom and Robert P. Goodman, "Private Demands for Public Goods," *American Economic Review,* vol. 63 (June 1973), pp. 280–96; and Thomas E. Borcherding and Robert T. Deacon, "The Demand for the Services of Non-Federal Governments," ibid., vol. 62 (December 1972), pp. 891–901.

66. For reviews of the literature on expenditure determinants see Roy W. Bahl, "Studies on Determinants of Public Expenditures: A Review," in Selma J. Mushkin and John F. Cotton, *Functional Federalism: Grants-in-Aid and PPB Systems,* State-Local Finances Project of the George Washington University (GWU, 1968), pp. 184–207, and "Quantitative Public Expenditure Analysis and Public Policy," in NTA-TIA, *Proceedings, 1969,* pp. 547–69; Richard M. Bird, *The Growth of Government Spending in Canada,* Canadian Tax Paper 51 (Toronto: Canadian Tax Foundation, 1970), pp. 209–24; John Eric Fredland, "Determinants of State and Local Expenditures: An Annotated Bibliography" (Washington: Urban Institute, 1974).

67. Stephen M. Barro, *The Urban Impacts of Federal Policies,* vol. 3: *Fiscal Conditions* (Rand Corp., 1978), pp. 131–55; Edward M. Gramlich, "Intergovernmental Grants: A Review of the Empirical Literature," in Wallace E. Oates, ed., *The Political Economy of Fiscal Federalism* (Lexington Books, 1977), pp. 219–39; Deacon, "Private Choice and Collective Outcomes," pp. 371–86.

OUTPUT MEASURES. A basic, unanswered question about local governments is whether differences in their spending levels should be attributed to differences in the quality of the services provided, to unavoidable differences in input costs, or to differences in operational efficiency. Empirical studies of the determinants of local government expenditures sometimes demonstrate, but more often simply assume, that in the sample examined, differences in costs and operational efficiency are small enough to make expenditures a good proxy for the quality of local government services. Other studies separate local government expenditures into two major components—employment levels and wage rates—arguing that public employment is a better proxy for quality of output than total expenditures are, particularly when there are few differences in the quality of workers hired or in the capital intensity of production. Using this approach to examine police expenditures in seventy-nine metropolitan area city governments in 1972, Bahl, Gustely, and Wasylenko found both demand and supply factors to be important.[68] In cities where both per capita incomes and the wage rates that government employees could command in the private sector were higher than average, spending on police services was typically substantially higher, mostly because of differences in the wage rate rather than in employment levels. If, as the authors suggest, the higher wage rates do not reflect a higher quality of service, the higher spending on police may be said to result from supply rather than demand factors. Thus a positive income elasticity of demand for local government expenditures should be interpreted with care, for differences between communities may be due in greater part to wage costs than to tastes for public services.

Another useful distinction in measuring public output, formulated by Bradford, Malt, and Oates, is the difference between the services or outcomes that local consumer-taxpayers desire and the measurable inputs and activities that presumably determine the quality of those services.[69] The message here is that local governments' output can only be measured indirectly through detailed analyses of production functions in the public sector. No one would maintain that this is an

68. Roy W. Bahl, Richard D. Gustely, and Michael J. Wasylenko, "The Determinants of Local Government Police Expenditures: A Public Employment Approach," *National Tax Journal*, vol. 31 (March 1978), pp. 67–79.
69. "The Rising Cost of Local Public Services," pp. 186–89.

easy task. The long and passionate debate over what scores on school achievement tests really mean and what school inputs, if any, affect them is all too familiar.[70] Even if all communities in an area agreed that the scores on particular tests do measure well the student achievement levels sought, the measurement of the relative outputs of schools in the area would not be easy. A school district with low test scores might have a high output because of the stimulus its program gave to the students it had to work with, while a high-scoring district might have done little to produce that result. What matters in school output, in other words, is not the value turned out at graduation but rather the value added during the school year.

The analysis of other local public services is similarly complex. Consider, for example, a city that has relatively high crime rates and also relatively high police expenditures for its area. For nonresidents considering moving there, two obvious disamenities to be considered would be the crime rates and the impact of police costs on city tax burdens and on the quality of other local services. For residents the above-average police expenditures might result from a deliberate choice to spend extra money to avoid the even more costly effects of still higher crime rates. Yet the facts might easily be misinterpreted to mean either that the high expenditures resulted from high costs or operational inefficiencies, or that the quality of police services is not an important factor in decisions to live or not live in that urban area. It is true that potential migrants might not perceive the police services as being above average, but if they were not, the still higher crime rates would act as a strong deterrent to newcomers.

The elusive character of many local government services may well be an ineradicable fact of urban life. If so, it greatly complicates things not only for the voters and taxpayers who live there but also for those who wish to analyze their behavior.

LOCAL PUBLIC CHOICE MODELS. A serious weakness of early studies of the determinants of local expenditures was their lack of any systematic theory of how the public sector operates. In 1968, however, several studies appeared that extended to the state and local sector the standard economic model of consumer choice based on the

70. See, for example, Henry J. Aaron, *Politics and the Professors: The Great Society in Perspective* (Brookings Institution, 1978), chap. 3.

maximization of utility subject to a budget constraint.[71] Once introduced, this model, with its emphasis on the tastes and resources of the median voter, quickly established a monopoly in its area. The model has been improved and refined, but future progress may require testing alternative theories of public choice.[72]

The narrowness of the model has been evident from the beginning —besides consumer-voters there are, after all, other groups operating in the local public sector that have different utility functions—but the model is appealing because it consistently generates coefficient estimates with correct signs and plausible sizes.[73] The model's predictions of local government behavior under changing conditions have begun to show serious signs of weakness, however. Unrestricted federal grants that stimulate much more state and local spending than would an equal-sized reduction in federal individual income taxes raise questions. A more dramatic development, suggesting considerable voter distrust of traditional public choice mechanisms, is the whole movement to limit taxes and expenditures.[74] Its future is hard to pre-

71. Edward M. Gramlich, "Alternative Federal Policies for Stimulating State and Local Expenditures: A Comparison of Their Effects," *National Tax Journal*, vol. 21 (June 1968), pp. 119–29, and "State and Local Governments and Their Budget Constraint," *International Economic Review*, vol. 10 (June 1969), pp. 163–82; James M. Henderson, "Local Government Expenditures: A Social Welfare Analysis," *Review of Economics and Statistics*, vol. 50 (May 1968), pp. 156–63; Ann R. Horowitz, "A Simultaneous-Equation Approach to the Problem of Explaining Interstate Differences in State and Local Government Expenditures," *Southern Economic Journal*, vol. 34 (April 1968), pp. 459–76.

72. Early analyses that stressed the political aspects of state and local spending behavior typically adopted an individualistic theory of the state in which politicians, at least in the long run, acted to satisfy the tastes and demands of coalitions and groups of voters and not to satisfy the desires of bureaucrats or to articulate some independent concept of the public good. See, for example, James L. Barr and Otto A. Davis, "An Elementary Political and Economic Theory of the Expenditures of Local Governments," *Southern Economic Journal*, vol. 32 (October 1966), pp. 149–65; Otto A. Davis and George H. Haines, Jr., "A Political Approach to a Theory of Public Expenditure: The Case of Municipalities," *National Tax Journal*, vol. 19 (September 1966), pp. 259–75. Alternative theories of the state are discussed in James M. Buchanan, *Fiscal Theory and Political Economy: Selected Essays* (University of North Carolina Press, 1960).

73. Robert P. Inman, "Testing Political Economy's 'As If' Proposition: Is the Median Income Voter Really Decisive?" *Public Policy*, vol. 26 (Winter 1978).

74. See the ACIR's issue on the balanced budget movement, *Intergovernmental Perspective*, vol. 5 (Spring 1979); NTA-TIA, *National Tax Journal*, Supplement: "Proceedings of a Conference on Tax and Expenditure Limitations," vol. 32 (June 1979); Aaron Wildavsky, *How to Limit Government Spending* (Los Angeles: University of California Press, forthcoming).

dict, as the evidence so far produced is ambiguous. California's Proposition 13, for example, may be interpreted in two very different ways.[75] Voters there may have been reacting mainly to a rapid increase in the share of local property tax burden falling upon single-family homes and to a state school grant formula that increased the local cost of schools as assessed values rose.[76] If so, their support for Proposition 13 indicated not disenchantment with the size of local government but a desire to reduce the importance of the property tax as a source of local finance. In the short run, people of that persuasion have had their wishes fulfilled as state government surpluses have been used to increase state shares of both welfare and school costs so that only moderate reductions in most local government services have been needed. Though the true significance of Proposition 13 may not be clear for some time,[77] there is mounting evidence throughout the country of widespread activity aimed at restraining government spending.[78] Before 1970 only one state (Arizona) had a limit on local government spending, but by November 1979 eight had them. Whereas before 1970 only three states imposed constraints on local property tax levies, by late 1979 twenty states did so. Before the adoption of Proposition 13, four states had restrictions on state government spending powers. In the following year and a half, voters in six

75. It has also been seen as a desire for less waste and inefficiency in the public sector rather than for fewer government services. See, for example, Selma J. Mushkin, ed., *Proposition Thirteen and Its Consequences for Public Management,* Council for Applied Social Research (Cambridge, Mass.: Abt Associates, 1979). The size of the revenue reduction—57 percent of local property tax revenues—suggests that voters either had a highly inflated idea of the amount of waste in local government operations or were influenced by other objectives.

76. Single-family homes' share of total asssessed valuation of property in California rose from 32 percent in 1973–74 to 41 percent in 1977–78. It is estimated that shortly before Proposition 13 passed, an increase of 1 percent in assessed values per capita implied a 0.4 percent increase in property taxes per capita just to maintain the real level of school services. Perry Shapiro, David Puryear, and John Ross, "Tax and Expenditure Limitation in Retrospect and in Prospect," *National Tax Journal,* Supplement: "Proceedings," vol. 32 (June 1979), pp. 1–10.

77. Frank Levy, "On Understanding Proposition 13," *Public Interest,* no. 56 (Summer 1979), pp. 66–89.

78. John Shannon and Chris Cooper, *The Tax Revolt—It Has Hurried History Along,* speech delivered to the Public Securities Association Panel Discussion, Proposition 13, One Year Later, Colorado Springs, October 8, 1979. The data on state expenditure-restraining measures given in the text are from ACIR staff compilations provided by John Shannon.

states, including California itself,[79] approved limits on state expenditures, and six other state legislatures enacted them directly.

In any case, it may well be that the time has come for a significant change in the structure of expenditure determinant studies, comparable to the early breakthroughs of the 1960s. Then it was the addition of explicit theories of local public choice that raised the whole development to a higher level of productivity. In the future a more vigorous competition among alternative theories may add realism to empirical analyses of government behavior and provide policymakers with more reliable guides and evidence.[80]

ELASTICITIES OF DEMAND FOR LOCAL GOVERNMENT SERVICES. The two basic economic determinants to be studied in models of consumer behavior in the private sector are product prices and household incomes. So it is also in the public sector, where the relative sizes of income and price elasticities matter especially. In the Baumol model of unbalanced growth, for example, a growing economy generates both rising real incomes and rising relative prices of government services. Output therefore rises or falls in the public sector as the income elasticity of demand for public goods exceeds or falls short of the price elasticity of demand. Future growth in the public sector can thus be predicted from knowledge of the relevant income and price elasticities of demand and from the estimated rate of technological progress in the private sector. These predictions could cover both absolute and relative rates of growth in the public sector, as well as growth rates in particular program areas. Comparisons of the predictions with actual government behavior provide an empirical test of the Baumol model.[81]

Estimates of the income and price elasticity parameters can also be used to evaluate local tax systems. In general, if the levels of services offered and the distribution of the tax burden are to satisfy most voters, household tax burdens should be set so as to balance the

79. Proposition 4, which limits the growth in both state and local expenditures to future rates of inflation and population growth, passed in the November 1979 elections by a wider margin than had Proposition 13.

80. Robert P. Inman, "The Fiscal Performance of Local Governments: An Interpretative Review," in Mieszkowski and Straszheim, *Current Issues in Urban Economics,* pp. 270–321.

81. Robert M. Spann, "The Macroeconomics of Unbalanced Growth and the Expanding Public Sector: Some Simple Tests of a Model of Government Growth," *Journal of Public Economics,* vol. 8 (December 1977), pp. 397–404.

positive effects that higher incomes have on the willingness to contribute to the cost of collective services against the negative effects of the higher price (tax share) paid for them. More precisely, if a consensus is to be reached on problems of local public choice, effective household tax burdens should be set so that the income elasticity of demand for local government services exactly equals the absolute value of the product of the price (tax share) elasticity of demand and the income elasticity of household tax shares.[82] This means, for example, that if the income and price elasticities of demand are equal (in absolute value), the local tax system should be proportional to household incomes. Higher income than price elasticities support progressive local tax systems, and higher price elasticities support regressive systems.

Empirical evidence on the relative sizes of the income and price elasticities of demand for local public goods is difficult to evaluate. The range of estimates by different investigators for different samples of data and for different local government services is still very wide, and measurement problems are severe.[83] In this situation it is difficult to avoid seeing one's own prejudices confirmed by the data. Agnos-

82. The optimal local tax structure would be one for which $x + yz = 0$, where x is the income elasticity and y the price elasticity of demand for local public goods, and z is the income elasticity of tax shares under the optimal structure. The tax policy parameter, z, should then be set so that $z = -x/y$. See Bergstrom and Goodman, "Private Demands for Public Goods," p. 293. Their data for general municipal expenditures show an income elasticity of 0.64 and price elasticity of -0.23; z therefore would be equal to 2.78, a value that indicates a highly progressive tax burden structure.

83. For the income parameter there are the familiar problems of identifying and measuring permanent rather than current income and the infrequently considered problem of separating the measured income elasticity of government expenditures into its demand and supply components. Even in a completely residential community using only a property tax to finance its services, measurement of the perceived price of those services is complicated if any renters are present. What fraction of the property tax burden on their dwellings do they see themselves bearing, and what fraction do they believe is borne by landlords or some other group? That renters do not behave as if they bore the entire property tax burden themselves is the consistent message of empirical studies of local government spending. George E. Peterson, for example, concludes "that the rental population of a community provides a strong voting impetus for higher public service levels." "Voter Demand for Public School Expenditures," in Jackson, *Public Needs and Private Behavior*, p. 110. Bergstrom and Goodman, like numerous other researchers, included the percent of housing that is owner-occupied as one of their determining variables and found the expected statistically significant negative coefficients, indicating an inverse net relationship between that variable and local government spending. "Private Demands for Public Goods," pp. 288–90.

ticism and an experimental bent appear to be the qualities most needed by designers of optimal local tax systems.

Another potential use of local government income and price elasticities of demand is in the design of matching school grants that would vary the local tax costs of schools inversely with district wealth to achieve greater equality in spending levels among districts. Here again measurement problems loom large. Few existing school grants have a significant price effect at the margin of choice, and when they do it is not clear whose price elasticity of demand really matters. Is it that of the median voter, or the local school bureaucracy, or some other person or group? Whatever the answer to this question, it is clear that price incentives and disincentives are important and that proposals for reforming school finance that generate them, as district power-equalizing grants do, may achieve their goals under some circumstances but fail to do so under others.[84]

THE PUBLICNESS OF LOCAL PUBLIC GOODS. Two intriguing questions about the nature of local government services concern the extent to which private services are capable of generating the same benefits and the extent to which the local public services themselves combine the attributes of private and public goods. Both questions have been receiving increasing attention in recent years.

Shoup, using crime protection as an example of group-consumption goods, stressed the interactions between the use of such private goods as burglar alarms and reliance on the traditional activities of police departments.[85] Similar interactions between the two sectors of the economy have long interested scholars in the field of education. Are society's goals best served by a mixed public-private system or by some other institutional arrangement?[86] School-finance reform-

84. Another use for empirical estimates of the price and income elasticities of demand for school services is to determine whether or not use of the property tax leads to an optimal level of school expenditures. See Robin Barlow, "Efficiency Aspects of Local School Finance," *Journal of Political Economy*, vol. 78 (September-October 1970), pp. 1028–40; Daniel L. Rubinfeld, "Voting in a Local School Election: A Micro Analysis," *Review of Economics and Statistics*, vol. 59 (February 1977), pp. 30–42.

85. Carl S. Shoup, *Public Finance* (Aldine, 1969), p. 68. Shoup defines group-consumption goods as those that can be provided more efficiently to people by the public sector's nonmarketing techniques than by individualistic private markets. Ibid., pp. 66–67.

86. Yoram Barzel, "Private Schools and Public School Finance," *Journal of Political Economy*, vol. 81 (January-February 1973), pp. 174–86; Joseph E. Stiglitz, "The Demand for Education in Public and Private School Systems," *Journal of Public Economics*, vol. 3 (November 1974), pp. 349–85.

ers must pay close attention to the impact their proposals may have on incentives to shift students from public to private schools.[87] If, because of unionism and other factors in the public sector, the costs of government programs increase faster than the costs of providing the same services in the private sector, substitutions will occur. Clotfelter has developed a theoretical model of the trade-offs between private and public provision of services and has applied it to an explanation of variations between states in the ratio of public police employees to private protective employees in 1970.[88]

The other important question, which is directly relevant to the debate over consolidation or decentralization of local governments, concerns the degree to which local government services may be said to be pure public goods, pure private goods, or something in between. If they are pure public goods, each person in a community enjoys the benefits of the total output, X, that is produced. The addition of more people to the jurisdiction would then reduce per capita costs but not per capita benefits. There would be, in other words, no crowding or congestion effects that reduce the quality of service as it is extended to more recipients. At the other extreme, local government services would be like a pure private good if each household's consumption were not X but X/n, where n is the number of households sharing the service. In this case the quality of service is reduced proportionately as it goes to more people, and no economies of scale exist. Some mixture of these two pure elements, finally, would produce the familiar U-shaped average cost curves for local government programs as the size of the population base increased.[89]

An important empirical question, then, concerns the minimum-cost sizes of community for different local public goods. As both Shoup and Hirsch have emphasized, the answers will depend on

87. Robert P. Inman, "Optimal Fiscal Reform of Metropolitan Schools: Some Simulation Results," *American Economic Review*, vol. 68 (March 1978), pp. 107–22.

88. Charles T. Clotfelter, "Public Services, Private Substitutes, and the Demand for Protection Against Crime," *American Economic Review*, vol. 67 (December 1977), pp. 867–77.

89. Increases from a small population base, in other words, would be expected to reduce per capita costs with little or no change in the quality of output. Beyond some population size, however, increasing congestion would lower the quality of service faster than it lowered per capita costs. See William F. Fox and others, *Economies of Size in Local Government: An Annotated Bibliography*, Rural Development Research Report 9 (U.S. Department of Agriculture, Economic Statistics Cooperative Service, 1979); David Segal, "Are There Returns to Scale in City Size?" *Review of Economics and Statistics*, vol. 58 (August 1976), pp. 339–50; Shoup, *Public Finance*, pp. 80–84, chap. 5.

exactly how the output of a given program is defined,[90] and on how well changes in output are measured.[91] What is striking about empirical studies of economies of scale in the provision of local government services is the consistency with which none have been found in medium-sized or large cities (apart from such obvious exceptions as water supply and sewers and sanitation). This is true whether municipal expenditures are simply related to city size,[92] whether per capita expenditures on services of a given scope and quality are related to population,[93] or whether a special crowding parameter is included among the determinants of per capita expenditures.[94] Indeed, using a crowding parameter, Bergstrom and Goodman found that in a sample of cities with populations between 10,000 and 150,000, police protection, parks and recreation, and current general municipal expenditures (excluding education and welfare) were indistinguishable from pure private goods, as far as the distribution of per capita benefits was concerned.[95] This finding not only weakens the case for any consolidation of metropolitan governments in the provision of the standard housekeeping services,[96] but also strengthens the case for benefits-received, rather than ability-to-pay, financing of those services.

Urban Revenue Systems

Although property taxes still supply the preponderance of own-source revenue for local governments, many cities have become so

90. Shoup, *Public Finance*, pp. 129–33, discusses the cost implications of defining a unit of school services as the amount by which a person is educated or as the amount of opportunity the person is offered to become educated.

91. Werner Z. Hirsch, "Quality of Government Services," in Howard G. Schaller, ed., *Public Expenditure Decisions in the Urban Community* (distributed by Johns Hopkins Press for Resources for the Future, 1963), pp. 163–79; Werner Z. Hirsch, "Expenditure Implications of Metropolitan Growth and Consolidation," *Review of Economics and Statistics*, vol. 41 (May 1959), pp. 232–40.

92. Harvey E. Brazer, *City Expenditures in the United States,* Occasional Paper 66 (New York: National Bureau of Economic Research, 1959).

93. Hirsch, "Expenditure Implications of Metropolitan Growth."

94. Bergstrom and Goodman, "Private Demands for Public Goods"; Borcherding and Deacon, "Demand for the Services of Non-Federal Governments."

95. "Private Demands for Public Goods," pp. 293–94.

96. For an analysis of the effects of size on the responsiveness and efficiency of local governments' provision of both housekeeping and education services in California, see William Niskanen and Mickey Levy, "Cities and Schools: A Case for Community Government in California," Working Paper 14 (Graduate School of Public Policy, University of California—Berkeley, June 1974).

Table 5-4. Sources of Local Government General Revenue, Fiscal 1942, 1952, and 1977

	1942		1952		1977	
Revenue	*Amount (billions of dollars)*	*Percent of total*	*Amount (billions of dollars)*	*Percent of total*	*Amount (billions of dollars)*	*Percent of total*
Own source	5.3	100	11.7	100	102.0	100
Property taxes	4.3	82	8.3	71	60.3	59
Other taxes	0.4	7	1.2	10	14.5	14
Charges and miscellaneous	0.6	11	2.2	19	27.2	27
General	7.0	100	17.0	100	179.0	100
Intergovernmental transfers	1.8	25	5.3	31	76.9	43
Taxes	4.7	67	9.5	56	74.8	42
Charges and miscellaneous	0.6	8	2.2	13	27.2	15

Source: U.S. Census Bureau, *Governmental Finances in the United States, 1942* (GPO, 1945), p. 14; *Census of Governments, 1972*, vol. 6, *Topical Studies*, no. 4: *Historical Statistics on Governmental Finances and Employment* (GPO, 1974), p. 45; and *Governmental Finances in 1976–77*, series GF77, no. 5 (GPO, 1978), p. 19. Figures are rounded.

dependent on federal aid that many experts doubt their ability to free themselves of this dependency or to survive without it. In 1942, property taxes provided 82 percent of local own-source revenues and over 90 percent of tax receipts; by 1977 these figures had dropped significantly, but property taxes still accounted for nearly 60 percent of own-source revenues and over 80 percent of tax receipts (table 5-4). Over the same period, intergovernmental grants increased from 25 percent of total local government revenues to 43 percent. Heavy reliance on outside aid has, in particular, become a distinguishing feature of the nation's largest cities. In fiscal 1977, intergovernmental revenue was $456 per capita in cities with over one million people but only $104 per capita in those with less than fifty thousand people. Outside aid ranged from 75 percent of own-source revenue in the largest cities to 46 percent in some of the smallest, in sharp contrast with the degree of dependency prevailing as recently as 1962 (table 5-5). In 1978 it is estimated that direct federal aid alone provided over 75 percent of own-source general revenue in three of the nation's largest cities (Buffalo, Detroit, and Pittsburgh) and 50–75 percent

Table 5-5. Intergovernmental Aid Per Capita and as a Percent of Own-Source Revenue, by Size of Municipality, 1962 and 1977

Size of population	Total inter-governmental aid per capita, 1976–77 (dollars)	Intergovernmental aid as percent of own-source revenue	
		1962	1977
Less than 50,000	104	21	64
50,000–99,000	105	22	46
100,000–199,000	145	24	54
200,000–299,000	184	24	67
300,000–499,000	196	27	62
500,000–999,000	268	32	74
1,000,000 or more	456	29	75
All municipalities	177	26	66

Source: Census Bureau, *Compendium of City Government Finances in 1962*, series G-CF62, no. 62 (GPO, 1963), p. 7, and *1976–77*, series GF77, no. 4 (GPO, 1979), p. 8.

in twenty-two others.[97] These percentages have been doubling about every five years for the last two decades.

That these trends in intergovernmental aid have added a new dimension to fiscal federalism in the United States is beyond dispute. What is less clear is whether federal aid has created a high-spending environment from which it will be difficult for the nation's cities to escape. Will the federal government be forced to continue its steady infusion of more and more aid, making it the dominant partner in urban public affairs and relegating at least some cities to the frustrating, debilitating status of chronic fiscal dependency? Of central importance to local governments' efforts to help themselves is the quality of their existing revenue systems and the amenability of those systems to improvement. As with all Gaul and the federal grant system, local fiscal reforms seem to be divided into three parts, in this case reflecting the main areas of responsibility of local governments—the standard housekeeping services, education, and welfare.

To find some viable solution amid the growing mass of conflicting opinion as to how these activities should be financed it is essential to establish some rational and consistent guidelines. Since the goals to be achieved are as controversial as the means, however, no single set of guidelines will suffice. It becomes the task of urban fiscal reformers,

97. ACIR, *Countercyclical Aid and Economic Stabilization*, Report A-69 (GPO, 1978), pp. 22–23.

therefore, to begin with some general theoretical model of what a superior local revenue system would be like, evaluate existing systems in that light, and then propose appropriate changes. The major alternatives that appear to exist for this purpose—naturally, three in number—include the benefits-received and the ability-to-pay models that have long been familiar to fiscal economists. Highly idealistic and philosophic in nature, they are beautifully appealing theories in search of a pragmatic solution. The third model, in contrast, resembles more a set of ad hoc and unintegrated solutions in search of a theory. The solutions all seek to curb or control governmental activities in various ways, indicating that they share the common belief that governments, left to their own unregulated devices, will not act to maximize the general welfare. Because of this unanimity of purpose they are called the restraining-rules-and-process model.

The Benefits-Received Model

The goal of benefits-received financing is to have taxes play the same role in the public sector as prices play in the private. For the last unit of each local government service received, each person would be required to pay a tax that just equaled the utility, or benefit, that he received from the unit. This nice balancing of marginal benefits and costs is equitable in the sense that no one pays less than he would willingly contribute, and no one is coerced into paying more. The system's efficiency derives from the expectation that paying for what they receive will lead people to direct the allocation of society's scarce resources to their highest and best uses. Specifically, voters will support increases in government spending as long as the benefit of any further output exceeds the tax they have to pay for it and will demand reductions when taxes exceed benefits. Learning in this way what people are really willing to pay for different local services, governments would choose to provide the optimal amount of each. Everyone would agree on an efficient allocation of resources, and urban fiscal systems would live happily ever after.

There is no denying either the long-standing logic of benefits-received financing[98] or its current lack of political appeal. Tax-reform plans for any level of government are invariably formulated on ability-

98. Musgrave, *Theory of Public Finance,* chap. 4.

to-pay principles, and financing systems are usually criticized from the same point of view.[99] Yet there clearly is a pervasive and persistent air of fiscal malaise in the nation. Does its source lie simply in the inadequacies of the specific plans and programs that have been proposed for local governments, or does it reflect something much more fundamental? It is certainly possible that the ability-to-pay model has been overused and that, as Richard Bird put it, the time is ripe for a new look at an old idea.[100]

One of the major difficulties with benefits-received financing of local government services that critics typically stress is its supposition that there is a just distribution of income and wealth in the society. In such a world no taxpayer would be called on to make any undue sacrifices nor would high-priority public needs go unfulfilled. In a less perfect world, but one in which there was a broad national consensus on what constitutes an equitable distribution of income, the federal government could achieve such a distribution with the use of tax-transfer programs, leaving state and local governments free to adopt benefit financing for all of their operations. Since such consensus seems unlikely, the redistribution functions of government might be decentralized so that people with similar tastes could satisfy them by living in the same political jurisdiction and voting into being the appropriate redistribution policies. Thus benefit and ability taxation would compete as goals of state and local revenue systems, and benefits-received financing could, in theory at least, become a viable model for local revenue systems.

Applying this model to the design of general tax instruments is another problem, however. Pursuit of the optimal goal of getting people to reveal their true preferences for public goods is likely to lead to much frustration.[101] Making local tax burdens depend on each person's declared willingness to contribute to local government does indeed seem a fine way to create widespread failures of will and to maximize incentives for the self-interested to try to become free riders. These difficulties could possibly be obviated, however, by devising institutional and other choice mechanisms to induce people to

99. Inman and Rubinfeld, for example, use only the ability-to-pay model of local finance in their "Judicial Pursuit of Local Fiscal Equity."

100. Richard M. Bird, *Charging for Public Services: A New Look at an Old Idea,* Canadian Tax Papers 59 (Toronto: Canadian Tax Foundation, 1976).

101. Randall Bartlett, *Economic Foundations of Political Power* (Free Press, 1973), p. 84.

reveal their true preferences for public goods. Though the theoretical literature on this topic is considerable,[102] no imminent implementation seems likely. Nevertheless, a pragmatic solution to the problems of local financing is well worth study and debate. The search for objectively measurable tax bases that would serve as reasonable proxies for the unobservable benefits people receive from local government services seems particularly worthwhile because the problems of designing and implementing an ability-to-pay model are, if anything, even more intractable.

Functional Reassignments

The benefits-received model has both a geographical and an individual taxpayer dimension. The former has to do with the *right* to tax and establishes the basic jurisdictional rule that taxing and benefit areas should be coterminous. In the urban economy this means that areawide programs, such as pollution control and intercommunity transportation, should be administered and financed by areawide units of government. Public services whose benefits are highly localized, in contrast, can equitably be assigned to small towns and even to neighborhoods within large cities.

The benefit principle has long provided a strong argument for moving at least the financing, and possibly also the operation, of elementary and secondary schools and all welfare programs up from the local to the state and federal levels of government. For education this proposition is based on the idea that the public benefits that better educated people contribute to society are broadly disseminated throughout the country by highly mobile households. An alternative rationale, which favors both local operation and financing of public schools on a private benefit basis, is that children have a right to a basic minimum of educational services. Any major shift of local school financing to tuition or user charges would, of course, increase

102. In addition to works cited in Deacon, "Private Choice and Collective Outcomes," pp. 372–73, see David F. Bradford and Gregory G. Hildebrandt, "Observable Preferences for Public Goods," *Journal of Public Economics*, vol. 8 (October 1977), pp. 111–31; Jerry Green and Jean-Jacques Laffont, "On the Revelation of Preferences for Public Goods," ibid., vol. 8 (August 1977), pp. 79–93; Theodore Groves and Martin Loeb, "Incentives and Public Inputs," ibid., vol. 4 (August 1975), pp. 211–26; Mordecai Kurz, "Experimental Approach to the Determination of the Demand for Public Goods," ibid., vol. 3 (November 1974), pp. 329–48; Dennis C. Mueller, "Voting by Veto," ibid., vol. 10 (August 1978), pp. 57–75.

the responsibility of higher levels of government for income support payments to low-income families. If the poverty-line budget for a family with two children were $7,000 a year and schools cost local taxpayers $1,000 per pupil per year, a shift of schooling costs from the local property tax to parents could raise poverty-line budgets by as much as $2,000 a year for a family of four.[103] Either rationale for a public interest in schools would justify removal of their financing from the general taxing powers of local governments. If income support responsibilities were also transferred to higher levels of government, local governments would confine their activities to the provision of the basic collective services required by urban living. The question would then concern the *amounts* of taxes that each family should pay to finance these public housekeeping services. This is the individual taxpayer dimension of the benefits-received model.

User Charges

The most direct and efficient way to implement the benefit principle would be to price, via user charges and fees, all local government services that flow to clearly identifiable consumers and not to other people. Doing this would narrow the bounds of the old political game of getting someone else to pay for one's own special benefits. If the charges were well designed and kept in line with changing economic circumstances such as inflation, they would provide local governments with a clear indication of how to allocate their resources among the programs in question. Such public pricing has the advantage over taxation of reducing the risks that local programs are either oversupported, because beneficiaries perceive their tax costs to be well below the resource costs of providing them, or undersupported, because of the opposition of nonbeneficiaries to high local taxes. In some cases, however, user charges are relatively inefficient fiscal devices.[104]

There is, of course, the nagging concern that wider use of public pricing would unduly burden low-income consumers of local government services. Unfortunately, no clear answer is possible here

103. The increase would be less if lower property taxes reduced consumer good prices so that the basic nonschool poverty-line budget fell below $7,000.

104. Bird, *Charging for Public Services;* Selma Mushkin, ed., *Public Prices for Public Products* (Washington: Urban Institute, 1972); Martin O. Stern, "User Charges as a Planning Tool" (McLean, Va.: International Research and Technology Corp., October 17, 1975).

because there is no precise definition of the family income levels required to support some "health and decency" standard of living. Nevertheless, both state and federal governments could create a fiscal environment more conducive to the use of pricing by those local governments that found the option attractive. In the allocation formulas for shared revenue, measures of tax effort could be replaced by revenue measures that included user charges and fees. Federal income tax deductibility rules could be tightened to remove all local taxes from the category of allowable personal deductions.[105] Federal or state transfer payments related to income could compensate for area differences in the cost of living, including the cost of buying local public goods. Or yet another federal subsidy, local public service stamps, could be added to the arsenal of in-kind welfare programs.

No one regards user charges as the urban financing panacea.[106] They can, however, give important assistance to hard-pressed local governments and in general offer one route toward a more efficient and equitable revenue system.

Earmarking

Restriction of the use of the revenue from a particular tax to the financing of a particular local government program is another well-known avenue to a benefits-received revenue system. Whether such earmarking of funds increases efficiency by tying benefits to costs or reduces it by interfering with normal budgetary procedures has been vigorously debated for some time.[107] The general conditions under which earmarking is likely to work well are not in serious dispute. They occur when consumer tastes for government services are diverse and when there is good reason to believe that the burdens of the earmarked tax are distributed among families in close relation to benefits enjoyed from the financed government activities. Earmarking is then

105. The role of intergovernmental tax deductibility is discussed in George F. Break, "Tax Principles in a Federal System," in Henry J. Aaron and Michael J. Boskin, eds., *The Economics of Taxation* (Brookings Institution, 1980).

106. Charles J. Goetz, "The Revenue Potential of User-Related Charges in State and Local Governments," in Richard A. Musgrave, ed., *Broad-Based Taxes: New Options and Sources* (Johns Hopkins University Press, 1973), pp. 113–29.

107. Bird, *Charging for Public Services*, chap. 3. The theoretical case for earmarking is presented in James M. Buchanan, "The Economics of Earmarked Taxes," *Journal of Political Economy*, vol. 71 (October 1963), pp. 457–69; Charles Goetz, "Earmarked Taxes and Majority Rule Budgetary Processes," *American Economic Review*, vol. 58 (March 1968), pp. 128–36.

likely to be superior to general fund financing.[108] Which taxes satisfy this requirement is the critical question to be answered before any wide application of the benefit principle to urban revenue systems can be made.

Benefit Taxes for Intermediate Services to Business

In any search for a good local benefit tax four candidates, depending on the kind of government service to be financed, deserve consideration. Three would finance final services for consumers. The fourth, for intermediate services rendered to business enterprises, may be regarded as the dark horse of the group.[109] It is a value-added tax (VAT) to finance local government services to business. Its rationale for this purpose rests on the assumption that the benefits of local collective housekeeping services are closely related to the amount of private productive activity carried out in the taxing jurisdiction. Though that relationship can never be exactly quantified, it is a plausible assumption on which to base local business taxation, and particularly so when compared to the rationales underlying other kinds of business tax base. Gross receipts from sales are unsatisfactory because they include varying amounts of economic activity carried on outside the jurisdiction, depending on the type of business. Business profits are unsatisfactory because unprofitable firms benefit from local public services as much as do profitable firms. Neither business property nor payroll alone is satisfactory because there is no evidence that public service benefits are closely related to only one of those two factors of production. The virtue of the value-added tax is that it treats all factors of production equally.

If the notion of a local business VAT is appealing,[110] the next question concerns its administrative feasibility. Piggybacking a local VAT

108. When public opposition to higher general fund tax rates is strong, earmarking is a means of generating support for higher taxes that finance programs whose benefits are especially sought.

109. See, however, Harvey E. Brazer, "The Value of Industrial Property as a Subject of Taxation," *Canadian Public Administration,* vol. 4 (June 1961), pp. 146–47; George F. Break, *Agenda for Local Tax Reform* (Institute of Governmental Studies, University of California—Berkeley, 1970), chap. 5.

110. It must be admitted that there is a strongly held popular belief that it is unfair to tax unprofitable, or low-profit, business for local intermediate services. Collective good inputs, in other words, are placed in a different category from private good inputs. In essence, this means choosing the ability-to-pay financing model over the benefits-received one.

on the tax bases used by higher levels of government is, unfortunately, not now a widely available option. No federal VAT exists,[111] and only in Michigan is there a state VAT base that could be used.[112] A do-it-yourself approach to local value-added taxation, however, is by no means outside the realm of possibility. If a VAT is to be inaugurated directly, the main problems will be in the measurement of local business profits, particularly those of large enterprises operating in different parts of the country. Some allocation formula similar to those used for the interstate division of multistate corporate profits would be needed.

A local business VAT could also be imposed indirectly simply by adding a payroll tax to existing business property taxes and setting the rates of both taxes so as to approximate the burdens of a single-rate VAT. The goal would be to add to existing property taxes (which impose an implicit tax burden on business profits) a tax on payrolls set at an equivalent rate and to keep business tax revenues constant in the process. Suppose, for example, that the effective property tax rate is 2 percent of full market value, the average profits rate is 10 percent, and wages are two-thirds of total value added. The implicit tax rate on business profits, therefore, is 20 percent on the average. Since adding payrolls will double the available business tax base, the implicit VAT rate sought is 6.67 percent, one-third of the former

111. But see Felix Kessler, "Controversial Levy: Experience with VAT in Europe Leads Some to Propose It for U.S.," *Wall Street Journal*, February 2, 1979, and "The Renewed Appeal of VAT," *Business Week*, February 12, 1979, pp. 63–64. On the VAT generally see Shoup, *Public Finance*, chap. 9; Clara K. Sullivan, *The Tax on Value Added* (Columbia University Press, 1965); Charles E. McLure, Jr., "Economic Effects of Taxing Value Added," in Musgrave, *Broad-Based Taxes*, pp. 155–204. For debates on the desirability of enacting a federal VAT and on its merits compared to those of a federal retail sales tax see Dan Throop Smith, "Value-Added Tax: The Case For," *Harvard Business Review*, vol. 48 (November-December 1970), pp. 77–85, and Stanley S. Surrey, "Value Added Tax: The Case Against," ibid., pp. 86–94; John F. Due, "The Case for the Use of the Retail Form of Sales Tax in Preference to the Value-Added Tax," in Musgrave, *Broad-Based Taxes*, pp. 205–13, and Carl S. Shoup, "Factors Bearing on an Assumed Choice Between a Federal Retail-Sales Tax and a Federal Value-Added Tax," in ibid., pp. 215–26.

112. See Sydney D. Goodman, "Administrative Aspects of Michigan's Single Business Tax," John E. Gessert, "The Michigan Single Business Tax—The Business View," and Harvey E. Brazer, "Michigan's Single Business Tax—Theory and Background," in NTA-TIA, *Proceedings, 1976*, pp. 55–59, 60–62, 62–69; ACIR, *The Michigan Single Business Tax: A Different Approach to State Business Taxation*, Report M-114 (GPO, 1978).

implicit profits tax rate. This can be achieved by taxing payrolls at 6.67 percent and by reducing the effective property tax rate from 2 percent to 0.67 percent.[113] Thus the time path of local business tax revenues would not change until the tax adjustments caused some alteration in either component of the new base.

There would, of course, be many details to be settled in drawing up any local VAT law. Before those problems need be faced, however, both the basic philosophy of the tax and the general way in which its base could be measured by a local government acting on its own must be understood. Adding a payroll tax to an existing business property tax in the ways just described would produce a VAT with an implicit, variable rate on profits.[114] Clearly, there are arbitrary elements in such a levy. Because of the need to allocate multijurisdictional profits, however, there are also arbitrary elements in any directly imposed VAT. The policy question, then, is how the two approaches to the enactment of a local VAT compare in this and in all other respects.

If a VAT is a good benefit levy for the financing of intermediate local government services to business, including rental residential enterprises, it should serve equally well for the same services rendered to owner-occupied homes. Owner-occupants, in other words, can be regarded as being in the business of renting homes to themselves. Since payrolls are typically a very small part of the value added in that sector, residential property taxes could simply be allowed to stand (with the rate adjusted to equal the altered effective rate on other business property);[115] their equity would be judged on a benefit

113. If e is the effective property tax rate, B is the market value of business property, r is the average rate of return on business property, i is the implicit property tax rate on profits, t is the value-added tax rate, and W is wages or krB, where k is the ratio of wages to profits, then $i = eB/rB = e/r$. An equal-revenue shift from the property tax to a VAT requires that $tW + trB = eB$ or $trB(k + 1) = eB$, since $W = krB$, whence $t = e/r(k+1)$. When $e = 0.02$, $r = 0.10$, and $k = 2.0$, the required VAT rate is $t = 0.02/0.3 = 0.067$, and the post-shift effective property tax rate is $e' = 0.067 \times 0.1 = 0.0067$.

114. This occurs because for various reasons rates of return on taxable property differ across industries and among individual firms. Whether the levy would be an income- or consumption-type VAT is debatable, depending on whether property tax burdens show a closer relation to gross profits net of depreciation or to gross profits net of capital expenditures.

115. Expanding the VAT plan to cover owner-occupied homes would, of course, change the calculation of the equal-yield VAT rate discussed above.

rather than an ability basis, however. Thus the regressivity or progressivity of the property tax burden in relation to homeowner and renter incomes would become an irrelevant policy issue. Judged on a benefit basis, equity requires that it be proportional to the benefits received by homeowners from local government housekeeping services.

Benefit Taxes for Final Services to Consumers

If the financing of welfare programs were completely shifted to state and federal governments, and if payment for schools were split between higher level governments and parents, as the benefit principle suggests they should be, there would be no further problems in the design of benefits-received local tax systems. Until that shift occurs, however, the question to be answered is which, if any, local taxes can reasonably be regarded as benefit levies for the financing of the local share of school and welfare program costs. The three major candidates here—income, retail sales, and residential property taxes—are all well-established sources of local revenue. The public benefits of schools and welfare, however, all fall in the intangible quality-of-life category, and hence no clear-cut answer to the question posed is to be expected. Empirical evidence concerning the closeness of the relationship between the demand for local school and welfare expenditures and household incomes, consumption, and residential wealth might help, but it is difficult to obtain because of the high correlation among the three alternative tax bases. For researchers this is a highly frustrating state of affairs. For policymakers, however, it greatly simplifies matters by suggesting that, judged by the closeness of their relation to benefits received, there is little reason to prefer any one tax base to either of the other two. Choices may then be made on the basis of other considerations.

One option is to reject benefit taxation for final local government services to consumers and go to an ability-to-pay model. If the benefit approach is chosen, the field can quickly be reduced to two candidates. Personal spending on private consumer goods and services may well be more closely related to demand for public consumer services than either personal income or residential property. Because of shopper mobility in large urban areas, however, a local retail sales tax is not a feasible means by which one community can charge its own residents for the benefits of the services it provides to them.[116] Moreover, a retail sales tax is not a flexible source of local revenue since sales tax rates in any one urban community cannot be allowed to get very far out of line with those in other communities without generating adverse economic effects.

What remains, then, is a difficult choice between a residential property and a personal income tax. A major weakness of the property tax is that for renters it is an indirect tax that will perform its benefit role well only if its burdens are fully and convincingly shifted from landlords to tenants. Few fiscal experts believe that to be the case, and apparently few tenants act as if they believed it either. A local personal income tax would have the great advantage of placing its burdens as directly on renters as on owner-occupants, and should, for that reason alone, rank higher on both equity and efficiency grounds.

The property tax, however, does have the important advantage of having a firmly established position both as the principal source of tax revenue for most local governments and as a recognized benefits-received levy.[117] A well-established position has obvious attractions, but those can be overcome if the replacement tax promises gains in efficiency and equity that clearly outweigh the transitional costs. Moreover, many of the benefit qualities attributed to the property tax apply equally well to a local personal income tax. The use of either levy to finance local public services that would make the community in question more attractive, relative to its neighbors, would increase property values in the taxing community. In that sense either is a benefit levy and to the same degree.

116. Of course, if the federal government were ever to adopt a personal spendings tax, a piggybacking arrangement with it, similar to the one now available for the federal individual income tax, would permit local government use of that base at low administrative and compliance costs as either a benefit or an ability tax. For a discussion of the issues involved in either adding a personal expenditure tax to the federal tax system or in adopting it as a replacement for present federal income taxes, see Joseph A. Pechman, ed., *What Should Be Taxed: Income or Expenditure?* (Brookings Institution, 1980).

117. For an analysis of the conditions under which the property tax would serve as a true benefit levy see Bruce W. Hamilton, "Property Taxes and the Tiebout Hypothesis: Some Empirical Evidence," in Mills and Oates, *Fiscal Zoning*, pp. 13–29; Bruce W. Hamilton, "Capitalization of Intrajurisdictional Differences in Local Tax Prices," *American Economic Review*, vol. 66 (December 1976), pp. 743–53.

Another desirable attribute of a good benefit levy would be a clear distinction between it and any related ability-to-pay tax. Here again the choice is difficult. A benefit income tax should, in the absence of convincing evidence of a different vertical distribution of public benefits, be levied at a single rate on the total net income of all taxpayers. Strong pressures would inevitably arise, however, to convert any such levy into a progressive tax of the usual kind, in which case there would be no way of saying whether the tax was playing a benefits-received or an ability-to-pay role. Similar problems arise in the case of the residential property tax. Whether a well-administered tax that imposed its burdens at the same rate on all dwelling units should be regarded as a good benefit levy is debatable. On the one hand, there is no a priori reason to expect a close relation between consumer tastes for housing and for school or welfare services. On the other hand, housing expenditures may in fact be a reasonably good proxy for a family's permanent income status, and permanent income may be an important determinant of family demands for local education and redistributive benefits. The choice is further complicated by the widespread existence of circuit breakers and other structural adjustments designed to reduce property tax burdens on the lowest income groups. These are ability-to-pay tax reliefs with no justification under a benefit rationale.[118]

Conclusion

The benefit principle has important attractions as a guide for local revenue reform. It offers a particular kind of equity that is attractive to many, and it promises efficiency gains that its main rival, the ability-to-pay principle, cannot hope to match. Adopting the benefit model as the theoretical foundation of urban revenue systems would involve changes not only in specific revenue sources but also in some comfortably entrenched public attitudes.

Two widely held views are that local tax systems are regressive in the incidence of their burdens on persons and inequitable when their

118. In an ability-to-pay model, property tax circuit breakers are a way of providing relief from excessive tax burdens. In a benefits-received context, however, they provide a straight income supplement whose amount is not closely related to any widely accepted measure of family need. Remission of a benefit tax, in other words, does not permit the recipient to purchase more of some merit good at a reduced price, as does the standard kind of price subsidy.

burdens fall on small businesses or on unprofitable enterprises. These beliefs, which are based on the ability principle, have no relevance to the evaluation of benefit principle revenue systems. What matters there is the relation of tax burdens to benefits received, which is a very different question. Benefit taxes, in other words, should be levied with an even hand on all beneficiaries. One practical implication, which will not be without interest to local governments, is that there would be no reason to exempt nonprofit enterprises from a local tax system based on benefit principles.

The revenue redesigning that is suggested by the benefit model has four main features: the shift of all financing responsibility for welfare to state and federal governments and the split of school financing between those governments and parents, a restructuring of local government units to improve the geographical matching of program benefits and tax burdens, an expanded use of public pricing for non-collective local government services and some school services, and the shift of general fund financing to a local value-added tax (this shift would relate the costs of intermediate services to business enterprises, broadly defined to include home owner-occupants, to the amount of productive activity carried out in the taxing jurisdiction). Given the slow pace at which the financing of schools and welfare is being shifted to higher levels of government, local revenues for these programs are likely to be needed for some time. The two leading candidates for this role are local personal income and residential property taxes, and the choice between them is a close one. Moreover, their qualifications as benefit levies are open to serious question. It remains to be seen how well they conform to ability-to-pay principles.

The Ability-to-Pay Model

The great popular appeal of ability-based local tax systems derives from the belief that if the government does something, it is for the general good and that all citizens should therefore contribute according to their individual abilities to do so. In more technical terms the proposition is that pure public goods, whose benefits are intangible and enjoyed by all, are best financed by the ability principle. Their financing can be regarded as one of the basic responsibilities of citizenship and should not depend on individual likes or dislikes. Someone who placed no value on education, for example, should not on that account be relieved of any responsibility to help pay for public schools.

Acceptance of such logic is likely to make the opposing benefit principle of taxation highly unattractive to many. Yet the benefit concept can still play an important role in the financing of pure public goods by serving as a constraint on the progressivity of the vertical distribution of ability-based tax burdens. If these depart too sharply from the probable vertical distribution of the perceived benefits of pure public goods, opposition to high taxes may keep the level of these services too low.

It seems clear that the ability principle may be regarded as the main model for the financing of pure public goods. Many government services, however, have attributes of both private and public goods, and the applicability of the ability model to these impure public goods, which are especially important at the local level of government, is more open to debate.

Like its major competitor, the ability-to-pay model has two serious drawbacks, but of a quite different nature. One is a problem of definition, the other of effects. While the idea of benefits received from government services is relatively clear and unambiguous, the concept of ability to pay is not. There is no objective way either to measure individual abilities or to determine how tax burdens should vary among people with different abilities, however measured.[119] Of course, absolute precision is not required, as the widespread use of ability tax systems eloquently testifies. As the level of tax burdens rises, however, rough approximations become less and less satisfac-

119. The long-continued debate over the nature and merits of the comprehensive income tax base illustrates the difficulties involved in defining the ideal ability measure. See, for example, Boris I. Bittker, Charles O. Galvin, Richard A. Musgrave, and Joseph A. Pechman, *A Comprehensive Income Tax Base? A Debate* (Branford, Conn.: Federal Tax Press, 1968); Joseph A. Pechman, ed., *Comprehensive Income Taxation* (Brookings Institution, 1977). In addition, a new debate may be developing over the relative merits of personal consumption expenditures and personal income as ability measures. See Pechman, *What Should Be Taxed?* U.S. Treasury Department, *Blueprints for Basic Tax Reform* (GPO, 1977); Institute for Fiscal Studies, *The Structure and Reform of Direct Taxation,* Report of a Committee Chaired by Professor J. E. Meade (London: Allen and Unwin, 1978); Sven-Olof Lodin, *Progressive Expenditure Tax—An Alternative?* Report of the 1972 Government Commission on Taxation (Stockholm: LiberFörlag, 1978). On the difficulties involved in determining the best allocation of tax burdens among people with differing abilities to pay see Walter J. Blum and Harry Kalven, Jr., *The Uneasy Case for Progressive Taxation* (University of Chicago Press, 1953).

tory. Worse still, high tax rates induce widespread shifting of activities from those that produce measurable ability-to-pay attributes to those that do not.[120] If the resulting erosion of the tax base becomes severe enough, either government spending must be cut, or new sources of revenue found, or existing tax rates reduced in the hope that this will induce such an increase in the size of the tax base that revenues will not fall significantly.[121]

Serious conceptual difficulties, then, are an inherent quality of the ability principle of taxation. Their presence greatly strengthens the case for diversification both in the basic theoretical models by which revenue systems are designed and in the specific levies chosen to implement the ability model itself.

The second major problem with ability taxation has to do with incentives and general economic efficiency. Unlike the benefit principle, which is capable of achieving equity and efficiency goals simultaneously, the ability principle requires some difficult trade-offs between the two.[122] Tax burdens that are well above perceived benefit levels can waste resources by shifting taxpayers' energies to tax avoidance and evasion and slow the rate of progress by generating disincentives to work, to save, or to invest. Even the equity goal itself will be missed if opposition to high tax burdens keeps government spending below levels that a benefit-oriented tax system would support. This can hap-

120. High tax rates stimulate the growth of "the underground economy" where transactions are made on a nonmonetary basis or for hard-to-trace cash transfers. See Peter M. Gutmann, "Off the Books," *Across the Board,* vol. 15 (August 1978), pp. 8–15; Irwin Ross, "Why the Underground Economy Is Booming," *Fortune,* October 1978, pp. 92–98.

121. That tax rates can be pushed so high that revenues are thereby reduced, rather than increased, has long been recognized in public finance literature. Interest in the stimulating powers of tax cuts has been rekindled by Arthur B. Laffer, and by the professional debate that his "Laffer curve" has precipitated. See Alfred L. Malabre, Jr., *Wall Street Journal,* December 1, 1978, and Letters to the Editor, ibid., December 21, 1978. For a comprehensive sampling of professional opinion on these issues see *Tax Reductions—Economists' Comments on H.R. 8333 and S. 1860 (The Kemp-Roth Bills) Bills to Provide for Permanent Tax Rate Reductions for Individuals and Businesses,* House Committee on Ways and Means, Committee Print, 95 Cong. 2 sess. (GPO, 1978); and *Leading Economists' Views of Kemp-Roth,* House Committee on the Budget, Committee Print, 95 Cong. 2 sess. (GPO, 1978); also published for the Senate Committee on the Budget (GPO, 1978).

122. Arthur M. Okun, *Equality and Efficiency: The Big Tradeoff* (Brookings Institution, 1975), and "Further Thoughts on Equality and Efficiency," in Colin D. Campbell, ed., *Income Redistribution* (Washington: American Enterprise Institute for Public Policy Research, 1977) (Brookings Reprint 325).

pen because the distribution of government expenditure benefits is more progressively distributed by income group than are tax burdens,[123] though the differences are less at the state and local than at the federal level. Suppose, however, that a 10 percent increase in all state and local programs whose benefits can be allocated to specific income groups is financed by a tax measure that raises state and local tax burdens by the same proportion in each income class. Even this change, which on its face is proportional, would have a distinctly progressive incidence: in 1968, it would have raised the net fiscal benefits of the lowest income groups by more than 1 percent of total family income while reducing them at the top by about 0.5 percent.[124]

In addition to these two inherent problems of the ability tax model, local governments face some special dilemmas that arise from the openness of the urban economic environment. Jurisdictions imposing relatively high onerous tax burdens—those not matched by correspondingly high local benefits—will have to pay more to attract mobile workers and capital unless land prices within their boundaries adjust downward sufficiently to counteract their relative fiscal disadvantages. Fear of generating such adverse economic effects, in turn, may either keep local spending levels too low or overstimulate the use of intergovernmental grants so that local fiscal autonomy is sacrificed. Alternatively, hidden concessions and favors may convert what appears to be an ability tax system into one that is not close to any normative model of local finance.

Need for Reform

Public perceptions both of the need for local revenue reform and of the direction it should take are heavily dependent on which reference model is used to evaluate existing revenue laws. A local revenue system that scores well under the ability test will generally do badly under the benefit test, and vice versa. A system that meets neither

123. "Progressive" here refers to any distribution of fiscal benefits or burdens that systematically favors lower, relative to higher, income groups. The ratio of government benefits to family incomes is highest at the lowest levels of income and falls off steeply as income rises. Strictly speaking, this indicates a regressive distribution of benefits, but such terminology is likely to be confusing to many.

124. Musgrave and Musgrave, *Public Finance in Theory and Practice*, pp. 389–401; derived from lines 16 and 15 in tables 16-1 and 16-3, respectively. For a similar calculation for the federal government see Gerard M. Brannon, "Tax Reform: Justice, Efficiency and Politics," *Tax Notes*, vol. 5 (November 7, 1977), p. 6.

test should be changed, but the kinds of reforms called for by the two models are quite different.

A good illustration of the kinds of problems involved here is provided by Inman and Rubinfeld's analysis of the distribution of fiscal burdens and benefits, by family income group, in typical U.S. metropolitan areas.[125] Two performance parameters are used to judge the equity of local fiscal systems. One is the income elasticity of local government expenditures which, if spending differences are a good proxy for differences in quality of service, summarizes the vertical distribution of public good benefits in urban economies. The other is the income elasticity of after-tax family income which measures the progressiveness of local tax systems. This "residual income" measure of tax progression takes values of less than unity for progressive taxes, of greater than unity for regressive levies, and of one for a proportional tax.[126] Local fiscal systems judged by ability to pay should have an expenditure elasticity of either zero (indicating that the flow of service benefits is unrelated to recipients' incomes) or one in the negative range (indicating that the distribution of services favors the poor). The elasticity of residual income should be unity or less. Point *A* in figure 5-2 indicates a fiscal system with a neutral distribution of benefits and a proportional tax structure. Communities at *A* or in the quadrant to the southwest of *A* would be rated high by the ability model.

A good benefit fiscal system, on the other hand, would show precisely the opposite range for the two performance parameters. Taxes that are proportional to benefits received will typically be regressive in relation to income, and the elasticity of residual income therefore should show values greater than unity. Expenditures on public goods, like those on private goods, may be expected to increase, on the average, with family incomes, thus setting the range of targets for the expenditure elasticity parameter in a benefit system somewhere above zero. The estimated values that would prevail if local government services in metropolitan areas were allocated to consumers by private market mechanisms are shown by the line *BR* in figure 5-2.

The two opposing reference points, *A* and *BR*, by which the equity performance of local governments can be evaluated lie on either side

125. "Judicial Pursuit of Local Fiscal Equity."
126. Alternative measures of tax progression are discussed in Musgrave and Musgrave, *Public Finance in Theory and Practice*, pp. 285–87.

Figure 5-2. Measures of Fiscal Equity in U.S. Metropolitan Areas

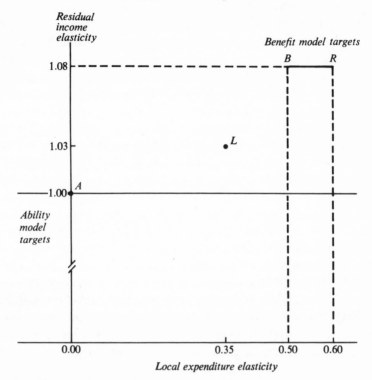

Source: Robert P. Inman and Daniel L. Rubinfeld, "The Judicial Pursuit of Local Fiscal Equity," *Harvard Law Review*, vol. 92 (June 1979), pp. 1662–1750.

of point *L,* which represents the elasticities that Inman and Rubinfeld found for the typical metropolitan area. Clearly, local fiscal systems do not meet either test of fiscal equity. Some kind of reform program is desirable, but proponents of the ability model would support measures that move the point *L* southwestward toward *A,* while supporters of the benefit model would wish to move *L* northeastward toward *BR.* To evaluate reform measures intelligently, in short, the public must first decide whether it prefers an ability-to-pay or a benefits-received model.

Property Tax Reform

Local tax systems based on the ability-to-pay model have been the dominant goal of fiscal reformers for some time. The two major policy packages that compete for public attention are property tax reform and increased use of local income taxes.

Much has been written about various ways and means of improving the local property tax.[127] A good deal less has been said, however, about whether the tax is a suitable source of local government revenues, and if so, under what circumstances. The crux of the matter is the degree of accuracy that can be achieved in the assessment of property for tax purposes. Under a general tax, properties should all be assessed at full market value, or at some specified ratio to full value. Given the distinctive characteristics of many kinds of property, the thinness of many real estate markets, and the uncertain profit prospects of long-lived assets, highly precise assessed values are not to be expected. Rather, the goal should be a range of potential sales prices and not one single value. Considerable disagreement, therefore, will always surround the assignment of market values to seldom-sold properties with few close substitutes. Imperfect interpersonal equity, in short, is the hallmark of any general property tax, and the basic question is how much imperfection is acceptable.[128]

In the first of three distinct phases in the development of local property taxes, effective rates are low and administrative inequities numerous,[129] but neither shortcoming is large enough to matter much. The second phase begins when rising tax rates cross the threshold at which most taxpayers perceive their burdens as something to be actively concerned about. Public interest in assessment practices at that point increases, and as a result specific improvements are likely to be made.[130] The third phase, though only a distant threat for many communities, begins whenever effective tax rates rise to the point where

127. See, for example, Dick Netzer, *Economics of the Property Tax* (Brookings Institution, 1966); George E. Peterson, ed., *Property Tax Reform* (Washington: Urban Institute, 1973); ACIR, *The Role of the States in Strengthening the Property Tax,* Report A-17 (GPO, 1963).

128. For an analysis of urban property markets see Ralph Turvey, *The Economics of Real Property: An Analysis of Property Values and Patterns of Use* (London: Allen and Unwin, 1957), pp. 8–54.

129. Measures of both horizontal and vertical administrative inequities are developed and tested empirically for the Portland metropolitan area by Morton Paglin and Michael Fogarty, "Equity and the Property Tax: A New Conceptual Focus," *National Tax Journal,* vol. 25 (December 1972), pp. 557–65.

130. Evidence of this kind of development is provided by John H. Bowman and John L. Mikesell, "Uniform Assessment of Property: Returns from Institutional Remedies," *National Tax Journal,* vol. 31 (June 1978), pp. 137–52. However, there is also evidence that inflation tends to impede progress toward improved assessments. Census Bureau measures, for example, show significant improvements in administrative equity between 1956 and 1966, but a reversal apparently occurred between 1966 and 1971 and accelerated in the next five-year period. Allen D. Manvel, "Slippage in Assessment Uniformity," *Tax Notes,* vol. 8 (January 8, 1979), pp. 44–45.

most people regard the property tax as unacceptably inequitable even under the best-attainable assessment practices. Whether the passage of Proposition 13 in California signals such a situation there is one of the many mysteries surrounding that tax revolt.

It is to communities in the second phase that reform of property valuation offers the greatest potential gains.[131] That the benefits are important is clearly indicated by the disparities in assessment ratios found by researchers both across different kinds of property and among owners of the same kind of property, notably homes, with different market values.[132] Achieving greater horizontal equity, however, involves substantial costs. Apart from the time and effort required to develop, sell, and implement any fiscal reform, a move toward uniform assessment ratios would generate large windfall gains and losses as property values reacted to changed tax burdens.[133] The political costs of such developments could be an important barrier to improvements in assessment practice, as the ACIR has stressed.[134] Certainly their incidence and importance should be part of any benefit-cost analysis made of proposed reforms.

Apart from these basic administrative improvements, three kinds of structural change in the property tax are of continuing policy importance.

131. Bowman and Mikesell, "Uniform Assessment"; Vincent J. Geraci, "Measuring the Benefits from Property Tax Assessment Reform," *National Tax Journal*, vol. 30 (June 1977), pp. 195–205; Paul V. Corusy, "Improving Assessment Performance: Key Findings of Recent Research," in NTA-TIA, *Proceedings, 1976*, pp. 125–29. A more radical change in assessment practice, which has not attracted much popular interest, would be the shift to a self-assessed property tax that would employ the same tax filing and auditing procedures as are now used with the individual income tax. Daniel M. Holland and William M. Vaughn, "An Evaluation of Self-Assessment Under a Property Tax," in Arthur D. Lynn, Jr., ed., *The Property Tax and Its Administration* (University of Wisconsin Press for the Committee on Taxation, Resources and Economic Development, 1969), pp. 79–118; T. R. Swartz and Lawrence C. Marsh, "A Self-Assessed Property Tax Revisited Once Again," in NTA-TIA, *Proceedings, 1977*, pp. 191–99.

132. A pioneering study in this area is Oliver Oldman and Henry Aaron, "Assessment-Sales Ratios Under the Boston Property Tax," *National Tax Journal*, vol. 18 (March 1965), pp. 36–49.

133. Daniel M. Holland and Oliver Oldman, "Estimating the Impact of Full Value Assessment on Taxes and Value of Real Estate in Boston," in Break, *Metropolitan Financing*, pp. 195–241; Henry J. Aaron, *Who Pays the Property Tax? A New Look* (Brookings Institution, 1975), chap. 4.

134. ACIR, *The Property Tax in a Changing Environment: Selected State Studies*, Information Report M-83 (GPO, 1974), p. 1.

SCOPE OF THE TAX. Should the property tax be levied uniformly on all tangible property, classified by type of property so as to impose differential tax burdens, or confined to site values only?[135] The long debate over classification seems to have entered a phase of strong interest in statutory classifications of property,[136] either as an incentive for open space and farmland preservation[137] or as a means of reducing property tax burdens on residential property.[138] The main problem faced by reformers is that some kinds of property tax classification make sense and some do not. Badly defined departures from uniformity, moreover, are likely to create political pressure for further tax favors, and the process may continue until the tax becomes a complex mixture of differential tax rates or assessment ratios with no economic justification at all.

Some classification proposals are simply an attempt to bring the law into conformity with assessment practice.[139] Others, being justified by the existence of differential rates of return on different kinds of property, are in reality an attempt to create a local income tax by

135. Another controversial issue has centered on the types of tangible property that should be exempt from taxation. Some of the disagreements here arise from the use of different reference models—the benefit model calls for the taxation of all property owners who receive value from local government services, and the ability model calls for the exemption of all property that makes no contribution to personal net wealth positions. See Alfred Balk, "The Extent and Economic Effect of Property Tax Exemptions," Dick Netzer, "Property Tax Exemptions and Their Effects: A Dissenting View," and Ronald B. Welch, "The States' Concern Over Property Tax Exemptions," in NTA-TIA, *Proceedings, 1972,* pp. 263–67, 268–74, and 275–82; John M. Quigley and Roger W. Schmenner, "Property Tax Exemption and Public Policy," *Public Policy,* vol. 23 (Summer 1975), pp. 259–97.

136. A general property tax can, of course, be converted into a classified one simply by systematically assessing different kinds of property at different ratios to true market value. Statutory classification may combine a single tax rate with variable assessment ratios or a single assessment ratio with variable rates.

137. See, for example, Robert E. Coughlin, David Berry, and Thomas Plaut, "Differential Assessment of Real Property as an Incentive to Open Space Preservation and Farmland Retention," *National Tax Journal,* vol. 31 (June 1978), pp. 165–79; Helen F. Ladd, "Tax Policy Considerations Underlying Preferential Tax Treatment of Open Space and Agricultural Land," Discussion Paper D78-20 (Harvard University, Department of City and Regional Planning, September 1978).

138. Jon Sonstelie, "Should Business Pay More Taxes Than Individuals?" *Taxing and Spending,* October-November 1978, pp. 16–19; Sonstelie, "The Classified Property Tax," in *Technical Aspects of the District's Tax System,* Studies and Papers Prepared for the District of Columbia Tax Revision Commission, House Committee on the District of Columbia, 95 Cong. 2 sess. (GPO, 1978), pp. 233–60.

139. Some examples are given in Sonstelie, "Should Business Pay More Taxes?" p. 17.

indirection. A more sophisticated argument for classification, though one of dubious practical significance, is that owners of different kinds of property have varying abilities to shift their burdens to others. This may well be so, but to use classification to achieve a uniform pattern of property tax burdens means that only partial shifting must occur and also that the extent of that shifting must be known within reasonable margins of error.[140] Even if such a procedure could achieve equity with respect to the unshifted parts of the tax, the shifted parts remain a problem. What is gained on the one hand by classification may mostly be lost on the other.[141]

One kind of property tax classification that does make economic sense in an ability model of local finance is the elimination of business property from the base and the restriction of the levy to residential property. As Brazer has forcefully argued, the local taxation of business property, other than land, is justified only to the extent that the tax approximates "a user charge which the firm, if offered the choice between tax-and-service and no-tax-no-service, voluntarily would accept."[142] Ability to pay is a personal attribute, and business property or income, though an obvious component of individual net wealth, is not by itself a good ability-oriented base for taxation at any level of government.[143] It is especially unsuitable at the state or local level

140. Assume that property type A has no power to shift tax burdens placed on it, type B can shift one quarter of its burdens, and type C can shift half of its burdens. A classified property tax that imposes a 1.00 percent statutory rate on A should then impose a rate of 1.33 percent on B and 2.00 percent on C. If property type D can shift all of its burdens to others, however, there is no way to reach its owners by any property tax.

141. If the shifted portions of the property tax mainly burden consumers, as is commonly supposed, adoption of the kind of classified property tax discussed in the preceding footnote would shift local tax burdens away from property owners onto consumers. Jon Sonstelie, "The Incidence of a Classified Property Tax," Working Paper in Economics 93 (Department of Economics, University of California—Santa Barbara, November 1977).

142. Brazer, "Value of Industrial Property," p. 144.

143. While there may be strong support for a federal income tax system that did not contain a separate tax on corporation profits, there is considerable difference of opinion about how best to move the present system toward that goal or, indeed, whether such a change would be desirable. Charles E. McLure, Jr., "Integration of the Personal and Corporate Income Taxes: The Missing Element in Recent Tax Reform Proposals," *Harvard Law Review*, vol. 88 (January 1975), pp. 532–82, and *Must Corporate Income Be Taxed Twice?* (Brookings Institution, 1979). See also the NTA-TIA symposium, "The Taxation of Income From Corporate Shareholding," *National Tax Journal*, vol. 28 (September 1975).

because a significant portion of the burdens of business taxes levied by one jurisdiction falls on the residents of other areas. Judged by the ability model, therefore, local business property taxes are both inequitable and productive of numerous economic distortions.

So far as property taxes are concerned, then, local governments have two basic options. One is to fold them into a benefits-received system of local finance. The other is to finance intermediate services to business on a benefit basis and final services to residents on an ability basis. A residential property tax qualifies for the latter role if it indeed is a good proxy for the permanent income levels of households or at least as good a proxy as its major competitor, a local tax on households' current incomes.

Lowering local tax burdens on business property and raising them on residential property is, of course, precisely the opposite goal to the one sought by many advocates of a classified property tax. Given these political pressures, the second-best solution may well be to stick with existing uniform and general property taxes rather than to embark on the stormy seas of ill-defined property tax classifications.

Another logical but even more radical kind of classification would confine the levy to the site value of land. Highly attractive in principle because of its potential ability to capture windfall gains without generating serious taxpayer disincentives, the land tax has been the subject of much passionate controversy. Seen as the ideal source of government revenue by devotees of Henry George,[144] the levy has been criticized on both theoretical and pragmatic grounds. How equitable, critics have asked, would it be to shift to a land tax that would impose large capital losses on owners who had purchased their properties on the reasonable assumption that no such radical change in local tax systems would ever be made? A land tax that is imposed from the beginning of the development of an urban area would indeed capture for public benefit the private windfall gains that land-

---

144. Henry George, *Progress and Poverty: An Inquiry into the Cause of Industrial Depressions and of Increase of Want with Increase of Wealth: The Remedy,* 50th Anniversary ed. (New York: Robert Schalkenbach Foundation, 1939); Harold M. Groves, *Tax Philosophers: Two Hundred Years of Thought in Great Britain and the United States,* ed. Donald J. Curran (University of Wisconsin Press, 1974), pp. 126–30; Richard W. Lindholm and Arthur D. Lynn, Jr., eds., *Land Value Taxation in Thought and Practice* (University of Wisconsin Press, forthcoming). For economic analyses of the effects of site value taxation see Netzer, *Economics of the Property Tax,* pp. 197–212; Turvey, *Economics of Real Property,* pp. 76–92.

owners would otherwise enjoy. One imposed at some later date, however, would miss many of those windfall gains and would impose windfall losses on many current owners. As Brazer has aptly put it, "One is tempted to suggest that if land values were to be taxed more intensively than they are now, we should have started before this!"[145]

Similar disagreements arise over the effects, or rather noneffects, of site value taxation on the allocation of resources.[146] Proponents stress the economic neutrality of the tax toward new construction or property rehabilitation and argue that it would not affect the optimal intensity of land use in urban areas. Neutrality, however, is a controversial tax principle. The case for it assumes either well-functioning private markets or well-designed and -executed public policies that counteract market imperfections. Critics are not willing to accept these assumptions in principle and, as a result, predict that a shift to land taxation would worsen rather than improve resource allocation. Greater intensity of urban land use, for example, is not to everyone's taste.

Pragmatic criticisms of the land tax center on the accuracy with which site values could be determined in different kinds of communities.[147] Some regard land valuation as more manageable than property valuation. Others stress the need in highly developed urban areas, where few vacant lots exist, to derive site values from observed or hypothetical sales price data by subtracting the estimated value of buildings and other improvements.[148] Such a standard of tax assessment would rate low by the criteria of taxpayer certainty and convenience and might or might not score well on administrative equity. Taxpayers would have no objective evidence against which to mea-

145. Brazer, "Value of Industrial Property," p. 144. See "Three Lectures on Progress and Poverty by Alfred Marshall," *Journal of Law and Economics,* vol. 12 (April 1969), especially pp. 200–01, 205; Aaron, *Who Pays the Property Tax?* pp. 87–90. For a general discussion of the case for compensating people who lose from tax reforms see Martin Feldstein, "Compensation in Tax Reform," *National Tax Journal,* vol. 29 (June 1976), pp. 123–30.

146. The major effects are discussed in Netzer, *Economics of the Property Tax,* pp. 204–08.

147. Daniel M. Holland, ed., *The Assessment of Land Value* (University of Wisconsin Press for the Committee on Taxation, Resources and Economic Development, 1970); Oliver Oldman and Mary Miles Teachout, "Land Valuation Under a Separate Tax on Land," in NTA-TIA, *Proceedings, 1977,* pp. 182–86; Brazer, "Value of Industrial Property," pp. 141–44.

148. On the complexities involved in computing such residual site values see Turvey, *Economics of Real Property,* pp. 80–83.

sure the accuracy of their assessments, the appeal process would be complicated because of its heavy reliance on expert opinions, and equity would depend on how well assessors managed to do their job. It seems questionable whether there would be greater public satisfaction with theoretical land valuation than with values derived from sales data and subject in the final analysis to the market test.

Land value taxation is no panacea for urban ills. It will, however, continue as a policy issue, and classification plans that tax buildings less heavily than site values may well gain in popularity.[149] Since assessment practices now frequently favor land over buildings, any reform aimed at greater property tax uniformity will raise the relative burdens on land.[150]

PROPERTY-TAX CIRCUIT BREAKERS. Plans aimed mainly at relieving the tax burdens of low-income households by automatically breaking the property tax circuit at points where it becomes overloaded first appeared in Wisconsin in 1964, received strong early support from the ACIR,[151] and spread rapidly during the next ten years. By 1978 there were thirty-one circuit-breaker programs in operation, some only for the elderly, others for all low-income families. Such kinds of property tax relief clearly have broad popular appeal.

However good their intentions, circuit breakers do involve some troublesome subjective choices. Not only must personal abilities to pay be measured, with all of the attendant difficulties, but excessive tax burdens must be identified as well. Is the residential property tax really a highly regressive levy, as is widely believed, or are its burdens roughly proportional to each household's lifetime income status, which many regard as the best measure of ability to pay?[152] Should

149. Pennsylvania first authorized this kind of property tax in 1913. See Netzer, *Economics of the Property Tax*, pp. 202–04.

150. See, for example, Frederick D. Stocker, "Property Taxation, Land Use, and Rationality in Urban Growth Policy," in Arthur D. Lynn, Jr., ed., *Property Taxation, Land Use, and Public Policy* (University of Wisconsin Press for the Committee on Taxation, Resources and Economic Development, 1976), pp. 190–92; Robert Edelstein, "The Determinants of Value in the Philadelphia Housing Market: A Case Study of the Main Line, 1967–1969," *Review of Economics and Statistics*, vol. 56 (August 1974), p. 325.

151. The commission went on record in support of circuit breakers in 1967. ACIR, *Property Tax Circuit-Breakers: Current Status and Policy Issues*, Information Report M-87 (GPO, 1975).

152. Aaron, *Who Pays the Property Tax?* chap. 3.

assistance be given to families simply because they have unusually strong tastes for housing? What proportion of property tax burdens do renters bear, and hence what degree of relief should they be granted? Do high property taxes that purchase services of high quality impose excessive burdens? The ambiguities inherent in these questions counsel caution in the adoption and design of circuit-breaker plans.[153]

Circuit breakers may also be seen as contributing to a number of other fiscal goals. Indeed, they were originally viewed not as structural improvements in the property tax but as a means of alleviating the liquidity problems of elderly homeowners whose current incomes had fallen below their lifetime status levels or whose pensions were reduced in value by inflation. For this purpose, circuit breakers are very much a second-best instrument. Benefits are not precisely targeted on the elderly but are extended as well to their heirs who need not qualify for public assistance at all. One obvious solution is the kind of tax deferral plan adopted by California that enables the elderly to postpone payment of part of their property taxes as long as they continue to live in their houses. The state can recoup the value of the deferred taxes, with or without an interest charge on the accrued amount, when the property is sold or transferred at death or by gift.

State-financed circuit-breaker plans provide local governments with a kind of unrestricted grant that is allocated on the basis of tax effort and the number of resident low-income families. Under a few plans, state funds flow directly to local governments; in most, reimbursement for excess property taxes is made to qualifying individuals, either as a cash payment or as a refundable credit against state income tax liabilities.[154] If the flypaper hypothesis is correct, the two reimbursement arrangements will have different effects on local spending patterns. Reimbursement to individuals should stimulate local government spending less, although in the longer term as more and more voters are affected, opposition to increases in tax rates may be significantly weakened.

An additional effect of circuit breakers is to serve as a means of imposing lower tax burdens on residential than on business property.

153. Ibid., pp. 71–79.
154. ACIR, *Property Tax Circuit-Breakers,* pp. 20–25.

In this respect they resemble homestead exemptions. If their use defuses the move toward a classified property tax, critics of that kind of local levy will be well pleased.

Circuit breakers have, for a number of reasons, established themselves rather widely. Nevertheless, state and local governments, whether they have such devices in operation or not, would do well to weigh the costs of alternative designs and of other kinds of relief programs, such as tax deferral plans, by which their goals might be accomplished.[155]

BUSINESS BASE SHARING PLANS. A structural reform in property taxes authorized in the Minneapolis-St. Paul metropolitan area in 1971 and implemented in 1974 constitutes a kind of share-the-growth plan for urban communities. Conceived as a means of moderating incentives for fiscal zoning, it calls for sharing throughout the metropolitan area the fiscal surpluses created by rapid business growth in some parts. A portion of the increase in assessed values of business property in each community is assigned to a common pool which is then distributed to all communities on the basis of relative fiscal capacity and need. The designers of this bold and innovative arrangement had to deal with a problem for which no reliable guidelines exist —setting the shared portion of business property growth high enough to capture most fiscal surpluses but low enough to preserve community incentives to incur the intangible costs of congestion and pollution often associated with new commercial and industrial development.[156] They had also to define an allocation formula that would create few undeserving gainers and few unjustly deprived losers from the redirection of property tax revenues. Again no foolproof rules are available. Only time and any insights gained from

155. Marc Bendick, Jr., "Designing Circuit Breaker Property Tax Relief," *National Tax Journal*, vol. 27 (March 1974), pp. 19–28; Steven D. Gold, "A Note on the Design of Property Tax Circuitbreakers," ibid., vol. 29 (December 1976), pp. 477–81; W. Norton Grubb and E. Gareth Hoachlander, "Circuit-Breaker Schedules and Their Application in California," *Policy Analysis*, vol. 4 (Summer 1978), pp. 317–37.

156. Proposition 13 in California greatly reduced, if it did not eliminate or reverse, the property tax surpluses obtainable from new business development. Point-of-sale allocation of local sales tax revenues, however, does tend to stimulate competition among communities for shopping centers and other retail business. These incentives would be increased if some of the lost property tax revenue were to be made up by an increase in the local sales tax rate, as some have proposed.

experience with variations that may be tried elsewhere can prove the efficacy of the Minnesota plan.[157]

Another way to share the tax base among urban communities is to shift to an areawide tax on business property. This would eliminate onerous property tax differentials as a factor in location decisions, but it might also eliminate the willingness of communities to accept certain kinds of new business. Its distributional effects would also have to be studied carefully. Helen Ladd, for example, found that shifting to areawide taxation of business property in the Boston area would have made the gap between rich and poor communities worse rather than better. Even a strongly redistributive formula aimed at school districts would have failed to improve equity in school finance.[158] How an areawide business tax might affect district spending levels would also bear close watching. In communities with a large business sector the implicit tax price of local government services would be increased—an effect that could improve the economic efficiency of local public choices by moving tax costs closer to real resource costs. Such equity and efficiency effects are too uncertain to count on, however, and may vary greatly from one area to another.

CONCLUSION. Like many things in life, local property taxation is fine when used in moderation and in the right ways. Held within reasonable limits, the tax has an important fiscal role to play, and in many communities that role can be enhanced by well-designed structural and administrative reforms. In communities operating at or beyond the inherent limits of property taxation the alternative candidate based on ability to pay is a local income tax.[159]

Local Income Taxation

The fact that the income tax is firmly established as the basic ability-to-pay component of the U.S. tax system somewhat ironically presents one of the two main barriers to its widespread use at the

157. Andrew Reschovsky, "New Strategies for Metropolitan Area Cooperation: Sharing Rather Than Competing for Business Tax Base," in NTA-TIA, *Proceedings, 1977*, pp. 155–62.

158. Helen F. Ladd, "State-Wide Taxation of Commercial and Industrial Property for Education," *National Tax Journal*, vol. 29 (June 1976), pp. 143–53.

159. L. R. Gabler, "A Reconsideration of Local Sales and Income Taxes," in NTA-TIA, *Proceedings, 1974*, pp. 281–88, and Robert D. Reischauer, "In Defense of the Property Tax: The Case Against an Increased Reliance on Local Non-Property Taxes," ibid., pp. 288–306.

local level. Admittedly, the existence of both federal and state individual income taxes greatly simplifies the administrative problems
for local users by offering them a variety of piggybacking arrangements. On the other hand, heavy reliance on the income tax, particularly by the federal government, does limit the attractiveness of that
levy to local governments. The inherent ambiguities of ability-based
tax principles create a strong case for a diversified system that makes
relatively balanced use of income, consumption, and wealth taxes.
How close the United States comes to such a balanced system will
probably always be a matter of dispute.[160] Greater use of local income
taxes would clearly move the nation as a whole away from balanced
tax diversity.[161] In the eyes of the general public it would apparently

160. Three sets of ambiguities greatly complicate the search for balance in the
use of different ability taxes. A tax on personal net wealth cannot serve as a comprehensive source of ability-based revenues unless the value of human capital is
included in its base, and that seems clearly impractical. A balanced ability system
should make about equal use of income and consumption taxes, with wealth taxes
in a supplementary role, but there is no precise set of optimal weights for the three
levies. Another difficulty arises in effectively separating benefit from ability taxes.
Some important components of the U.S. tax system—notably the payroll tax for
social security—play both roles, and no clear-cut separation is possible for them.
Uncertainties about the true incidence of some major taxes also pose problems. In
1975, for example, a survey of member countries by the Organization for Economic
Cooperation and Development showed that 44 percent of U.S. tax revenue came
from income taxes, 24 percent from social security contributions, 18 percent from
taxes on goods and services, and 14 percent from taxes on property. If social security
contributions are put aside as mainly benefit levies, and if property taxes are regarded
as equivalent to a national wealth tax, this would mean that 58 percent of the revenue
drawn from ability-based taxes in the U.S. system was then derived from income
taxes, 24 percent from consumption taxes, and 18 percent from wealth taxes. Need-
less to say, these determinations are controversial. Moreover, many would regard
the indicated shares of consumption taxes as too low because of the consumer burdens
believed to result from the corporation income tax, property taxes, and payroll levies
on employers. The data from all twenty-three OECD member countries showed
the United States to be just above the median (ranking ninth) in its relative use of
income taxes, at the top of the group in reliance on wealth and property taxes, and
at the bottom of the group in its use of taxes on goods and services. Organization
for Economic Cooperation and Development, *Revenue Statistics of OECD Member
Countries, 1965–75* (Paris: OECD, 1977), p. 82.

161. At the state and local level it would continue the trend toward greater
diversity, but ability tax systems should be judged from the national point of view.
Whereas in fiscal 1954, property taxes provided 45 percent of total state and local
tax revenue, sales taxes brought in 33 percent, and income taxes 9 percent, by fiscal
1978 those three tax shares were 34 percent, 35 percent, and 23 percent, respectively.
ACIR, *Significant Features of Fiscal Federalism, 1978–79 Edition,* Report M-115
(GPO, 1979), p. 46.

be a shift from one unpopular form of taxation to another. In the annual ACIR opinion polls the local property tax and the federal income tax have run neck and neck since 1972 for the dubious distinction of being considered the worst tax in the country.[162]

Of course, the unpopularity of the federal income tax might or might not carry over to a local income tax with much lower tax rates.[163] There is, however, a stronger reason for doubting the popularity of a shift from property taxes to an ability-based local income tax. Whereas property taxes are imposed on both businesses and households and generate burdens that fall on outsiders as well as on insiders, the ability model calls for a local individual income tax imposed on the total income of community residents only. A tax policy proposal that in most communities with important business sectors would raise the general taxpayer's share of the cost of existing government services is not likely to win the hearts of many voters.[164] While a theoretically sound, ability-based local tax system would appeal to some, others would be more attracted to the pragmatic maxim: "Export to others at least as many tax burdens as they are already exporting to you."

162. ACIR, *Changing Public Attitudes on Governments and Taxes, 1979,* Report S-8 (GPO, 1979), p. 2. In 1972 the local property tax was rated worst by a 45–19 percent margin, but after five years of very close competition this was reversed to a 27–37 percent relative rating.

163. The fact that state income taxes, which have basically the same structure as the federal income tax, consistently draw a less unfavorable rating—8 percent in 1979 compared to 37 percent who thought the federal income tax was the worst and 27 percent who picked the property tax—indicates that the intensity of use of a tax is an important determinant of its unpopularity. The relatively low worst-tax ratings enjoyed by state sales taxes—13 percent in 1972 and 15 percent in 1979—should be interpreted cautiously for this reason. Ibid.

164. Because the incidence of local taxes on business depends critically on the nature of each community's business sector, the effects of a shift from property to income taxation must be determined empirically for each different urban area. See, for example, Arthur P. Becker and Hans R. Isakson, "The Burden on the City of Milwaukee and Its Residents of the Real Property Tax Compared with the Individual Income Tax," in Break, *Metropolitan Financing,* pp. 243–99; Larry D. Schroeder and David L. Sjoquist, *The Property Tax and Alternative Local Taxes: An Economic Analysis* (Praeger, 1975); R. Stafford Smith, *Local Income Taxes: Economic Effects and Equity* (Institute of Governmental Studies, University of California—Berkeley, 1972). The size of the potential shift of tax burdens between residents and outsiders may be judged from Schroeder and Sjoquist's estimates that 48 percent of property taxes are exported, as are 50 percent of sales taxes, and 18–21 percent of residence-based individual income taxes. *Property Tax,* p. 49.

There are, then, some important difficulties in the way of any large-scale shift of local revenue systems toward individual income taxes, at least those modeled on ability principles. One possibility, of course, would be to forgo theoretical purity by adopting the standard local income tax plan that assesses residents on their total income from all sources and nonresidents on all income originating in the taxing jurisdiction. By seeking to satisfy both benefit and ability goals with one instrument, however, local governments may sacrifice the attainment of either objective. The tax on nonresidents might be higher than benefit considerations would support while the tax on residents was lower, and less progressive, than ability principles suggest. More satisfactory local ability systems clearly exist, but their achievement may require a high degree of intergovernmental cooperation.

Intergovernmental Tax Plans

One solution to the difficulties of using ability taxation at the local level would be simply to eliminate any need for it by shifting the financing of education, welfare, and other social services to state and federal governments. In the absence of such a move, local ability-based revenue systems could be improved by enactment of federal incentives for the adoption of resident-based local property or individual income taxes; authorization of areawide taxes on retail sales, levied at each area's chosen rate on the state base, with the proceeds distributed to individual communities in the area on the basis of per capita income;[165] establishment of a federal tax on personal expenditures, allowing state and local supplements similar to those authorized for the individual income tax.

No intergovernmental tax plan for local governments, whether based on benefit or ability principles, can be developed overnight. Much time and effort will be required, and assurances are needed that it will all be worthwhile. The model that stresses restraints on urban revenue systems suggests that those assurances may be hard to come by.

---

165. Uniform areawide sales taxes are needed to avoid the disruptive economic effects of sales tax rates that differ among communities in the same urban area. Distribution of the proceeds should in principle be based on taxable consumption of all residents of each jurisdiction. Per capita income is suggested as the closest available proxy.

The Restraining-Rules-and-Process Model

That government powers need to be restrained one way or another has been a fundamental belief in the United States from the very beginning. Popular interest in tax and expenditure limitations as one means of restraint has waxed and waned over the years, but it now appears to have entered a new expansionary phase.[166] This suggests that the proper goal for urban governments in the eyes of many is not a local revenue system based on benefit or ability principles but one that keeps the size of government within tolerable limits. As Paul Gann, coauthor of California's Proposition 13, put it: "I don't want the Legislature to live within *their* means. I want them to live within *my* means."[167]

Such popular attitudes do not lack for theoretical support. The analysis of government behavior, however, is exceedingly complicated and, like economic theories of the operation of concentrated, oligopolistic markets, has yet to produce many definitive results. It may therefore serve more to satisfy the already convinced than to convert the skeptical.

Theories of public choice do, however, raise some important policy questions. If government is widely perceived to be too big or too inefficient, what is the best remedy? Would it be a change in bureaucratic and political incentive systems and institutions, or a change in power relations in the public sector? Systematic analysis of both of these aspects of government behavior is the hallmark of the growing

166. For a discussion of state limitations on local government operations see ACIR, *State Constitutional and Statutory Restrictions on Local Taxing Powers*, Report A-14 (GPO, 1962), and *State Limitations on Local Taxes and Expenditures*, Report A-64 (GPO, 1977). For a proposal and discussion of a limit on the taxes of all levels of government equal to 25 percent of national income, see Colin Clark, "Public Finance and the Value of Money," *Economic Journal*, vol. 55 (December 1945), pp. 371–89; Joseph A. Pechman and Thomas Mayer, "Mr. Colin Clark on the Limits of Taxation," *Review of Economics and Statistics*, vol. 34 (August 1952), pp. 232–42; *The Limits of Taxable Capacity*, Symposium Conducted by the Tax Institute (Princeton, N.J.: Tax Institute, 1953), reviewed by E. Cary Brown, *American Economic Review*, vol. 44 (June 1954), pp. 448–50; Amotz Morag, "The Limits of Taxation," *Public Finance*, vol. 14, no. 1 (1959), pp. 68–84.

167. *North East Bay Independent and Gazette* (Richmond, California), March 10, 1978.

body of literature on public choice.[168] In the behavioral models typically proposed, several competing groups operate and interact, each maximizing its own utility subject to the constraints placed upon it by the behavior of the others.[169] Conflicting pressures are endemic, and choices concerning the use of society's resources and the design of tax-transfer programs are based on negotiation and compromise. This bargaining mechanism, as McKean has stressed, is the "unseen hand in government" that "tends to harness individual interests within government to carry out broader objectives."[170] What these objectives are in practice and whose interests they serve are the critical questions.

In such a theoretical framework the quality of performance in the public sector depends very much on the nature of the institutions and on the incentives to which the various actors in the drama respond. Bureaucrats, for example, are rewarded less for increasing the efficiency of their agencies than for expanding their size.[171] Ambitious civil servants work unusually hard for the public good, or at least for their conception of it, while the unambitious do very little, secure in the knowledge that they are unlikely to be fired.[172] Special interest groups engage in what may well be a negative-sum game of maximizing their own benefits and shifting the costs onto others. The public good need not be well served by such activities. Voters are bombarded with biased and misleading information designed to profit the disseminators. The media and various public interest groups may provide more objective data, but the individual voter has only weak incentives to spend time and effort to sort out all the conflicting evidence. Politicians respond to well-informed interest groups pushing

168. Dennis C. Mueller, "Public Choice: A Survey," *Journal of Economic Literature*, vol. 14 (June 1976), pp. 395–433; *Public Choice* (Cambridge University Press, 1979).

169. See, for example, Bartlett, *Economic Foundations of Political Power;* Douglas G. Hartle, *A Theory of the Expenditure Budgetary Process,* Ontario Economic Research series 5 (University of Toronto Press for Ontario Economic Council, 1976); Morris P. Fiorina and Roger G. Noll, "Voters, Bureaucrats and Legislators: A Rational Choice Perspective on the Growth of Bureaucracy," *Journal of Public Economics,* vol. 9 (April 1978), pp. 239–54.

170. *Public Spending,* p. 29.

171. William A. Niskanen, Jr., *Bureaucracy and Representative Government* (Aldine-Atherton, 1971).

172. Hartle, *Theory of the Expenditure Budgetary Process,* pp. 73–74.

programs with carefully disguised benefits for themselves and relatively invisible costs spread widely over the general public.[173]

Redirecting these complex incentive-disincentive systems toward economic efficiency and consumer satisfaction is a task that few attempt and fewer complete.[174] Political processes can also be improved, but results are uncertain and progress is slow. If improvement in the process by which public choices are made is a vain hope, the alternative is to change the power relations prevailing in the government sector.[175] Specifically, controls on the amount or composition of expenditures and taxes may succeed in reducing the discretionary power of politicians and bureaucrats and increasing that of the ordinary voter-taxpayer. Indeed, such a shift of power may be necessary before any significant improvements can be made in incentive systems or decisionmaking processes in the public sector. That at least is the hope of many of the supporters of tax and expenditure limitations. Whether these measures are simple and direct avenues toward more efficient and responsive urban fiscal systems or only simplistic, counterproductive fiscal aberrations is the key question to be answered. Application of this philosophy to local governments does, however, have sufficient potential appeal to warrant its treatment as a model for the design of urban revenue systems.

Problems

Like its two competitors, the restraining-rules-and-process model has its own inherent problems. One difficulty faced by anyone wishing to evaluate the possibilities of tax and expenditure limitations is to

173. Gordon Tullock, "Why Politicians Won't Cut Taxes," *Taxing and Spending,* October-November 1978, pp. 12–14.

174. President Carter made such a task a primary commitment both before and after his election to office. Alan K. Campbell, "Why the Civil Service Doesn't Work," *Taxing and Spending,* October-November 1978, pp. 33–36.

175. Just as conventional and radical economists see the private sector in starkly different lights and recommend equally different solutions, some experts see the public sector as basically competitive and responsive, hence needing only ameliorative reform measures, while others view it as monopolistic and unresponsive, requiring radical controls or changes. On the former school of thought see Helen F. Ladd, "An Economic Evaluation of State Limitations on Local Taxing and Spending Powers," *National Tax Journal,* vol. 31 (March 1978), pp. 1–18; on the latter see Richard E. Wagner and Warren E. Weber, "Competition, Monopoly, and the Organization of Government in Metropolitan Areas," *Journal of Law and Economics,* vol. 18 (December 1975), pp. 661–84.

discern exactly what the public has in mind in passing them.[176] Are
such limits seen as the only reliable route to increased government
efficiency, as a means of changing the tax or intergovernmental structure by limiting some sources of revenue so that others can expand
to take their place, or as a curb on the size of government so that
private goods and services can supplant public ones?[177] Public opinion polls, not surprisingly, give conflicting answers to these questions.
Various measures of attitudes clearly show increasing disenchantment with government and alienation from it.[178] When asked whether
government spending in general is too high, people typically respond
that it is, but when asked about spending on particular programs, the
majority agree on only a few as overexpanded.[179] People also appear
to have an exaggerated view of the amount of waste in government.
Asked in a Gallup poll how many cents were wasted out of each
dollar spent, for example, people responded: 48 cents by the federal
government, 32 cents by state governments, and 25 cents by local
governments.[180] Of course, waste to some may mean doing the wrong
things rather than doing things inefficiently. If so, the poll may be
interpreted less as a naive longing for the proverbial free lunch than
as a dissatisfaction with the results of governments dominated by
special interests.[181]

Using tax and expenditure limitations to restrain, or even reduce,
the size of government is like trying to lower the level of the water in
one of several connected ponds by pressing down on its surface. Put-

176. For evidence of the electorate's voting largely in its economic self-interest
see Mickey Levy, "Voting on California's Tax and Expenditure Limitation Initiative,"
National Tax Journal, vol. 28 (December 1975), pp. 426–36.

177. Evidence that high rates of local expenditure growth and high property tax
burdens in relation to personal income both increased the probability that a state
would adopt some limiting measure during the 1970s is given in Ladd, "Economic
Evaluation," pp. 2–3.

178. Jacob Citrin, "The Alienated Voter," *Taxing and Spending*, October-
November 1978, pp. 7–11, and "Do People Want Something for Nothing: Public
Opinion on Taxes and Government Spending," *National Tax Journal*, vol. 32, Sup-
plement (June 1979), pp. 113–29; Everett Carll Ladd, Jr., "What the Voters Really
Want," *Fortune*, December 1978, pp. 40–48.

179. The least popular program areas are welfare, space, and foreign aid. See
Ladd, "What the Voters Really Want," pp. 44–46; Robert Cameron Mitchell, "The
Public Speaks Again: A New Environmental Survey," *Resources*, no. 60 (September-
November 1978), p. 3.

180. *Tax Revolt Digest* (Sacramento, California), January 1979, p. 4.

181. Kevin Phillips, "The Balkanization of America," *Harper's*, May 1978, pp.
37–47.

ting a limit on one tax may simply increase use of another. Curbing the expenditures of one level of government may expand those of other levels. Restricting the expenditures of all levels of government may induce greater use of regulatory powers, of off-budget lending and loan-guaranteeing agencies, or of tax subsidies and incentives.[182]

Using these limitations to improve the quality of government services depends on the assumption that monopolies respond to their customers only when forced to do so, and that tight budgets will provide the needed pressure. The initial reaction to Proposition 13, however, was not to reduce employment by terminating the least effective workers and programs but by freezing salaries and thereby inducing some of the most effective workers to go elsewhere. It may be that increased competition, from both the private sector and other parts of the public sector, is a better check on excessive monopoly powers than regulation and controls.

Process Controls

One method of control aims at improving the processes by which local taxing and spending decisions are made. Full disclosure laws, pioneered by Florida in 1971,[183] focus on the quality of the information made available to voters. Each year a standard property tax rate is established that yields some stated percentage of the previous year's revenue. This could be set in a 95–100 percent range if a gradually shrinking public sector is desired, or at 100–110 percent, say, if stability in an inflationary economy is the goal. Any rate above the standard one must be set by explicit vote of the local governing body after the electorate has been notified and public hearings held.

Another type of control seeks to raise the level of the hurdles that proposals for increasing taxes must surmount. One way is to mandate direct public votes on all such measures; another is to allow legislative bodies to enact them, but only by a 60, a 67, or even an 80 percent vote. Similarly large majorities may also be required for the passage of ballot measures dealing with tax increases.

Improvement may also be sought by changing the design of local

182. See Geoffrey Brennan and James M. Buchanan, "The Logic of Tax Limits: Alternative Constitutional Constraints on the Power to Tax," *National Tax Journal*, vol. 32, Supplement, pp. 11–22; Stephen Lile, Don Soule, and James Wead, *Limiting State Taxes and Expenditures* (Lexington, Ky.: Council of State Governments, 1978), pp. 17–22.

183. ACIR, *State Limitations on Local Taxes and Expenditures*, pp. 14–17.

tax structures. Efficiency gains may be achieved by bringing the prices for public goods, as perceived by local voters, more in line with the real resource costs of the services to be financed. Reforms in the local taxation of business property are a good example of this kind of approach. Constraints on the growth of the public sector can be applied indirectly by making local taxes more visible to voters, thereby raising the perceived price of public goods, or by taxes with lower built-in growth sensitivities, so as to reduce easily spent fiscal dividends. Such structural changes have highly uncertain effects.

That some taxes are more visible than others is plausible enough, but it is not easy to make even a rough ranking.[184] Among local taxes a residence-based individual income tax would probably rate at the top. A residential property tax would be somewhat less visible, on the average, because of its uncertain incidence on renters. A general property tax would be likely to be still lower on the scale because business tax burdens are probably even less visible to the ordinary voter than renter burdens. A retail sales tax is hard to rank. Most people know it is there, but only those who itemize their federal tax deductions are likely to have a very accurate impression of how much they pay over the year.[185] Whatever the relative visibility of local revenue sources may be, the property tax seems to evoke particularly pained responses. Ironically, Proposition 13 and similar measures may, by relieving this pressure point and lowering the perceived prices of state and local government services, move government spending levels up instead of down.[186]

One of the testable hypotheses produced by theories of bureaucratic behavior is that government expenditures will tend to grow, apart from cyclical fluctuations, at least as rapidly as the fiscal dividends produced by a growth- and inflation-elastic revenue system.[187] Empirical analyses by Oates confirm a positive relation between the

184. Tax visibility is a part of the general theory of fiscal illusion. See Buchanan, *Fiscal Theory*, pp. 59–64; Charles J. Goetz, "Fiscal Illusion in State and Local Finance," in Thomas E. Borcherding, ed., *Budgets and Bureaucrats: The Sources of Government Growth* (Duke University Press, 1977), pp. 176–87; Richard E. Wagner, "Revenue Structure, Fiscal Illusion, and Budgetary Choice," *Public Choice*, vol. 25 (Spring 1976), pp. 45–61.

185. Even itemizers may know only what the sales tax tables, based on budget studies of average spending patterns of different families, say they paid in sales taxes during the year.

186. Colin D. Campbell and Rosemary G. Campbell, *Property Taxes in New Hampshire* (Hampton, N.H.: Wheelabrator Foundation, 1978).

187. Hartle, *Theory of the Expenditure Budgetary Process*, p. 94.

growth elasticity of tax systems and the size of the public sector.[188] On this basis, then, the restraining-rules-and-process model would dictate the choice of relatively inelastic local tax sources. Here again only a rough ranking is possible. The personal income tax is usually placed at the top of any sensitivity scale, with the retail sales tax next, the general property tax third, and specific excises last.[189] This ranking for the property tax is questionable, however. Statutory requirements that assessors value all taxable property at full market value or at some stated percentage thereof imply a high target elasticity for the tax, especially in an inflationary economy where residential property offers one of the few inflation-proof investments available to most people. The actual elasticity of the tax, of course, depends on how frequently and how well assessors revalue existing properties. Where they do come close to statutory targets, as appears to have been the case in California before the passage of Proposition 13, the property tax will not be highly regarded by supporters of the restraining-rules-and-process model. The individual income tax, however, may well be worse, especially if it has a progressive structure that is not indexed for inflation. That means that both of the general ability taxes available for independent use by urban governments may prove too elastic for their purposes. In 1978 and 1979, however, six states indexed the structure of their personal income taxes against inflation.

Process reforms and controls, then, provide one main route to greater efficiency both in the operation of government programs and in the allocation of resources between the private and public sectors. Their potential accomplishments, however, are uncertain enough to keep the search for alternative control measures going on apace.

Tax and Expenditure Limits

Though not the first measure limiting local taxing or spending powers to be adopted in the 1970s,[190] Proposition 13 gained national

188. Wallace E. Oates, " 'Automatic' Increases in Tax Revenues—The Effect on the Size of the Public Budget," in *Financing the New Federalism: Revenue Sharing, Conditional Grants, and Taxation,* Papers by Robert P. Inman and others, The Governance of Metropolitan Regions no. 5, ed. Wallace E. Oates (Johns Hopkins University Press for Resources for the Future, 1975), pp. 139–60.

189. For estimated income elasticities of the main state and local taxes see ACIR, *Significant Features of Fiscal Federalism, 1976–77 Edition,* vol. 2: *Revenue and Debt,* Report M-110 (GPO, 1977), p. 254.

190. Between 1970 and 1976 fourteen states and the District of Columbia enacted some form of control on local taxes or expenditures. ACIR, *State Limitations on Local Taxes and Expenditures,* p. 2.

attention because of the stringency of its terms—a statewide average 57 percent mandated reduction in local property tax revenues plus a two-thirds vote requirement for future tax increases—and the strength, surprising to many, of the popular support it attracted. The mystery about it is what people thought they were voting for. Such limits on local governments' use of the property tax can be aimed at two quite different fiscal goals. One seeks to alter the structure of state and local revenues without a change in spending levels, and the other aims to reduce, or at least restrict the future growth of, government spending. The tax-shift goal could be accomplished by increasing local reliance on public service user charges and nonproperty taxes and simultaneously shifting welfare and school financing responsibilities to the state level. Essentially this would represent a substitution of income and sales taxes for the property tax and might or might not involve an increase in intergovernmental grants.[191] In either case, some increase in state controls could be expected.

The adoption of property tax limits could push local revenue systems in a number of different directions. If the role of user charges were expanded, in spite of the disincentives currently provided in the deductibility rules of the federal individual income tax and by the allocation formulas for general revenue sharing, the result would be a move away from ability and toward benefit financing. If the role of intergovernmental grants were expanded, in spite of current prospects that federal grant monies will expand less rapidly than the general price level,[192] the result would be a reduced degree of local fiscal independence. If reliance on local income taxes were increased, in spite of the current heavy use of that revenue source by federal and state governments, ability elements in local revenue structures would be strengthened. If the pressures on single-purpose local governments heavily dependent on the property tax were relieved by consolidating

191. The two main competing models of school finance are full state financing of a centralized school system, on the one hand, and state grants to equalize district powers in a decentralized system, on the other. See Robert W. Hartman and Robert D. Reischauer, "The Effect of Reform in School Finance on the Level and Distribution of Tax Burdens," in John Pincus, ed., *School Finance in Transition: The Courts and Educational Reform*, A Rand Educational Policy Study (Ballinger, 1974), pp. 107–50 (Brookings Reprint 296).

192. See, for example, "A Crunch Is Coming for State and Local Budgets," *Fortune*, February 1979, p. 12; John Shannon, "The Politics of Fiscal Containment—Its Effects on State and Local Governments and on the Federal Aid System," paper presented to the Faculty, Bureau of Governmental Research and Service, University of South Carolina, March 17, 1980.

them into general-purpose jurisdictions, in spite of the well-known barriers to governmental reorganization, a less fragmented local government structure would be created. Whether that would improve or impair the effective performance of urban governments continues to be a hotly debated issue.[193]

Important questions also arise about the future role of local business taxation. Some tax and expenditure limitations explicitly shift property tax burdens from residential to business property.[194] Attractive as such a change may be to those who prefer invisible to visible tax burdens, it is basically inconsistent with the goals of all three of the financing models discussed here. Other limiting measures maintain the uniform taxation of residential and business property but shift it to a lower level. If the result is a uniform statewide rate on business property, it is likely to have some important, though potentially conflicting, locational effects. Economic efficiency may be improved by the elimination of property tax burden differentials as a factor in businesses' choice of location, but it may be adversely affected by the loss of the fiscal incentives needed to induce communities to admit businesses that threaten the quality of urban life. In California the combination of a low and uniform business property tax with local sales tax revenues distributed on a point-of-sale basis promises to shift community preferences away from manufacturing and wholesaling enterprises toward shopping centers and other large retail businesses.[195]

In several respects Proposition 13 should serve as a warning to voters in other states considering similar measures, for it vividly illustrates some of the difficulties and paradoxes inherent in trying to achieve tax reform by this means. Although the simplistic terms in which the initiative was couched may well have enhanced its political

193. "Special Districts—Victims of Prop. 13," *Tax Revolt Digest*, January 1979, p. 6.

194. Sonstelie, "Should Business Pay More Taxes?" In November 1978, Oregon voters defeated a measure that would have granted property tax reductions only to homeowners and renters, but Massachusetts passed a proposal authorizing the legislature to establish separate assessment ratios for different categories of property. Howard S. Bloom, "Public Choice and Private Interest: Explaining the Vote for Property Tax Classification in Massachusetts," *National Tax Journal*, vol. 32 (December 1979), pp. 527–34; *Tax Revolt Digest*, December 1978, pp. 2–3.

195. "California's Construction Crimp," *Tax Revolt Digest*, January 1979, pp. 1, 5. Residential development has also been made less attractive, leading some municipalities to impose special fees on private developers and others to increase their existing charges substantially.

appeal, they are already producing effects patently not intended by most of the people who voted for it. One of these effects will be a steady reduction of the business share of total property tax burdens. This comes from the stipulation that the assessed value of existing property is permitted to increase at only 2 percent a year (from a 1975–76 base of full market value) until the property is sold or transferred, at which time it must be reassessed at current market value. (Current value is also applied to new construction.) Given a rate of increase in property values greater than 2 percent a year and a higher turnover rate for single-family homes than for business property, property tax burdens can be expected to shift gradually toward homeowners.[196] Furthermore, over time the widely differing assessment ratios this process will create will produce serious horizontal inequities and provide an obvious disincentive for Californians to move from one home to another within the state.

Reactions to these effects are gradually beginning to reveal themselves as urban governments consider ways to squeeze more revenue out of business by increasing license fees and other such levies, thereby adding to the uncertainties surrounding business locational choices. Because Proposition 13 requires a two-thirds vote of the electorate for new taxes or increases in old ones, city councils have tended to turn to user charges, which do not need voter approval. Some communities, however, especially small upper-income suburban ones with few revenue sources other than the property tax, have voted tax overrides to prevent cuts in basic services. These observed reactions do not suggest that this measure, at least, is a particularly effective way of limiting the growth of government spending or of making it more efficient. Moreover, it adds some new problems of its own, such as the equity issue, which will become more and more troublesome until corrected.

In contrast to the tax limitation approach followed by Proposition

196. The importance of newly built or transferred property in the California tax base is indicated by the fact that total property assessed values rose by 13.8 percent in 1978–79, compared to an increase of 14.2 percent in 1977–78, the last year before imposition of the 2 percent limit. In Los Angeles County, according to the speaker of the California Assembly, Leo T. McCarthy, the business share of total assessed valuation fell from 36 percent in 1978 to 28 percent in 1979 and was expected to drop to 20 percent by 1984. *North East Bay Independent and Gazette*, August 27, 1979. Whereas the average holding period for residential property in California is six years, that for business property may be as high as thirty years. David J. Levin, "Proposition 13: One Year Later," *Survey of Current Business*, vol. 59 (November 1979), p. 15.

13, measures passed by Arizona, Hawaii, Michigan, and Texas in the same year (1978) placed limits on state expenditures, with one (Michigan's) extended also to local spending. California enacted spending limits for both state and local governments in 1979. The parade continues. Most of these impose their ceilings in the form of holding expenditures to some stated percentage of state personal income or tying them to the size of the population served plus some general inflation factor. An earlier attempt in Florida to limit state employment levels was defeated. The search for the perfect formula has a long way to go.

Taxing and spending limitations are of interest here not for their own sake but for their potential impact on the design of urban revenue systems. By shifting financial responsibilities to the local level, state limitations may increase the urgency of local revenue reform. Local limitations, in contrast, may move local revenue systems toward a greater reliance on intergovernmental grants or benefits-received financing in general. The more effective such limiting measures at any level of government, the less important revenue reform will be as a major fiscal goal. However, by stimulating the achievement of public sector goals through tax incentives rather than through spending programs, expenditure limitations may help create what many would regard as a less equitable and efficient tax system.

Conclusion

It remains to be seen whether process controls and limitations on either taxes or expenditures are more than a temporary phenomenon, serving to nudge the public sector toward greater efficiency and urban revenue systems closer to either the ability or the benefit models. If their tenure is firmer, as it may well be, the big question is what the effect will be on the general quality of life. Is it better to make a drastic change, as California has chosen to do, in the hope that adjustments can be worked out without serious side effects and the good life attained with all deliberate speed? Or would a more gradual approach, by way of restraining rules and processes, be a better alternative? One of the great strengths of the U.S. federal system is that it affords vast space for laying out avenues to fiscal reform and ample opportunities for comparing the efficacy of their design.

Index

Aaron, Henry, 24, 41n, 136n, 145n, 216n, 230n, 244n, 248n, 249n
Ability-to-pay taxes: arguments for, 237–38; and business property, 246–47; equity of, 241–42; problems, 228, 238–40; taxes regarded as, 41–42, 44; tax reform based on, 226–27
ACIR. See Advisory Commission on Intergovernmental Relations
Adams, Charles F., Jr., 154n, 161n, 162n, 163n, 191n, 193
Advisory Commission on Intergovernmental Relations (ACIR), 8n, 31n, 34n, 36n, 38n, 39n, 45n, 53n, 54n, 60n, 61n, 62, 64n, 70n, 73n, 126n, 137n, 164n, 166n, 167n, 168n, 176n, 177n, 180n, 187n, 188n, 190n, 211n, 217n, 225n, 232n, 243n, 244, 249n, 250n, 253n, 254, 256n, 260n, 262n, 263n; block grants, 170, 171, 175n; cigarette tax proposal, 48; creation of, 21; optimal government structure, 16n; fiscal balance, 21, 22; representative revenue system, 109–11, 113n, 116, 149–50; revenue sharing, 143; state grants, 181–85; federal and state tax coordination, 48; transfer of local government functions, 19–20; grant system, 21, 127, 130, 132n, 133n, 134n, 138, 139, 141, 142n; regional growth problems, 26
Aid to families with dependent children (AFDC), 103
Ainsworth, Kenneth G., 69

Akin, John S., 109n, 111n, 113n
Anderson, William, 1n
Andrews, William D., 60n
A-95 reviews, 19
Antirecession fiscal assistance (ARFA), 164–68, 196
Anton, Thomas J., 160, 164n
Appalachia, 139
Appalachian Regional Development Act of 1965, 139n
ARFA. See Antirecession fiscal assistance
Aronson, J. Richard, 4n, 36n, 205n
Arrow, Kenneth J., 90n
Auld, D. A. L., 201n
Auletta, Ken, 25n

Bahl, Roy W., 17n, 166n, 200n, 214n, 215
Balk, Alfred, 245n
Barber, Arthur B., 64n, 67n
Barlow, Robin, 221n
Barr, James L., 90n, 217n
Barro, Stephen M., 149n, 150n, 214n
Bartel, Ann P., 211n
Bartlett, Randall, 227n, 257n
Barzel, Yoram, 78n, 221n
Baumol, William J., 92n, 197–99, 219
BEA. See Bureau of Economic Analysis
Becker, Arthur P., 254n
Behavioral models, 111–13
Bell, Daniel, 189n
Bendick, Marc, Jr., 251n
Benefit spillout programs, 77, 128, 129;